Schoenberg's Error

William Thomson

University of Pennsylvania Press

Philadelphia

Library of Congress Cataloging-in-Publication Data
Thomson, William, 1927–
     Schoenberg's error / William Thomson.
         p.   cm. — (Studies in the criticism and theory of music)
     Includes bibliographical references and index.
     ISBN 0-8122-3088-4
     1. Schoenberg, Arnold, 1874–1951—Criticism and interpretation.
2. Music—Theory—20th century   3. Music—Philosophy and
aesthetics.   4. Twelve-tone system.   I. Title.   II. Series.
ML410.S283T6   1991
781.2'68'092—dc20   90-28313
                                                        CIP
                                                        MN

To Walter Robert:
Impeccable Musician and Model Scholar,
my First and Best Theory Teacher

CONTENTS

PREFACE

Toward the end of 1924 one of the world's great music publishers, Universal of Vienna, released Arnold Schoenberg's *Suite für Klavier* Op. 25. By usual standards this was not an auspicious event, even in the sedate circles of classical music publishing. In fact, few persons in addition to Schoenberg himself—some close friends from his circle of present and past students like Erwin Stein and Alban Berg— were even aware that this collection of short piano pieces had been committed to print, much less that it could, in time, come to signify something far greater than just the music it contained.

Even Stravinsky's notorious *Sacre,* older by some dozen years, could not match this slight composition's eventual symbolic power. In some ways its release was the public revelation of what would become one of the dominant forces in twentieth-century music. Inauspicious at birth, perhaps, its compelling role in history was nonetheless confirmed by developments during the next fifty years.

Even today, most serious music lovers do not find Schoenberg's suite of little pieces especially delightful. In fact, the composition's principal claim to fame was not its substance but Schoenberg's use of his "method of composing with twelve notes" as a controlling agent throughout all six movements. He had composed music earlier that made use of the same method, but not to the degree incorporated in the *Suite.* This latest piece signaled an epochal point in the composer's creative life, one of those deliberate turns in a personal road that ultimately changes the direction of many others as well. From that time in 1924 to now, professionals and non-professionals alike have argued the musical validity, the artistic propriety, the historical justification of Schoenberg's contribution to how we think about music. Ironically, like the *Suite,* Schoenberg himself seems destined to endure mainly as a mythic symbol of musical revolution. Posterity seems intent upon neglecting both.

Schoenberg's quick and brilliant mind sought ultimate answers; but he now seems more an extension of intellectual beliefs of nineteenth-century Romanticism than an oracle for an ineluctable evolution. Early in his maturity, he was consumed by the intoxicating ideas of his troubled times, some of which he did not fully comprehend (like Darwin's version of evolution), and others which even in their original formulations were of doubtful credibility (like Nietzsche's idea of the artist as cosmic prophet). Historian Donald Grout could have had Schoenberg rather than Berlioz in mind when, in defining the essential Romantic stance, he speaks of "this conception of the composer as prophet, a lone heroic figure struggling against a hostile environment."

Only Schoenberg's theories of music and of history, not his compositions, occupy us in this study. One of the most articulate composers of history, he left a record that enables us to trace and assess his reasons for choosing the particular trail that he blazed. Those reasons are likely to be more valuable to cultural history than the conclusions he reached or the music he created. This study argues that those reasons are especially important to us and to the history of ideas because they represent a noble attempt to plant a revolutionary artistic movement in what turns out to have been shallow soil. As this chronicle confirms, errors left unchallenged by one generation tend to fertilize the minds of the next; and while they are catalytic for the boldest minds, they often lead to ever more tenuous concepts and procedures.

My focus is on Schoenberg as the principal author and apologist for many of the theoretical positions that have dominated our century, as well as the chief architect of rigorous atonality and a systematic means for achieving it. This focus is appropriate, because he fits the role better than any other twentieth-century musician. But our chronicle can also be understood in broader terms, as the tracings of roots of issues that extend beyond one man's wrestlings with artistic change. Schoenberg-as-figure-head is a revealing symptom of more widespread conflict within the twentieth century's arts and their explications as structure. In music it is a conflict that began to change the art's complex creation-production-marketing-consumption apparatus when Beethoven, early in the nineteenth century, helped music develop into a vehicle of ego expression, when the artist's unique creative stamp first began to be a dominating motive for creation rather than a welcome by-product. It was then that *style* and its differentiating facets began developing into the central issue it has become today, when an obsessive self-consciousness for one's stylistic uniqueness began to show that it could stunt the creative impulse, much as the centipede's concern for the succession of feet could destroy its locomotion. For music theory it was a time to emulate—or at least try to emulate—the impressive successes of the natural sciences.

As theorist and as composer, Schoenberg indirectly posed for us the biggest question of all: whether it is even fruitful to think of music as evolving. Are those surface stylistic differences that distinguish one culture or era or individual from another the products of an unswerving linear progression from "there" to "here," each stage marked by substantive changes, each later stage demonstrable as the necessary outgrowth of its precedent? Or do they instead represent only this or that audacious way of mixing an unchanging reservoir of ingredients, in which historical progression is a zig-zagging from one boundary of the same spectrum to another? Schoenberg's path to his own forceful answers to those questions reveals several object lessons in speculative thinking about any art and its basis in human action.

ACKNOWLEDGMENTS

As for a child, a book's conception is best a private matter, yet its full flowering can be achieved only through the generous sharing by many others.

A number of persons contributed to this book in unique ways at various stages in its development. Faced with my near-despair one critical weekend, Betsy Snyder generously loaned me her Selectric so the labor could continue unchecked. Arthur Darack, Maryellen McDonald, and Larry Livingston gave broad insight and guidance for an early version of the manuscript, and J. B. Floyd helped refine my conclusions about Scriabin's music that are discussed in Chapter 12. Especially hard readings and pithy comment came from Diana Deutsch, James Hopkins, Bryan Simms, and Fred Lerdahl, who took to task my next-to-last manuscript version and helped to put many matters in better shape than I had left them. And finally, Leonard B. Meyer made enormous contributions to the final manuscript, from being the original source of several conceptual elegancies that have fed my thinking to gently curbing my penchant for overripe metaphor, both straight and mixed.

WILLIAM THOMSON

PART I

The Context and its Predilections

CHAPTER I

Music, Change, and a Dawning Century

Every era has its unique preoccupations, its favorite obsessions, its special solutions for special problems. In the arts these recurrent testings of goals and means are often little more than local stirrings of limited import. Whether ancient Sparta's flurry over Terpander's added lyre string or modern New York's debates over Andy Warhol's affinity for soup can labels, skirmishes over tools and boundaries often generate more heady talk than lasting substance: subtle realignments rather than jarring revolutions mark their places in history.

Yet other polemics in the arts may cut to deeper tissue and leave uglier scars. They raise fundamental questions that penetrate to the marrow, so they become serious business for those who take a particular art seriously. Either category may sometimes consume more time and arouse stronger feelings than seems reasonable to humanity at large, but this is to be expected: it is true of the art experience itself.

The central issue of music during the first half of the twentieth century was of the latter kind. Although it generated considerable heat at times, it managed to persist, waxing and waning through the decades, well into the century's second half. It suffered little competition as the reigning musical issue during its seven-decade life. In the minds of thoughtful people of the world's music capitals, these were years dominated by a question raised by many imposing figures but argued most forcefully by one of history's most formidable musicians, Arnold Schoenberg. The question had to do with the role of tonality in music and whether, as Schoenberg claimed, its necessary and inevitable demise and replacement should not mark a departure and next step in music evolution. This was the twentieth-century issue destined to affect music's future most dramatically, to fuel more discussions than any other. Musicians are familiar with the basic story, but in a larger context Schoenberg's forceful role in the polemic ensured his place in the intellectual history of our time. Like the names of Einstein, Freud, Wright, and Picasso, his has endured—for the non-professional as well as the professional—as an icon of what was considered revolutionary about the revolutions of the early twentieth century.

By mid-century, tonality had become a notorious word in the lexicons of music's intellectual circles. Tempers flared over its definition, over its alleged presence or absence, its clarity or ambiguity. Like most issues of the art world, its economic and sociological and political power, as a rallying point outside music, was not impressive. But within the art, tonality was the supreme issue, the anvil on which a significant portion of modern music was shaped.

Eliminating tonality from music was a more wrenching matter for musicians than eliminating linear perspective seems to have been for painters, or abandoning the concept of cosmic ether was for physicists. Indeed, tonality had been around far longer than either of those concepts had been freight for their respective disciplines.

TONALITY IN MUSIC

What is tonality? It is a perceptual condition which everyone experiences, yet few seem to agree fully about its nature and causes. As a word it is bandied about in a multitude of different contexts. Our discussion can be made easier if we assign a bedrock meaning to it, a meaning unbedeviled by some of the accumulated connotations that often weigh it down. We will use the word to refer to how musical pitch is organized to yield structure from tones, to make collections of them add up to more than random sounds. It is a condition achieved by the way tones are related to one another, and it provides an elemental coherence not unlike the way linear perspective works in vision.

Lewis Rowell has found as many as five metaphorical descriptions of tonality from over the ages. As he notes with some humor, they have included "*focus,* as in optics; *homing,* as in pigeons; *attraction,* as in magnets; *vectoring,* as in airport approaches; and *vanishing point,* as in perspective." He then adds that recent times have brought us more abstract labels like *centricity, priority,* and *referentiality.*[1]

As any of these terms makes clear, the most important distinction within the setup of tonality is what we shall call *pitch focus* (or better, *pitch-class focus*), the way one pitch enacts the role of focal point, with all other pitches related to it in varying degrees of simplicity or complexity, directness or indirectness. Tonality is a set of pitches operating as a resolutional hierarchy. It is the pitch nucleus, the drawing together of the members of a pitch collection as aural vectors toward a tonic—the *keynote* or *Do* of musical pitch—that is the primal feature. Beyond this fundamental state tonality cannot be reduced. Everything else about it falls into place as a consequence of this inequitable relating of many pitches to one. We shall consider its other manifestations and causes as they become pertinent to our principal topic (especially in Chapter 8).

The causes of tonality as an experiential concept were not explored significantly until early in this century,[2] perhaps because tonality had been so central to music that it was taken for granted as much by composers and music theorists as by listeners. It was such an implicit part of the musical experience that it was largely ignored, except in terms of its direct musical consequences. In fact, the musicians most responsible for the word's adoption were the Frenchman Françoise-Henri-Joseph Blaze (1784–1857) and the Belgian François-Joseph Fétis (1784–1871). They recognized the concept, just before the mid-nineteenth century, only as it had meaning in the narrow major-minor key sense of the music of their time.[3] Tonality was too fundamental to be an object of direct concern. It persisted in the kind of basic yet concealed status Ludwig Wittgenstein had in mind when he once observed that the aspects of things which are most important for us are hidden because of their simplicity and familiarity, that the core of our wonderment rarely strikes us because it is too commonplace, too "understood," to be noticed. And such was the case with tonality.

Though bedrock to the musical experience, it is a fragile condition. The perspective of a prevailing focal pitch can be changed instantly or made tenuous by the intrusion of a single pitch or chord, or by a rhythmic emphasis that topples previous alignments, the accumulated strength of a particular tonal hierarchy reduced within milliseconds to the disquiet of ambiguity. On the other hand, the condition itself can be emphatically suggested rather than explicitly established, a tonic response evoked without its carrier even sounded.

NINETEENTH-CENTURY TONAL FLEXING

During the waning years of the nineteenth century, several of the most perceptive musicians seemed to agree that perhaps familiarity had bred stylistic saturation. The hierarchy of tonal relatedness had actually provided the backbone for music of every description since one knew not when; yet it was during this era of music's ascendency (perhaps the very brightest of music's golden ages) that this largely implicit ground rule of tonal ordering came to be questioned, especially by Schoenberg. The questioning was stimulated by two circumstances of the times. One was a consequence of music's development, especially since Beethoven, toward greater chromaticism. The other was the emerging prominence and intellectual influence of the theory of biological evolution.

There are several plausible ways to explain the main changes of musical style between Beethoven's late works (let us say from around 1815) and the year 1900. Certainly one of the more evident of these changes, and one that most music historians accept as a given, was a product of extensive tonal exploration in the music of some of that period's most influential composers. It involved the flexing of tonality, the occasional attenuation of the long-spanned sense of pitch focus that could be heard in earlier music. This came about especially through the packing together of all or most of the twelve pitch classes into ever shorter musical spans, whether through continuous modulations (as in Reger) or through the extensive use of non-diatonic chords (as in Scriabin). This well-chronicled ferment of tonal exploration was centered in Germany, but the dominance of that country's composers ensured that the idea spilled far beyond its borders.

It is important to observe, however, that not all composers between 1815 and 1901 were lurching headlong toward tonal oblivion. Indeed, the most famous factional dispute in music of the times, the Brahms-Wagner "War," testifies to the absence of uniformity in matters of compositional persuasion. A more symptomatic clash of Classical-Romantic, Apollonian-Dionysian, Conservative-Radical could not be found in music's history, as its issues were a good deal broader than egoistic spats between camp followers of the two great composers. Its issues pitted opposing aesthetic ideals against one another as much as they paraded the prejudices of two musical perspectives. Those issues brought into stark relief the "thing in itself," the music as non-representational sound views of Eduard Hanslick, who passionately and unequivocally supported Brahms's side against the revolutionary music-dramatic ideas of Wagner.

Well after the fact (1926), Schoenberg described these stirrings for liberated tonal expression (symptoms more of Wagner than of Brahms), noting that they were motivated by the wish to treat music less as mere sonic delight and more as a message of concentrated expression. He recognized the effect of this outcome in the music of his immediate predecessors.

> It is clear that all these tendencies which exert an eccentric pull, worked against the desire to fix, make sensorily perceptible, and keep effective an harmonic central point, and that the composers who succeeded Wagner were soon obliged to make fast their forms in a different way from that practised until then.[4]

It would be an error to forget that composers before Wagner occasionally composed passages of high chromatic content, music in which tonal equilibrium was thrown, momentarily at least, to the winds. For instance, Mozart's development sections often include patches of tonal ambivalence, tonal orientations steered decidedly in the direction of harmonic flux. Brief but striking instances of similar flights of tonal fancy occur in the music of J. S. Bach as well, and the claim has been made (perhaps a bit exaggerated) that Bach's most illustrious German predecessor, Heinrich Schütz, composed music that at times was veritably *twelve-tone*. Let us not forget as well that some of the brooding creations of late Renaissance masters, Marenzio, Monteverdi, Gesualdo, Rore, and Banchieri—the musical expressionists of their day—bear unmistakable signs of radical tonal ambiguity recruited in the service of greater emotional expression.[5] Of these we shall have more to say later, especially in Chapter 12.

But none of these excursions into chromaticism seems to have made as strong an impression on Schoenberg as did those of his most illustrious German forebears. And with Schoenberg, historians have generally recognized surer signs of an evolving tonal syntax in works such as Liszt's *Faust Symphony* (1857), in which the first movement's main theme emphatically and systematically employs the full complement of the chromatic scale, or in Wagner's *Tristan und Isolde* (1857–59), where unfocused harmonies initiate a human drama of uncommonly high passion. As Charles Rosen points out about the dramatic harmony of *Tristan:*

> The expansion of the crucial moment of ambiguity attained monumental proportions. There are many pages where no single phrase can be interpreted as belonging to a fixed key, and where certain chords have more than two possible interpretations. . . . This suspension of clear small-scale harmonic sense is what enabled Wagner to give the impression of long-range action, in which the music proceeds in a series of waves and not in small articulated steps.[6]

Hindsight tells us that by the time the nineteenth century was fading into the twentieth, the trendsetters of art music, through stretches of chromatic wanderings (at least in some of their music), had achieved an apparent point of no return. These can be found scattered among the works of Chopin, Liszt, Wagner, and, later, Richard Strauss. And passages from the music of Reger, Wolf, Scriabin, and the later works of Mahler only confirm the conventional wisdom: anarchic chromaticism was in the act of overturning the neat and simple controls of the major and minor scales and the modal musics of times past. Or so it seemed, at least.[7]

MUSIC AS AN EVOLVING ART

For those who earnestly sought new expression, following the slow path toward tonal complexity and harmonic ambiguity as means for expressing high emotion seemed to be made more urgent by one of the most powerful emerging ideas of modern times, the concept of evolution. For an educated class weaned on this provocative new-old idea, to which Charles Darwin gave the sanction of science as well as the comforting endorsement of homely observation, no fact of life seemed to be more patently evident than the simple equation, TIME = CHANGE.

Steeped in the ideas of Lamarck and Malthus as well as those of his contemporary Alfred Russell Wallace, Darwin had argued, in his *On the Origin of Species* of 1859, that the constant flux Heraclitus had found in his stream centuries before was not just idle metaphor and that it rang true for life itself. Darwin's concept of accidental variation, which was the basic idea of the theory of survival by "natural selection," provided the most plausible scenario yet devised to explain its process in biological terms, even though it was widely and passionately misunderstood.

Then why should the truths of biology not be the truths of art? Indeed, the same notion of inevitable but gradual change brought about through natural selection could be applied to architecture and painting or to jurisprudence and music. And an interesting corollary of the time always seemed to be that change was automatically and convincingly equated with improvement. It was a notion that had been instilled in the late eighteenth-century French and English intellectual thought by way of the popularization of Newton's theories. The modern period, it was confidently conjectured, must be an improvement over the periods of the past, from whose achievements it had sprung. History must involve, therefore, a self-perpetuating stream of improving conditions; *progress* must be the byproduct of what then was usually referred to not as *evolution* but as *descent modification* or *developmental theory*.

Progress became the slogan of the day. Does not something's very survival prove its "fittingfulness," its superiority over whatever it replaced? Did not the very grandeur reached in nineteenth-century music prove this thesis, as well as prove the necessity for decisive change, the demand for basic readjustments? If not, then what was the meaning of the pronounced ambiguities, the unsettling tonal uncertainties found in some of the monumental dramatic works of the second half of the century?[8] Or more subtly in several of Chopin's more enigmatic essays in tonal ambivalence?[9] Was it not clear that the line of evolution from 1865 (give or take a decade or so) through 1885 thrust unerringly toward greater harmonic complexity, the clouding of key, and the knotting of chords that separated Haydn's triadic insouciance from Wagner's chromatic heavy breathing?

But saddled with these tenuous cultural inferences from Darwin's well-documented leap of biological theory, a dilemma plagued those who assumed they had a precise sounding on the quality and dimension of what had occurred in music through Beethoven. The really tough question was "What comes next?" This question frequently became the overriding concern for artists during the first decades of the twentieth century, so much so that what artists are supposed to do, which is to create artful things, was on occasion lost in aesthetic anticipating, in unproductive style-searching. The cult of the avant-garde, the "What's New?" obsession of the first half of this century, affected the judgments of all those who concerned themselves with matters of art.

That unsettling time found many composers probing unrelentingly for *the* secret door to evolution's next corridor. If music's harmonic palette had expanded excessively, concealing in the process the tonic-dominant polarity, the Do-Sol cornerstone of the Western key system—a convention established by J. S. Bach and recycled in their own images by Haydn, Mozart, Beethoven, Schubert, Mendelssohn, and Brahms—then where might lie the next step toward musical salvation? Had not the existence of the harmonic series, confirmed and reconfirmed late in the seventeenth century by Mersenne and Sauveur, then later shown by Rameau to be the very fount of music, been exhausted? That being the case, where to go from here?

There is evidence of nearly as many different answers to that question as respondents. In 1907 one of the era's most respected musicians, Ferruccio Busoni, rhapsodized his own version of where the present should lead. What he had in mind seems to have revolved around a return to creative simplicity quite different from the strained excesses of late Romanticism. As he urged, in his "Sketch of a New Esthetic of Music,"

Let us take thought, how music may be restored to its primitive, natural essence; let us free it from architectonic, acoustic and esthetic dogmas; let it be pure invention and sentiment, in harmonies, in forms, in tone-colors . . .; let it follow the line of the rainbow and vie with the clouds in breaking sunbeams; let music be naught else than nature mirrored by and reflected from the human breast.[10]

HELPING THE INEVITABLE TO HAPPEN

It seems ironic that a kind of Calvinist determinism motivated these largely Jewish and Roman Catholic composers of the turn of the century. Darwin's distinct and crucial addition to evolutionary theory actually denied purpose and predictability to whatever might arise over the millennia of the natural selection process. But although the reality of individual arrival points in evolution's flux may be regarded as pre-destined by the evolutionary odds (as some composers seemed to think), one nonethe-less could hope to move it forward just a bit with some judicious nudgings.

Music had reached breathtaking sublimity of sonic expression. Yet as a style, as a developing continuity, occasional gargantuan textures and programmatic super-monumentality dwarfed the events of mere humanity. It is easy to see in music's state a corollary to the condition of Western Europe itself just after World War I, in which historian Barbara Tuchman saw a crumbling tower, "an edifice of grandeur and passion, of riches and beauties and dark cellars."[11]

The first two decades of this century churned with efforts both to predict the future that would replace those troubled times and to be the first to welcome and dominate it. The popular question, "What will it be like in the twenty-first century?" was asked in every domain of the fine arts as well as in city planning. More effort was devoted by more people in trying to be thoroughly modern—or, even better, to achieve that state of inherent contradiction called *ahead of the times*—than in any other period of human history. Being au courant became for the first time a preoccupa-tion, more prized in some circles than individualism, uniqueness, or creativity. And those two separate conditions of being, contemporaneity and creativity, were at times confusedly joined in minds otherwise wholly rational as if they were synonymous.

This passion to greet the future before its time grew logically from peculiarities of thought surrounding the idea of evolution itself. If one's goal is to express something through art—and the urge to express *something* was the prime mover of that era's artistic sensibility—then saturation with expressing the present can lead readily to one of two alternatives: depicting something of the fancied past or of a predicted future. As Donald Grout has noted, "Romantic art aspires to transcend immediate times or occasions, to seize eternity, to reach back into the past and forward into the future."[12] In the 1890–1920 lust to Be With It, the future won, hands down. It was especially the favored stance for those most convinced of the necessity of change. For many artists—Futurists,[13] Vorticists, Dadaists, Expressionists, Fauvists, et al.—the spirit of the day was most eloquently expressed some years later by the rather old-fashioned poet Stephen Vincent Benét, who characterized the blind drive of American pioneers with the cry, "We don't know where we're going, but we're on our way!"

SOMETHING IN THE AIR ABOUT CHANGE

Of course, wakes for the old and welcomes for the new were not confined to the music room during the fascinating period that concerns us here. Although too much can be made of what in hindsight appear to have been parallel conditions in music, literature, and painting around 1900, the later bursts of development pioneered by Schoenberg and Stravinsky in music, by Kandinsky, Picasso, and Braque in painting, by Stein and Joyce in literature, suggest at least comparable states of aesthetic agitation.

But one should regard such similarities with a measure of skepticism, mainly because music lacks (except in the most abstruse metaphysical sense), the power of representation so commonplace for words and for visual symbols and signs. Music has always been nonrepresentational. Only the naive expect music, in and of itself, to depict the specific, to denote the precise. In music, as Charles Ives once asked, "Where is the expression of late spring against early summer—of happiness against optimism?"[14]

And so the stakes and the structural problems for the visual and the verbal and the aural arts were and remain quite different from those of music. Expressionist painter Oskar Kokoshka and atonal composer Arnold Schoenberg may have "recognized each other as engaged in the same dangerous, lonely work, at once of liberation and of destruction," as historian Carl E. Schorske observes,[15] but the reasons for their separate probings in paint and tone, between 1900 and 1920, were far from identical. In fact Schoenberg, from his earliest atonal through his thoroughly dodecaphonic works, sought to *control* a demon whose unbridled freedom could, he feared, spell musical chaos. Kandinsky and his colleagues, on the other hand, sought to *unleash* their art's demons to roam streets formerly trafficked only by music in the comfort of its abstraction, impotent, as it is, for allegorical representation.

How strange! We find the visual and verbal artists struggling, early in the century, to make their wares more like music, just as music's strongest wills were intent to remodel their art according to new specifications.

The revolution of late-nineteenth-century architecture, which led directly into what we later learned to know as Bauhaus (sometimes as if it were an adjective) was yet a different response to a slightly different set of circumstances. Let us remember that in architecture (whose very being is inseparable from function, from everyday "practicality") there can be talk of Expressionism, of *l'art pour l'art*, of Surrealism, or of total anarchy only to the degree that one might be willing to throw baby out with bathwater.

In fin-de-siècle architecture, stylistic rumblings were concerned more with verity than with expression of feeling. The most direct statement of revolt was projected in the Viennese Secessionists' manifesto *Ver Sacrum*, formulated mainly by Adolph Loos.[16] This document's plaint (and thus the principal basis for reform) can be narrowed down to the unconscionable way Vienna's *Ringstrasse* buildings had been designed to hide their crass commercial functions behind false historical facades, the use of artifice as "cultural cosmetic." It was Loos's passion to ban ornamentation from architecture, to purify objects until only structural necessities remained, to recognize embellishment as a profanity. This was the first public incubation of an attitude that would later fix architect Mies van der Rohe in the public mind with the catchy slogan "Less is more." No less than Adolph Loos himself confirmed the utilitarian consideration that separated architecture from the fine arts, noting that while a work of art is answerable to no one, the house is answerable to everyone.[17]

Although motivations for change may have varied from art to art, a significant thread of unity nonetheless prevailed. For all, the constant unifier of the time was the clangor for change itself. It is unlikely that any era has witnessed a more outspoken, a more sustained effort by humanity to wrench more profound change from each of its expressive arts. In their separate ways the more creative individuals of each medium were restlessly striving toward a new peak in what was confidently seen as the landscape of a larger process of evolving. If a case can be made that art is metaphor for life, this 1890–1920 span yields unsurpassed supporting evidence; the whole of European culture would erupt, within the later days of this search for direction, into the widest conflict of history, the Great War.

NOTES

1. Rowell, in *Thinking About Music*, 235.

2. One of the earliest empirical studies of the perception of tonality, although not called that, was W. Van Dyke Bingham's "Studies in Melody."

3. Blaze in his *Dictionnaire de musique moderne*, 1821, Fétis in his *Esquisse de l'histoire de l'harmonie considerée comme art et comme science systématique*, 1840. Bryan Simms ("Choron, Fetis, and the Theory of Tonality") assures us that the term was in general use early in the century, especially in France, as a means of distinguishing between music of modal characteristics (*tonalité antique*) and essentially major-minor textures (*tonalité moderne*).

4. Schoenberg, *Style and Idea*, 260.

5. We shall say more about these remarkable composers and their dramatic use of chromaticism in later discussions.

6. In *Arnold Schoenberg*, 30.

7. Any discussion of this earnest search for a new musical expression would be incomplete without mentioning others who were far more newsworthy at the time than posterity suggests. Especially influential were Russians Vladimir Rebikov (1866–1920) and Nikolay Rosslavetz (1881–?); Pole Karol Szymanowski (1882–1937); Italians Ferruccio Busoni (1866–1924) and Alfredo Casella (1883–1947);

Dutch–English Bernard van Dieran (1884–1936); and German–American Bernard Ziehn (1845–1912). The creative ferment of the era is thoroughly documented in Jim Sampson's *Music in Transition*.

8. I note here in passing the programmatic origins of much of this music. More of this later in Chapters 12 and 13.

9. Such as the *Mazurka* Opus 17 No. 4. See Thomson, "Functional Ambiguity in Musical Structures," 17–27.

10. In *Three Classics in the Aesthetics of Music*.

11. Tuchman, *The Proud Tower*, 544.

12. In *A History of Music in Western Civilization*, 339.

13. It is instructive to recall Renao Poggioli's conclusion (in *The Theory of the Avant-Garde*) that the Italian Futurists were a critical symptom of widespread artistic agitation, not a singular manifestation of artistic revolt in one country. Everybody was doing it.

14. *Essays Before a Sonata*, 71.

15. *Fin-de-Siecle Vienna*, 362.

16. Early reviews in Vienna of Schoenberg's music were peppered with the designation *secessionist*, suggesting a relationship between the philosophical position of the composer and other revolutionary activists in the arts, especially in architecture. On the other hand, it may just be another indication of journalistic pigeonholing, much as *atonal* was in those years used to suggest everything from unpleasant to keyless to Bolshevist.

17. A thorough discussion of Loos's passionate views about function and ornamentation is in Janik and Toulmin's *Wittgenstein's Vienna*, 98–101.

CHAPTER 2

In Search of Prophets

WHICH ROAD TO PROGRESS?

While the chronicles of this era bear evidence of imminent and drastic change more conspicuously than those of any other, all artists did not rush for the same stylistic exit—especially not in music. Within this brief corridor to modernity one finds a bewildering variety of experimentation. It appears that at times every composer seemed to be engaged in his own solitary search for what he hoped would be the unswerving path to the next evolutionary plateau.

Music as ethnic expression, as represented by folk music, provided one option. It was a path that sanctioned simplification as an alternative to expansion. It was a route to the continued maturing of a musical fruit that ripened first with Catholic musicians incorporating chant in their polyphony, then later with J. S. Bach, who created a large part of his monumental oeuvre with the help of Lutheran chorale tunes. Perhaps—or so it seemed to some—periodic returns to the simplicity and earthiness of indigenous folksong could provide the means to ensure music's return to an even keel, a return to its "natural" state, uncorrupted by the degenerative preciousness imposed by high art.

But even folksong enthusiasms were stimulated in some measure by a hunger for new sounds and the desire to incorporate them in art works.[1] Neither nationalistic fervor nor pure scholarship were their sole motivations. This was the case with the extensive researches in Hungary of Bartók and Kodály (as two examples) whose earliest products were published just prior to World War I, at a time when Schoenberg and Scriabin and Debussy probed with others for a structural solution to art music's future through the homogenization of the chromatic scale.

On the other hand, some of the era's ablest minds, Carillo in Mexico, Busoni in Germany, Varese in America (and France), as well as Schoenberg in Austria saw the future differently. Their pronouncements and their actions implied that the pitch complexity reached in art music by 1900 was simply one stage of a longer trip.

Indeed, they seemed to reason, matters would get worse (meaning more complex) before they would get better (meaning simpler). Julian Carillo investigated the reasonableness of music incorporating microtones, thus packing the octave with as many as seventy-two different pitches where no more than twelve had sufficed in the past.[2]

Still another major route toward creative progress led to increasing complexity of another kind. Why not, for example, combine simplicities in ways to produce complexities? Why not add the total sound from one prosaic ensemble to that of another (each playing insistently different things at the same time, of course) and thus achieve an altogether unprosaic result? And this may have been the motivating question Charles Ives put to himself before he produced the Putnam's Camp movement of his *Three Places in New England* (1907–1914). In this way something new (and extraordinarily complex) could issue from the joining of two things old and, separately, simplistically benign.[3] Still another answer to that most pressing question of the day, "So where do we go from here?"

Perhaps one of F. T. Marinetti's colleagues in the Italian Futurist movement, Luigi Russolo (1885–1947), should be remembered as the most inventive of the lot. He attempted no less than the formalization of noise into a taxonomy of musical structure.[4]

I recall these historical matters here to emphasize an important point: whatever an individual composer's chosen path to the future might be, some of the most talented artists were obsessed for the first time in history with how their produce might fit into larger world-schemes, how their creations might correspond to art music as it could be observed evolving "out there" like a particular genus of fruitfly or salamander.

THE SEARCH FOR NEW MEANS OF PITCH CONTROL

Those who sought evolution's secrets in new and more thorough ways of organizing pitch, whether of twelve or fewer in number, were quick to claim respectable precedents for their ideas. Wagner and Liszt, whose names commanded reverential awe in the musical circles of 1900, had provided ample clues as to how tonal instability or ambiguity, created by a higher degree of chromaticism, could affect an engaging and fresh music and yet appear to be the continuation of a well-defined trend. It is fascinating to discover that several people of the early 1900s were thinking along similar yet often quite original lines in their search for a new pitch community and ways for legislating its members' actions. Although he published no evidence of theoretical speculations about such matters, several compositions by Scriabin unmistakably reveal preoccupation with complex note collections, pre-compositional processes that, even when not dodecaphonic, lead to textures of fully saturated chromaticism. Indeed, George Perle grants Scriabin the distinction of being the first systematic serial composer,[5] although Debussy's occasional use of a fixed set (as in

"Voiles" of the *Preludes*) reflects the same kind of processing. One of the most convincing atonal works Scriabin wrote is the third Prelude from Opus 74 (1914), which is scrupulously derived from a systematic juggling of an octatonic collection.[6]

EXAMPLE 1. Octatonic scale, Scriabin, Prelude No. 3, Op. 74.

And his renowned "Mystic Chord" of the earlier *Prometheus* (Op. 60, 1911) is nothing more than a chordal set whose pitch components act as a compound organizational matrix. But the pitch order found in Scriabin's *Piano Sonata* No. 7 (Op. 64) merits everything Perle claims for the composer; embedded there is a seven-note collection with two variants that is embryonic to the music's pitch structure.

EXAMPLE 2. Heptatonic scale, Scriabin, Piano Sonata No. 7, Op. 64.

The relatively obscure Hungarian composer-theorist Fritz Heinrich Klein (b. 1892), connected with Schoenberg's circle for a while through studies with Alban Berg, published a work for small orchestra in 1921 entitled *Die Maschine, eine Selbstsatire*. It hints of the kinds of chromatic orderings Schoenberg would shortly unveil to the world, and even boasts what may have been the world's first twelve-note chord (which Berg with amusement referred to as *Mutterakkord*).[7] A speculative treatise of Klein's, *Die Grenze der Halbtonwelt,* which appeared in the respected periodical *Die Musik* in 1925, further confirms a continuing commitment to harness the twelve notes as pitch basis for music of the future. With fellow Viennese Josef Matthias Hauer (1883–1959), Klein would become the butt of Schoenberg's developing fear, in later years, that posterity might not appropriately identify him (Schoenberg) as the indisputable parent of the twelve-note method.

HAUER AND THE TWELVE NOTES

It may have been Josef Hauer who first seriously considered the idea of organizing the twelve notes as a compositional precondition. Claims and counterclaims, comparable to those surrounding invention of the airplane, cloud the issue as history. Whatever his chronological advantages may or may not have been, he was a fascinating character about whom we still know too little. A composer and sometimes conductor with a special flare for mathematical tinkering and hyperbole, he made his living as a public school teacher in Vienna. A work by him for piano of 1912, *Nomos,* contains the controlled play of twelve-note collections that justified his claim, at least in his own mind, that he, not Arnold Schoenberg, was the originator of the dodecaphonic approach to musical composition. He jealously guarded his primacy over Schoenberg until his death in 1959 at the age of seventy-six. Like Schoenberg, whose music and ideas survive as the more influential, Hauer published ample testimony to his active role in these matters, from his *vom Wesen des Musicalischen* of 1922 to his most widely known work (in this country, at least), the *Zwolfton Technik* of 1926. Indeed, it is impossible (and somewhat beside the point) to determine with certainty which of these two men (if not yet another) was the first[8] to come up with what in essence is a rather simple idea: a scheme for pre-ordering the twelve chromatic notes, to be used so-ordered as the pitch matrix for an extended musical statement.[9]

There is no doubt that Schoenberg, through his own compositions and through his teaching of an illustrious group of talents, laid a more solid and influential foundation. Even a perfunctory examination of the next illustration, from one of Hauer's songs, eloquently confirms posterity's judgment that he was not a gifted composer. But dodecaphonic composer he was, certainly, as note collections A, B, C, and D of Example 3 confirm.

EXAMPLE 3. Hauer, *Halfte des Lebenslebens*, Op. 21, No. 2, first twelve measures.

Schoenberg met Hauer during World War I, probably around 1917.[10] There is evidence that the two knew each other's ideas quite well, yet these took rather different forms in spite of being derived from similar premises. In a letter to Hauer in 1923[11] Schoenberg exults:

> I have found no mistake and the method keeps on growing of its own accord, without my doing anything about it . . . in this way I find myself positively enabled to compose as freely and fantastically as one otherwise does only in one's youth.

The two lived out their years disputing from a distance their separate proprietary rights to the twelve-note method. In light of their tenacity, it is interesting to note that such a question—of just whose patents on creative ideas were most pending—seems to have risen to greatest prominence during the era of Romanticism, in the arts as well as in the sciences. Thus Jacques Barzun reminds us that Darwin, Marx, and Wagner each did everything he could to ignore or misrepresent his close rivals in order to claim an individual creative advantage. As he puts it, "So strongly do they feel themselves to be missionaries and pioneers that they have managed in the teeth of historical evidence to persuade us of their essential originality."[12]

Several historians agree that it was in 1921 that Schoenberg made his monumentally revealing remark, to his friend and student Josef Rufer, to the effect that he (Schoenberg) had made a discovery that could "guarantee the supremacy of German music for the next hundred years."[13] But dating the very moment of the Eureka experience *Dodecaphony!* is really secondary to the observation that compositional manifestations and theoretical statements of the basic approach gradually emerged between 1900 and 1920, the result of a felt need on the part of a number of persons.[14] Each early step was a limited windup toward the great leap that produced what the late Glenn Gould liked to call "legislated atonality." Schoenberg's music provides a ready bridge between the occasional tonal mutinies staged by Wagner and Liszt and the growing threat of twentieth-century tonal anarchy. The roving keys of *Verklärte Nacht* (1899), followed by the negations of tonal relationships in *Pierrot Lunaire* (1912), and on through the first completely twelve-tone work, the *Suite for Piano*, Opus 25, in which articulated system replaces tenuous freedom, outline one searcher's answer—indeed, the principal searcher's answer—to the biggest question twentieth-century composers thought they faced at the time.

Schoenberg's pivotal role as arbiter of musical progress was further secured by his talent for prolonged and profound and, on occasion, bitter polemic. A more likely person to conduct the search for direction in a new century, a tougher proponent for any point of view, could not have been found. He frequently joked about the accident of fate that had "selected" him to fill this uncompromising and thankless job. But the fact was that he early and self-consciously shouldered the responsibility of helping music to "progress." And he argued until his death, some half-century after first framing his own version of the question, for the self-evident rightness of his answer. His discovery became his crown of thorns as well as his garland of victory. The background for this conclusion is one of our time's most compelling stories.

Typecasting for the Starring Role

No cosmic law legislates that great artists be pleasant people. Indeed, the talent, the intellectual rigor, the motivation, the appetite for relentless work, and the lifelong perseverance required to achieve genius status in this world seem, as often as not, to associate with crabbed psyches. Arnold Schoenberg was a monumentally difficult man. Since his special craggy outlook and his affinity for polemic bear meaningfully on his artistic convictions and deeds and their subsequent persistence in the world of art, they are pertinent to our discussion.

A part of his testy disposition may have been genetic in origin.[15] But whatever its source, it was further intensified by the circumstances of his early professional development and propelled him toward a lifetime of affronts (both real and imagined), which in turn nourished a mild but disquieting sense of personal oppression. It is not an exaggeration to say that Schoenberg fed off his feelings of persecution, at times using them as a self-justifying rationale, as a twisted supportive proof of his own extraordinary powers. Malcolm MacDonald describes his unfortunate development toward distrust, noting that his "youthful resilience and high spirits gradually turned to suspicion and over-defensive pugnacity, an almost pathological tendency to look for and expect difficulties and opposition in every situation."[16]

Schoenberg operated under a covert conviction that the antagonisms directed toward his music and against his artistic tenets were, in a way, confirmations of his genius. For him they were proportional, if not directly causal, to the refusal by ordinary listeners to enjoy his music and to accept the methodological revolution he effected. One is tempted to wonder if he did not unconsciously believe in a novel syllogism that could carry him through the trying times ahead:

> All great artists are misunderstood in their time;
> I am misunderstood;
> Therefore, I am a great artist.

Confidence of his prominence in music's destiny was perhaps made overbearing because accompanied by a rather heavy personal style. He frequently turned to the Bible as a justification for his perspective, a major guide to his evaluation of reality. In addition to Schopenhauer and Kant and to his Viennese contemporary Karl Kraus, it was the Old and the New Testaments that he mined for a treasure of metaphors that colored his life and his attitudes. That he was deeply concerned with religious matters is strongly suggested by his prolonged conversion from Judaism to Christianity during the thirty-five years of 1898 to 1933. Although this radical but later reclaimed shift in religious allegiance was undoubtedly aided by his Christian friend, the opera singer Walter Pieau, who served as godfather at the composer's Lutheran baptism, it was also unquestionably a reflection of this profound man's search for universal ties and divine guidance.[17] A precocious letter of May 1891 (when he was only sixteen) confided to his cousin Melwina that he was in fact an unbeliever, albeit one who admired the cultural testament and moral and ethical persuasions provided by the theology of their mutual heritage.

This inclination toward intense gravity made him providentially right to play the part of savior for twentieth-century German music. He was a person of firm convictions and a tenacious persistence that could have built (or destroyed) cities. His sense of certainty and his indomitable will to prevail, whatever the circumstances or the odds, were wedded to an uncompromising metaphysic traceable back through the idealism of Schopenhauer-Kant-Plato. Looking back on the intellectual and emotional development of his formative years, we find a passionate bundle of complexities in search of an appropriate cause.

In spite of his characteristically heavy-handed arrogance in professional matters, students, for the most part, revered him. The apparent inconsistency is readily explained, I believe, by observing that his more amiable side was reserved for those who were incorruptibly subservient to him. His Old World charm could be captivating, his wry humor infectious, according to colleagues and students from his Los Angeles days like composer David Raksin.[18] But only so long as he was sure of being in charge, of prevailing.

It is small wonder that history can see him as a bristling weave of contradictions, one who, from shifting viewpoints, can be seen as scorned yet esteemed, shunned yet endured, celebrated yet despised. Although for rather different reasons, he was, with Wagner, one of history's most controversial figures.

THREE EARLY INFLUENCES: LOOS, KRAUS, AND GEORGE

Architect Loos did not wage unaided his holy war on visual excess that we mentioned in Chapter 1. He argued for his particular form of artistic puritanism in tandem with the battle for clean and honest prose fought by fellow citizen and cultural critic Karl Kraus (1874–1936). Kraus was a cult hero for an entire generation of Austrian and German intellectuals, a man Peter Demetz once characterized as combining the interests and energies of H. L. Mencken, Søren Kierkegaard, and Woody Allen within one psyche.[19] Essentially a pamphleteer (of immense talent, extraordinary learning, lofty aim, dogged courage, and unsurpassed arrogance), Kraus exerted a lasting influence on musician Schoenberg. In fact, the composer's gift copy to Kraus of his *Harmonielehre*, in 1911, carried an inscription claiming that he had learned so much from the writer that his own independence of thought might be in jeopardy.[20]

Kraus's principal source of provocation was similar to that of Loos. He insisted that all aesthetic pretension be voided from expository prose, that language be allowed to perform its communicational function without the overload of verbal convention and redundance that weakens its message, that it be kept free of the innuendo and implication which can be used for direct and indirect propaganda in the service of commerce as well as the confirmation of political power. The terse, epigrammatic style of Schoenberg's prose, along with his frequent lexical obstinacies (as with his rejection of the word *atonal,* which he abhorred), harks back to his captivation by "the Isaiah of decaying Europe," sardonic stylist Herr Kraus.[21] For Kraus, societal sanity could be achieved only through the honing of language to its sharpest edge, with the concomitant removal of all potentially dulling residues. In this respect he preceded the semanticist movement of such persons as Count Korsybski, among others of the 1930s and 1940s, people who at times seemed to hold that precise syntax and unerring vocabulary could curb headaches more effectively than aspirin.

Both Loos and Kraus, who exerted enormous intellectual influence on Schoenberg between 1895 and 1918, were intent on separating from their respective arts all aspects that were not innate to structure, excising whatever could be removed without either reducing the integrity or diluting the impact of the object. In this they came to make profound distinctions between "the thing itself" and its package, a distinction between idea and worldly manifestation of that idea. This notion of separating wheat from chaff made a profound impression on young Schoenberg; in fact, it became one of his several intellectual touchstones. As we shall see later, he sometimes encountered knotty ontological problems in his descriptions of music because he assumed that one can perceptually divide substance from style, discarding some aspects of the musical fabric as mere wrapping, thereby leaving the enclosed gift for direct contemplation.[22] He probably came across the idea in Kraus before finding it in its more original form in Schopenhauer or Kant. It seems unlikely that he would have known the problem in its Platonic garb.

Probably the most influential artist in Vienna around the turn of the century—certainly the most important to music history because of his direct and powerful influence on Schoenberg—was Stefan George (1868–1933). His ideas eloquently personified the turn to art by late-nineteenth-century European intellectuals as an escape from their unfulfilled political and social aspirations. It was he who most convincingly spread the gospel of art's holiness, of its value as an absolute human good. Those who argued *l' art pour l' art*[23] (and those who still do) shared George's enthusiasm for his principal Nietzschean message. Art, he maintained, is man's highest form of activity. And thus the artist—at least the artist who can rightfully claim the distinction of genius—is the highest rung of the human ladder. The rare *homo sapiens* who achieves this precious level is mystically unified with the cosmos. It is the artist of genius who expresses most clearly and most convincingly the artistic message, who is most intimately unified with the cosmos. In George's view art is a far cry from fun and games with sounds and words and pictures. Art is life at its highest ontological peak, and it is practiced exclusively by the supreme creatures of the universe.

This intoxicating perspective was not lost on the aspiring Schoenberg. He concluded early in life that he was by all means an artist, not just as composer but as writer and as painter (for one short period) as well. The act of creation, and especially the Georgean idea of *being* a creator, with all of its cosmic fringe benefits, was important to him, whatever the medium of expression.

L'ART POUR L'ART

Schoenberg was an ideal protégé for Stefan George's ideas. We find him in 1910 barely able to make ends meet (he was begging financial help from a round of acquaintances that included Gustav Mahler) yet devoting extensive time to his secondary passion of expression, painting. A more touching manifestation of a doubtful Romantic ideal would be hard to find, especially since he could barely control the most elementary techniques of the painter. This dark period of his life and its irrational tendencies can perhaps be fathomed best in the perspective of the will-to-expression he shared with several of his contemporaries, a motivation that comes from inner necessity rather than from external goal.

In a remarkably dispassionate discussion of Schoenberg's self-portraits of that bleak period in his life, Eberhard Freitag traces this motivating concept, this drive of inner necessity, as far back as the writer Wilhelm von Kugelgen (1802–1867), observing that it "appears in Schopenhauer and migrates from there into the vast abundance of late-nineteenth-century popular philosophy." He further notes that the concept embodies appealing ramifications, providing a ready and functional aid to Schoenberg in particular. Freitag even supplies a plausible relationship between the down-and-out and frustrated composer and this notion of inner compulsion to make one's deepest feelings public:

> It is not difficult to understand precisely why Schoenberg marshals this concept so frequently for, as an artist, he could point then neither to titles and diplomas, nor to great works, that is, those recognized and performed by the cultural authorities.[24]

And perhaps most pertinent, Freitag suggests that by marshalling this popular justification for his actions, the composer could legitimize his results "by invoking the inspiration of a higher authority and thereby excluding at the outset any possible criticism based on the standard traditional rules." With his marriage in jeopardy and his stark alienation from the musical public seemingly irreparable, the many self-portraits he produced during the 1909–1911 period reveal a profoundly troubled mind.[25]

Schoenberg's drive for self-expression and his inclination for truculent profundity coexisted in a personality that could charitably be characterized as "heavy." In this he was, as George Rochberg has observed, "the very epitome of the German intellectual of that epoch . . . one who has forgotten how to laugh at himself or life."[26] Except for dealings with his most trusted and beloved friends and colleagues, he lacked the light touch, once remarking to Mahler that "middle of the road experiences don't happen to me."[27]

Some twenty-five years later a similar imperiousness dominated the scene described by composer David Raksin, in a delightful memoir of his work with Charlie

Chaplin. It was Raksin's coveted honor and pleasure to bring these two vaunted personalities together for the first time, through the implausible mediation of pianist-raconteur Oscar Levant. The ebullient Mr. Raksin soon discovered to his dismay that a warm friendship had not been sparked. The scene took place at Chaplin's film studio in Hollywood.

> In no time at all it was evident that the conversation was heading for a stalemate. Schoenberg, with his strong sense of his own eminence and his intellectual rigor, seemed baffled by the disparity between Chaplin's pre-eminent position as a film artist and his casual urbanity. It was disconcerting for Schoenberg to find that the cinematic genius he admired so much did not affect the serious demeanor which is in some cultures the perquisite of greatness. And although Charlie was on his best gracious-host behavior, the feeling soon grew awkward and painful, and it was with a sense of relief that I saw the visit end.[28]

PARENTAL DUALITY

Schoenberg's perspective on the world and its events, and his responsive actions to them, were marked by an oscillating tension between poles of being, a highly charged non-mixture perhaps inherited from his sharply contrasting parents. On the one side there was the established convention of tradition, the side of his personality reflecting mother Pauline, which found him responsive to the Jewish heritage, reverent toward the classic German tradition, indeed, all of those aspects of life and culture that to him projected equilibrium, warmth, reasonable certainty, resolution, and solidity. But a contrasting streak, coming from father Samuel, was colored by the iconoclastic, prone to dismiss tradition in favor of novelty, ready for argument at the drop of an irreverent comment. It was this latter aspect of his psyche that admitted the propriety of drastic change, that accepted a leavening evolution as the way of this world and made him feel ennobled to add his bit to it.

In the light of these conflicting ingredients, it is not surprising for us to come on his frequent expressions of "continuing a tradition," of representing a musical *evolution* as opposed to the *revolution* alleged to have been his goal. Even his frequent equivocations concerning Wagner the avant-gardiste and/or Brahms the revolutionary-classicist suggest the depth of this inner conflict over alluring concepts which he regarded, rightly or wrongly, as incompatible. Which was his real idol of the immediate musical past? Was it Wagner, the revolutionary dramatist-composer, who showed that tonal indecisiveness performed admirably as an ingredient in the musical mix? Or was it Brahms, the symphonist who continued where Beethoven left off, perpetuator of the classicism begun with Haydn and Mozart?

In his public pronouncements he often disdains Wagner, appearing to share Hauer's colorful estimation of him as "that brothel musician," treasuring Brahms as his most worthy model. And yet the two predecessors seem to have been inextricably entwined in his thoughts and feelings, the irresolvable yet co-present oil and water, musical equivalents of the cultural, religious, and family dissonances which also were never wholly resolved nor sorted out in his mind. It was this considerable tension between irreconcilable values that led Alma Mahler, an adroit appraiser of human character as well as one of the world's all-time gossips, to observe that "Schoenberg delighted in paradox of the most violent description." It was these opposing tensions within him that justified one biographer's oxymoronic tag *conservative revolutionary.*[29]

SCHOENBERG'S VIENNA

Even Schoenberg's early environment, from the intimacy of his modest home to the urbanity of the great city of Vienna, was a perfect incubator for nourishing a major polemicist in the arts. Turn-of-the-century Vienna was an incomparable arena in which to come of age, particularly for one immersed in music. The city's character was dominated by a rare blend of intellectual fervor and moral uncertainty, an elegant decadence that blended cruelty with sentimentality. Its telltale symptoms would seem familiar to most big-city dwellers today. Historian Pamela White lumps together as a continuity the century's last decade and its first quarter-century aftermath as she marvels at the concealed irony of artistic and intellectual energy of those years. These occurred, she notes, in a "hysterical, suicide-prone culture reflecting its own imminent decay and death." She neatly encapsulates the incomparable decadence of the era by observing that its unique sickness was "spectacularly manifested in the suicide of the young Crown Prince Rudolf in 1889."[30]

And so we are confronted with an apparent inconsistency. This Vienna of Schoenberg's origins, scene of his first successes and failures, may have been a breeding ground for artists, scientists, and philosophers of strong convictions and high aims, but it was not the land of marathon gaiety and artistic piety that some superficial historical glosses have passed off as gospel truth. It was not the Vienna we might conjure up with a vision of one of Gustav Klimmt's porcelain beauties dancing with light feet but heavy heart to a Strauss waltz.

A layer of tough cynicism lay just below Vienna's frivolous skin. One cannot read its contemporary writers without coming away impressed by the pervasive concealed fear that dampens the surface effervescence of these ultra-sophisticates. Things were rarely what they appeared to be. Hidden agendas were normal—so much so that they became less and less hidden. And nowhere was this troubled liaison of appearance and reality more volatile than in the arts. These played such a significant role in the lives of upper class citizens that some of the most perceptive historians of the time see them becoming more an obsession than a delight. The arts became, in effect, an escape from the disheartening political and social realities that hovered over the populace. Hugo von Hofmansthal called it *das Gleitende,* in the sense of a "slipping away of the world." It was as if nature had failed to provide an adequate footing for civilized interaction, and thus humanity had to struggle to make up the difference that would bring the stability it craved. This was a notion pregnant with overtones for one who would go on to legislate, as Schoenberg did, a radical new approach to composing.

As historian Carl Schorske tells us,

> If the Viennese burghers had begun by supporting the temple of art as a surrogate form of assimilation into the aristocracy, they ended up by finding in it an escape, a refuge from the unpleasant world of increasingly threatening political reality.[31]

And he continues his description of art's dominant yet troubled role by noting that as well-meaning citizens' sense of futility increased,

> Art became almost a religion, the source of meaning and the food of the soul. Art became transformed from an ornament to an essence, from an expression of value to a source of value. . . . The affirmation of art and the life of the senses thereby became, in Austria's finest types, admixed with and crippled by guilt.[32]

THE CONSERVATIVE REVOLUTIONARY

By 1930 Schoenberg's revolutionary proposals and his provocative music had been widely, if superficially, covered in the international press. Like his equally misunderstood yet more universally honored contemporary Albert Einstein, he became an internationally known figure. And yet his perspective through life remained that of conservative Austrian burgher. Always a political monarchist (supporting the Kaiser in World War I, a "true believer in the House of Hapsburg"), one wonders whether he would not have been much happier back in the Mödling countryside just out of Vienna, where he spent his intellectual and emotional recharging years for a period of stability after the war, rather than established in the very foreign United States. His letters and his essays give the impression, a decade later, that he was relieved and grateful to share the joys of life in the Promised Land of America, but even the sybaritic allures of Southern California, where he eventually settled, could not erase his outlook: his values and his deepest longings were indissolubly Germanic, Old World, idiosyncratically absolutist.

In 1938, just four years after settling in the United States, Schoenberg responded to fellow refugee Hugo Leichtentritt's request about some books he had read whose influence had been propitious.[33] He recommended a few for American readers with the remark that they might "help to convert them away from their fossilized aesthetics."[34]

This unconcealed scorn reminds us of the kind of artistic chauvinism that is alien to most American artists, although it played a prominent role in Schoenberg's thinking. Ironically, he sounds a bit like Alfred Rosenberg himself when, in an essay of 1919, he pleads that "the most important task of the music section of a proposed new Ministry of Art is to ensure the German nation's superiority in the field of music, a superiority which has its roots in the people's talents."[35]

These blinders that championed things Teutonic, and especially German music of the previous one hundred and fifty years, remained a part of his perspective throughout his life. It was an explicit nationalism, an ironic yet not uncommon trait of many of the principals in the artistic ferment early in our century, especially unexpected in those whose lives had been uprooted and blighted by Nazi inhumanities. Art historian Marjorie Perloff has observed that it was a paradoxical condition of those who were most influential in the avant guerre. For her, "seventy years and two world wars later, it was almost impossible to understand the particular mixture of radicalism and patriotism, of a worldly, international outlook and a violently nationalist faith."[36]

These were the controlling personal inclinations of a musical genius who would exert greater influence on art music of our century's middle years than any other person. They are important to remember because they help to explain two otherwise imponderable aspects of Schoenberg's career: the force that kept his arguments alive, despite their ultimate basis in conjecture, and the powerful will that sustained his motivation until his death in 1951.

NOTES

1. For an extensive discussion of the influence Bartók's folk music researches had on his composing see Suchoff, "Ethnological Roots of Béla Bartók's Musical Language."

2. Carillo was only one of many, of course. As achievable technique, the microtonal potential goes back well into the nineteenth century. The harmonium used by Helmholtz (*On the Sensations of Tone,* 1863) could yield thirty-one pitches within an octave, and R. H. M. Bosanquet (*An Elementary Treatise on Musical Intervals and Temperament,* 1876) mentions an instrument capable of fifty-three per octave. William Austin (*Music in the Twentieth Century*) claims that Bizet's father-in-law, Jacques François Halévy (1799–1862), used "occasional quarter tones" in his *Prométhée,* but I can discover nothing about this work nor about Austin's claim. Alois Hába was the European composer most commonly acknowledged for microtonal advances during the early twentieth century.

3. This expedient of mixing simple elements to achieve highly complex ones was, of course, the basis for mixing triads or two keys to achieve rich chords of tonal ambiguity. An early example of bitonal mixtures can be found in Strauss's *Also sprach Zarathustra,* as we shall note in Chapter 12. Although associated today largely with the Frenchman Milhaud, textures of mixed simultaneous keys came from sources as widespread as the Russians Stravinsky and Prokofiev and the Mexican Revueltas.

4. Russolo's fascinating *Manifesto* appears in Slonimsky's *Music Since 1900,* 3rd ed., 642–648.

5. In *Serial Composition and Atonality,* 38.

6. This is only one of many possible octatonic scales, in the generic sense of this term. It is the best known, perhaps because of its T–ST symmetry.

7. See Slonimsky's autobiography, *Perfect Pitch,* 176.

8. Abundant evidence shows, nonetheless, that Schoenberg began his first composition based on a

twelve-tone row in 1914. It was an unfinished symphony, parts of which ended up in *Jakobsleiter*. For an entertaining synopsis of the kinds of 12-note speculations that make the 1910–1925 era engaging, see Chapter 16 of Slonimsky, *Perfect Pitch*.

9. I assume my reader's understanding of dodecaphonic technique. A simple introduction to it can be found in the *Harvard Dictionary of Music*: "Twelve-tone Technique." The basis of Hauer's system of so-called *tropes* appears in his own works, in Carl Eschmann's *Changing Forms in Modern Music*, 1943, and in George Rochberg's "The Harmonic Tendency of the Hexachord." I trust that I can be forgiven for not mentioning every composer who employed some kind of series sub-structuring during the period in question. It was a popular solution to several problems.

10. Schoenberg biographer Stuckenschmidt disagrees, dating the first encounter, with Adolph Loos officiating, as 1919.

11. *Letters*, No. 79, 105–107.

12. Jacques Barzun, *Darwin, Marx, Wagner*, 14.

13. Stuckenschmidt, *Arnold Schoenberg*, 277.

14. In addition to the unfinished symphony mentioned earlier, Schoenberg certainly had composed dodecaphonic music before the *Suite*. For extensive discussion of this question see Hyde, "Musical Form and the Development of Schoenberg's Twelve-Tone Method"; Maegaard, *Studien zur Entwicklung des Dodekaphonen Satzes bei Arnold Schoenberg;* and Hamao, *The Origin and Development of Schoenberg's Twelve-Tone Method*. Opera 23, 24, and 25 were composed in complexly sporadic order during the same four-year period. Rufer, in *Composition with Twelve Tones*, 54–56, regarded 23 and 24 as dry runs for the more finished processes exemplified in Opus 25.

15. Stuckenschmidt, *Arnold Schoenberg*, 18 and 31.

16. MacDonald, *Schoenberg*, 60.

17. Schoenberg's conversion to Christianity preceded those of Karl Kraus and Gustav Mahler. See Alexander Ringer, "Arnold Schoenberg and the Prophetic Image," 26–38.

18. From conversations with Mr. Raksin.

19. In the introductory essay to Walter Benjamin's *Reflections*.

20. Mentioned in Joan Allen Smith, *Schoenberg and His Circle*, 41.

21. Kraus published a fortnightly newsletter in Vienna from 1899 to 1936. It was a kind of "*Wall Street Journal* of the arts and politics" called *Die Fackel* (*The Torch*). In addition, his essays could be read, along with the likes of such writers as Heinrich Mann and August Strindberg, in the influential arts weekly published in Berlin, *Die Sturm*.

22. To my knowledge this style-substance issue has been inexplicably ignored. While making sense in a literary object, where verbal accounts of extrinsic events occur, its application to the non-referential art of music remains at best problematic. It smacks of the Appearance-Reality dichotomy also treasured by Schoenberg.

23. John Wilcox argues ("The Beginnings of the *L'Art Pour L'Art*"), that the very idea of this intellectual cliché grew from a "fantastically careless and incompetent misreading" of Kantian aesthetic theory, especially the *Critique of Judgment* of 1790.

24. Freitag, "German Expressionism and Schoenberg's Self-Portrait."

25. Black and white reproductions of these can be seen in *Journal of the Arnold Schoenberg Institute* 2 (1978): 190–200.

26. Rochberg, *The Aesthetics of Survival*, 54.

27. Stuckenschmidt, *Arnold Schoenberg*, 88.

28. David Raksin, "Life with Charlie," 249.

29. Although the conjunction began, I suspect, with Rufer ("*Schönberg oder der konservativ Revolutionar*"), its aptness has led to repetition by many others. See Janik and Toulmin, *Wittgenstein's Vienna*, 250.

30. In *Schoenberg and the God Idea*, 52.

31. *Fin-de-Siecle Vienna*, 8.

32. Ibid., 9–10.

33. Professor Leichtentritt at the time was a faculty member in the Department of Music, Harvard University.

34. Letters, No. 180, 3 December 1938, from Los Angeles.

35. Printed in *Guidelines for a Ministry of Art*, ed. Adolph Loos, reprinted in *Style and Idea*, 369–373.

36. Perloff, *The Futurist Movement*, 6.

CHAPTER 3

Schoenberg's Controlling Assumptions

SEPARATING SOUL FROM SURFACE

Vigorous denial of an unacceptable status quo, and a struggle to rise above it, was a coveted principle passed on to Schoenberg by some of his most esteemed contemporaries. Architect Loos, together with painters Klimmt and Kokoshka (whose individual styles were quite different), and the literary badgerings of pundit Kraus, provided a strong influence for an individualistic approach to anything and everything. Indeed, it was probably Loos's cry for truth in architectural packaging (in his condemnation of the false facades of local Vienna) and Kraus's shrill lamentations over the dishonesty of contemporary prose that developed in the young composer a heightened sense of potential conflict between substance and ornamentation, between the elemental confrontation of what he would later discuss as style and idea. This problem plagued him. He was haunted by the difference he detected between the *Idea,* in the Platonic-Kantian sense, and its transmission, the contrast between what Heidiger would term Thing-in-Itself and its mere wrapping.

This strong will to separate the fruit from its husk had interesting consequences for the way he evaluated music. He was obsessed with discovering what he viewed as a work's ultimate qualities rather than be seduced by pretty surface trappings. Pianist Stefan Askenase once told Joan Allen Smith of Schoenberg's quaint preference for judging any orchestral composition in its piano arrangement, because in his mind "one could better find out what it really contained of musical quality."[1] In this we can detect echoes of Kraus, who as Schorske tells us "sought to restore the purity of the environment of many by removing all aesthetic pretensions from expository prose . . . by abolishing all embellishment."[2]

One cannot fail to recognize a certain puritanical streak in all of this, perhaps a grasping for purity and parsimony from the wont of embarrassing greed and waste that prevailed in pre-war Vienna. And perhaps most telling of all, Schoenberg shared with his older contemporaries, the intellectual pioneers of Vienna's elite—writer von Hofmansthal, psychiatrist Freud, painter Klimmt, philosopher Wittgenstein, physicist Mach—a diffuse sense that the border between the concerns of the individual and the external realities of the world could be negotiated.

Schoenberg was born a Jew. Vienna, like the Germany that would erupt in 1914 into what the Allies would call "the war to end all wars," smoldered with a persisting anti-semitism, on occasion breaking out into nasty incidents as revolting as they were unprovoked. Here was yet another burden this struggling composer could bear covert antagonism toward the religious heritage of his birth which, when added to the antipathy aroused by unfamiliar music in his fellow Viennese, could provide the motivation for a monumental life struggle.

ART AS BATTLE: THE IMPERATIVES OF CRUEL NECESSITY

Along with his powerfully felt premise of artistic progress and the abyss that seemed to separate the Idea from its Style, Schoenberg was convinced that the truly great artist—the genius, of whom there are precious few—must unquestioningly and unflinchingly suffer, Christlike, in the process of finding and revealing truth.[3]

There is a tinge of the Superman in Schoenberg's self-image and in his reverence for those whom he most admired, in an unmistakably Nietzschean ring to his ideas about the supreme artist, whose life goal must be to unmask and subdue the Philistines of this world. With Nietzsche his world was inhabited by Them and Us; the only acceptable regimen for Them was the struggle, an attempt to achieve the *Übermensch* condition of Us. For Schoenberg as for Nietzsche, the artist-genius was the top of this human pyramid, relating to ordinary humanity as humanity relates to the primates.

Schoenberg's public statements repeatedly rely on metaphors of struggle and battle in defining his function as a protagonist in the cause of modern music. Seldom did he miss an opportunity to observe that the way of art is not easy, that the way of the artist—again read *genius* or *chosen*—is pre-established for him to follow.[4] There are times when this path is too precious, too redolent of subtle perfection to be knowable by the casual or unprepared spectator, and it is above all fraught with deep anguish. In 1910 he identifies the true artists as those "who will wrestle with it; not those who blandly serve 'the dark powers', but of those who throw themselves into the machinery to grasp its construction."[5] And just nine years later, in the program notes for the first performance of his epochal Opus 11 piano pieces, he observes having passed a landmark on his journey toward artistic fulfillment in these deceptively tiny works, feeling that he has surpassed the conventions of an obsolete musical style (which, more simply put, alludes to textures in this music that are essentially amelodic, atonal).

In those notes he remarks that, in spite of the certainty of his goal, he can already feel the opposition he will have to overcome. And probably what seemed most depressing of all, he regrets that "even those who hitherto believed in me will not be willing to perceive the necessity of this development."[6] But undaunted, he had the same staying power Richard Elman found in James Joyce, the power to "read into his own inclinations the imperatives of cruel necessity."

Just after arriving in his adopted new home of the United States in 1934, Schoenberg refers to his "experiences from almost forty years in the battle of art."[7] On many subsequent occasions he projected the image of art itself as more ideological battle ground than sensory delight. This Schoenbergian will to suffer for artistic salvation has been remarked upon by Glenn Gould, whose assessment was that:

> In many a respect, indeed, Schoenberg was the stuff of which Ken Russell's screenplays are made. Despite a relatively quiet life on the domestic front . . . he gave full reign to an ego of Wagnerian proportions.[8]

This unceasing self-imposed struggle in the front-line trenches of art made close friendship with Schoenberg a succession of tests of loyalty, acerbic probes for tenuous allegiance, and purges of the unfaithful. Even Anton Webern and Erwin Stein, whose lives were in part committed to spreading the gospel of his greatness, were not spared his occasional wrath, his hurtful accusations of missteps from acceptable obeisance to the master. He was deeply troubled, rather than flattered, by the way Webern seemed to ape his every technical innovation, adding each new compositional trick to his own bag of creative resources.[9] It is embarrassing even now to read him lament, years later in a "putting-the-record-straight" essay, that "Webern immediately uses everything I do, plan, or say, so that . . . by now I haven't the slightest idea who I am."[10]

Schoenberg wished for, and expected, the same attitude of semiworship that he gave freely to those rare few, like Mahler, whom he considered to be of the exalted genius category. One of the most poignant disappointments in the documented history of the human ego is found in his letter to the younger Stein, long-time friend and devoted disciple, who had committed the egregious sin of writing an article praising a group of English composers without (for what would seem obvious reasons) even an indirect mention of A. Schoenberg. The affronted mentor bristles, asking: "Do you know if I am still alive? And if so, who told you? I would rather say that I belong to those whom people already want to forget."[11]

By nature and by early hard knocks he was, then, eminently prepared to do battle for what he saw as the future of music. That this struggle might alienate friends and colleagues, that it might lead to the derision of audiences and the abrasions of critics only served to confirm, for him, the rightness of his stand. He would prevail by the sheer force of intellectual, emotional, and moral conviction, wherever his assumptions might lead. For this monumentally talented man, these were the imperatives of cruel necessity. That his perspective might be based on tenuous data and false inference never seems to have entered his mind.

STRUCTURE AS ORGANISM

One of the dominant forces in Schoenberg's artistic outlook, and one consistent with his compositional practice, was the conviction that ultimate reality lurks beneath the surface of immediate experience. And it is tempting to see this "things are not quite what they seem to be" outlook as a metaphor for the Vienna of his day, where surface conditions of well-being concealed underlying decay. But for him the idea was more like the Platonic opposition of the Ideal and the Phenomenal. For the young Schoenberg, struggling to shape the future as well as his own career, it was the notion that the essence of reality is far more complex than our limited sensory machinery can directly absorb, too hidden to be perceived at first glance. And thus the value of truly great music could reside only in that which arose from hidden connecting links, the presence of ties divined from deep-seated wizardry. Too complex even for the artist's rational calculations, these kinds of embedded tissues of kinship were posited more through subconscious processes than through calculation. More than mere craft, they were the products of genius in touch with the divine.

This affinity for the concealed was manifested most forthrightly in Schoenberg's special regard for the potency of organicism in music, the idea that well-ordered music is like a complex biological structure, its parts organized in traceable, although frequently concealed, relationships. It was the great composer's job, in this view, to order sounds in systematic ways for which connections between parts, even if widely separated or tenuously related, could be found. These could in some cases be unashamedly arcane, and for Schoenberg so much the better, so much more the data of the deeply profound. With supreme effort and patience, however, one could nonetheless make the necessary discoveries of unimagined riches.

In part related to the public successes of contemporary biology and in part a product of his era's evolutionary perspective, he shared this predilection for subtle networks of relationships with several of his contemporaries.[12] At its best, this approach to understanding was a prized gift to his students. One from the Schwarzwald School in Berlin reported that painstaking, detailed analysis always preceded performance, "until the whole thing began to have a context—to have an organic development, to become an organic whole—before I realized that in the smallest detail of that sonata, the totality of that sonata is contained."[13] But at its worst, his outlook could lead him to find marvelous organic ties as an excuse for music otherwise short on justifying virtues; at other times it acted as the qualifying difference between the masterful and the pedestrian. The mere presence (or sometimes a *felt* presence that defied rational disclosure) of these subcutaneous affinities—a duplicated rhythm here, a returning pitch there, a camouflaged hint of an earlier motif somewhere else—was sufficient cause for the imprimatur of greatness.[14]

For Schoenberg, these remarkable structural ties were inexplicable by familiar compositional technique; they were instead the product of intuitive genius, or, as he so colorfully put it, as the "subconsciously received gift from the Supreme Com-

mander."[15] Their talismanic role for him was consonant with, and perhaps inseparable from, his more general notion that some connection bears between the complex
or difficult and truly great art. In this connection one can only wonder with biologist
Peter Medawar about "what was the origin of the philosophically self-destructive
belief that obscurity makes a prima-facie case for profundity."[16]

THE CASE OF THE TWO THEMES FROM OPUS 9

I can best illustrate Schoenberg's penchant for organicism by his discovery of
concealed unity he had always "felt" to be present, after some twenty years of
searching, within the themes of his *Kammersymphonie, Opus 9.* In revealing this
triumph of instinct over calculation, he shows the first two principal themes of the
work's movement.

EXAMPLE 4. First and second themes, Schoenberg, *Kammersymphonie,* Op. 9. Used
by permission of Belmont Music Publishers.

There follows one of the most provocative displays of analytical legerdemain
imaginable, remarkable intrathematic identities Schoenberg doubts could have been
crafted by deliberation of intellect. Let us note with care what he claims here, for
similar a posteriori reasoning underlies many recondite explanations of the dodecaphonic repertory, an organicism in an art so delicately poised at the time-bound limits
of our perceptual awareness.

His argument is basically simple and direct. It is that the primitive power of his
subconscious guided him to create an organically united set of themes. The second
theme, he holds, is demonstrable progeny of the first. Indeed, the second theme is
drawn from the principal notes of its antecedent, not directly but by melodic inversion, as shown in Example 5.

Faced with these derivations, we advisedly pause to reflect on several questions,
the kinds of questions that beg of asking when claims are made of any perceived
object. We shall pursue these questions only far enough to accomplish two ends: first
to reveal the potential speciousness of such an exercise, and second to suggest the
inherent weakness of representing the substance of musical reality as necessarily
more complex, more tedious, more deeply lined with structural mystery than raw
perception may lead one to expect.

EXAMPLE 5. Schoenberg's derivation of the second theme from the first, *Kammersymphonie*.

A hard look at Schoenberg's first theme leads to the first question: Why is G♯ so principal that it supersedes the other six notes of measure one and its preceding upbeat figure of a quarter-measure? Perhaps the G♯ was chosen because it is the first accented note of the measure (both metrically and agogically). But then we must wonder why the D, articulated five times in the first two measures and consuming one and two-thirds beats, is not at least equal in importance. In fact, the first five pulses here appear to form a straightforward decorative thrust within the space of the two Ds that frame the melody's opening (through the first beat of measure two). Then should D not be a principal tone also? And what about the designated F♯ (of sixteenth-note duration) in measure two? Is it really more principal than all of those Ds? If G♯ is a principal pitch in the first theme because of its rhythmic accentuation, why in the second theme is the pickup (and thus unaccented) A♭ a principal note? Should we reopen our questioning about the opening D of the first theme, since it provides the same metric function there?

These questions are not even obliquely considered by Schoenberg. They suggest that his discovery came from after-the-fact conceptual ruminations rather than from a summary of predictable melodic perception. An analysis of the second theme made according to principles consistent with those used in analyzing the first cannot yield the organic togetherness Schoenberg demanded of it. Even the dimmest shadow of organic ties vanishes when we compare principal notes from the first few measures of both melodies derived according to the same criteria (see Example 6).

In combing through his two themes to demonstrate obscure ties, Schoenberg overlooked the most imposing pitch feature of his first theme, a property that most audibly controls the theme's pitch structure. It is the whole tone progression of rising steps that channels the line's curve. This most salient encompassing pitch matrix for the theme was perhaps irrelevant for Schoenberg only because no such pattern is remotely concealed in his second theme.

EXAMPLE 6. Alternative reductions of the first and second themes, first three measures, *Kammersymphonie.*

ARTISTIC TRUTH AND THE COMMUNICATION BARRIER

Consistent with and related to his organicist bent was Schoenberg's conviction that the truth, the "right way," is not easily recognized or followed. Indeed, one of the ruling precepts of his life was the staggering difficulty, if not sheer impossibility, of communicating life's more profound truths, humanity's deeper feelings.

This notion of a frustrating barrier to communication, this unresolvable tension that divorces Idea from its worldly representation, can be traced, of course, to Platonic origins. It is dramatically embodied in Schoenberg's unfinished opera *Moses und Aron,* where the central dramatic conflict involves the disparity between the actuality of God and the people's knowledge of God. And one infers that this ultimate blockage or dilution of understanding is a direct product of the otherworldly nature of divine things—perhaps the music of geniuses as well as the thoughts in God's mind.

As Pamela White explains in her discussion of Schoenberg's God idea, this proposition is most directly stated just prior to the point where the composer left off his work on the opera, where at the end of Act II Moses addresses God as "Inconceivable God! Inexpressible, ambiguous Idea!" As White observes, the nominalism of Kant and Schopenhauer (with the contrast of *Vorstellung,* or Idea, and *Darstellung,* the Idea's representation) resonates loudly, equating Schoenberg's Ultimate Idea with Kantian *Noumena,* which can never be directly known in experience.[17]

And this disheartening state of affairs, wherein non-geniuses are doomed to a shadowy world of awareness without full comprehension, is implicit every time Schoenberg echoes the belief that "nothing can be known in its essence but only incompletely through the senses." Matters are even more complex, drearier. Like his literary mentor Karl Kraus (and not unlike the later Theodor Adorno), Schoenberg assumed that lofty thought must necessarily be expressed in commensurately complex ways: the more profound the substance the more obtuse its utterance.[18]

The unbridgeable chasm that separates the thing-in-itself from its representation is expressed in a less abstract way in Schoenberg's pitting of Style against Idea, an issue raised briefly in earlier discussions. In his 1946 essay "New Music, Outmoded Music, Style and Idea," he bares his central thesis which finds musical essence divided from its human presence, its existence in cognitive time. Style in this sense is regarded as the secondary (although essential) carrier of the musical gesture, not as part and parcel of the gesture itself. Note well that Schoenberg is not talking here about a musical analogue for the actual physical stuff of an Albert Ryder painting, whose surface of now-cracked pigment nonetheless projects the essence of the painting's original conception—its Idea—if in a flawed manner. Nor is he alluding to the blemished performance of a composition, wherein the inaccurate interpreter corrupts the composer's true conception, his pure Idea. On the contrary, he refers to the original message itself, that which the composer conceives for posterity, as a whole whose elements are somehow separable, that which is *Idea* from its sonic representation. Quite a different matter.

This distinction recalls that made between cognition and *Affekt,* a position briefly fashionable among academics during the later 1960s and early 1970s. (Today it seems patently clear that those who tinkered with such matters would have been hard pressed to show that they had on occasion experienced a cognition without an accompanying *Affekt,* or vice versa.) Yet any serious attempt to separate within an art object such things as pure Idea from mere carriers of its Style warrants skepticism, no matter how fetching the notion may at first seem to be in purely theoretical terms. Isolation of even the timbre of the clarinet from the Thing-in-itself that is Mozart's *Clarinet Concerto* does violence to the reality of the music, just as the neutralization of linear distortion in an El Greco painting would be a comical misrepresentation of structure. One might as well rob a sonnet of its adjectives. But Schoenberg persisted in his separation of style and idea; and this enabled him to argue for a musical content that was eternal, a content that, like his organicism, confirmed aesthetic superiority.

This was another facet of his character that bolstered the notion that he, as an artist and trafficker in Ideas rather than mere Styles, enjoyed contact with a realm of being which could be only dimly perceived by ordinary humanity. And we should not overlook that this artistic Messianism provided a powerful thrust in the turbulent intellectual circles of 1910–1950. When his music was met with hostility, or when his ideas failed to fit with the manifest realities of an external world, the very force of his conviction could still maintain his staying power. Like Aristotle's poetic truth, Schoenberg's Truth was conjured from a deeper and more privileged insight. And he furthermore assumed that the artist-genius's insights could reveal what ought to be, consistent with nature's *intentions,* rather than of nature's *actions,* which at times were misspent and flawed.[19]

Let us take stock of these disparate yet related aspects of Schoenberg's character and his perspective on the artistic and intellectual issues of his formative years. Our concern is primarily with these as they reflect on his role as the shaper of a larger musical culture.

Schoenberg was an activist. He cared deeply about issues of the mind and emotions; he especially cared about music, both as sonic object and as philosophical issue. He was one of a loosely knit tribe of Viennese intellectuals, one of an admirable faction whose members read and listened and talked and then acted in some purposeful way upon the most pressing matters of the day, who were prepared to lead rather than follow. He shared with many of his contemporaries the conviction that change was not just welcome: in art as in biology, change was inevitable. And it was his further conviction that it is the great artist's responsibility to control change, guiding the evolutionary process to ensure that the "higher" goals of an art are reached. It is the genius who effectively advances the evolutionary process, who rightly channels this inevitable change, who resolutely follows what Schoenberg, with his affinity for Christian metaphor, occasionally referred to as "the way of the cross."[20]

Both as a composer and as a defender of his perspective, he became by 1907 an embittered member of the "pure avant-garde," as William Gass defined it, joining ranks with some of his most auspicious contemporaries, a formidable group whose lot was not, by its nature, well-calculated for making friends and influencing people. In Gass's appraisal, they

> may pay a dreadful price for the role they have chosen to play, but if they are going to be a permanent part of 'the' avant-garde . . . they must remain wild and never neglect an opportunity to attack their trainers; above all, it is the hand that feeds them which must be bitten.[21]

Schoenberg provides a riveting case history of how an individual can fix on a cause, eventually so intertwining his personal anxieties and motivations and goals with external affairs that the two become indistinguishable. His early economic, personal, and professional suffering led him to adopt the "burden"—the "cross he must bear"—of preserving the Germanic domination of art music. Metaphorical or not, Schoenberg's allusions to suffering, to fighting the battle against indifference, untruth, and sham led to a creeping paranoia that could feed the beast, continually reconfirming the heady conviction that art music, thanks to his help, was progressing on schedule.

Unlike many artists who concentrate their total intellectual and emotional drives into producing actual works of art, Schoenberg proved early in his career that the battle he would mount would engage theory as well as practice. Thus he produced throughout his life a remarkable record of theoretical documents, some pedagogical, some descriptively speculative, others transparently defensive of his own innovations. His output was not of the prodigious bulk achieved by Richard Wagner, nor was his range of subject so expansive. But that these two successive musical giants shared a gift for literary expression, as well as musical innovation, is in itself an uncommon surprise of history.

Ideas were important to Schoenberg. His native mental sharpness and tendency toward abrasive profundity, his youthful contacts with ideas as the barter of intellectual negotiation, and the very intellectual richness of his native Vienna made philosophical and literary matters a central part of his makeup. In this respect he was music theorist as much as composer. Each role supported and fed off the other. Our main goal in what follows is to show that his theoretical claims—many of them formulated as apologia for his compositional actions—lacked basis in fact, whether historical, psychological, or physical. Whatever posterity may determine to have been the merit of his innovations as a composer, the rationale he devised for his music was derived from untenable hypotheses.

NOTES

1. Joan Allen Smith, *Schoenberg and His Circle*, 94. Also see page 85.

2. Schorske, *Fin-de-Siecle Vienna*, 339.

3. For Schoenberg, discovery of the beautiful was not the highest priority: he sought the truth. Just how the criterion of truth is meaningful and applicable to the music experience, as it can be to a verbal proposition, would make an interesting study in its own right. Schoenberg may have had an answer, but he did not share it.

4. See his essay "The Young and I," *Style and Idea*, 94.

5. In "Aphorismen," *Schöpferische Konfessionen*, Willi Reich, ed., 12.

6. Reported in Wellesz, *Arnold Schoenberg*, 27.

7. *Style and Idea*, 176.

8. In *The Glenn Gould Reader*, 142.

9. Schoenberg was especially rankled by the rumor that Webern rather than he had been the first to conceive of *Klangfarbenmelodie*.

10. *Style and Idea*, 484.

11. December 1947, as reported by Stuckenschmidt, *Arnold Schoenberg*, 486–487.

12. Rudolf Reti (1885–1957) is probably the most obvious, but Schenker's theory of the *Ursatz* is the most impressive example of the Romantic ardor for an elusive ultimate reality. Both his *Urlinie* and *Grundbrechung* are elaborate distillations of surface events whose discovery demands painstaking search following years of indoctrination in relevant conceptual prescriptions.

13. As told Joan Allen Smith by Lona Truding, *Schoenberg and His Circle*, 97.

14. Chief evidence for him of Brahms's progressiveness is the asymmetry of phrase structures often found, even in some of his earlier works. And Beethoven's mastery of organic tissue is for Schoenberg revealed thematically in such "prophetic" note successions as the Db, C, D figure in the first measure of the Opus 95 Quartet, which Schoenberg finds "reincarnated" as retrogrades and mirror images in the work's subsequent movements. See "Brahms the Progressive," *Style and Idea*, 416–424.

15. *Style and Idea*, 222. Also discussed in another essay of the same collection, page 85. The Platonic aura of Schoenberg's perspective is too evident to pass up. In the *Ion* dialogue Plato has Socrates saying: "For all good poets . . . compose their beautiful poems not by art, but because they are inspired and possessed." *The Dialogues of Plato*, 285–297.

16. Medawar, *Pluto's Republic*, 21.

17. White, *Schoenberg and the God Idea*, 70.

18. This is akin to his affinity for hidden or subtle organic relationships of the kind we discussed earlier.

19. See Richard McKeon's discussion of Aristotle's rhetoric and poetic in *The Basic Works of Aristotle*, xxix–xxxxii, or Peter Medawar's comments in *Pluto's Republic*, 52–58.

20. This was one of his favorite "hard times" metaphors. See *Style and Idea*, 258, for one notable instance.

21. Gass, "Vicissitudes of the Avant-Garde," 65.

PART II

Schoenberg as Theorist

CHAPTER 4

The Tonal Basis in Nature's Chord

Most people today who know Arnold Schoenberg at all know of him only as an influential composer, a *great composer*. And yet he left behind an imposing body of prose accounts of music: books, essays, and letters covering a wide range of matters dealing for the most part with aesthetics and aspects of musical structure. Many of these were apologia for his own special role in music, in that insuperable evolutionary chain he envisioned. In this he joined the ranks of music theorists, whose professional goals, although not incompatible with, are quite different from those of a composer. Keeping in mind this related but different professional hat worn by Schoenberg, we digress briefly here to provide some background perspective, ideas that for professional theorists will survey relevant but at times familiar territory.

THE THEORY OF MUSIC

Theories of music attempt to explain both the objective substance and the subjective response to the art, to whatever degree those presumed realms may be separable. Of all the disciplines of knowledge, none enjoys a more venerable history; it is hard to find an imposing intellectual figure of Western civilization who did not grapple at some time with the meaning of music, as object of human apprehension or as one of the significant trappings of culture. Scratch the surface of most philosophers from any period of history and you will uncover traces of musing about the nature of music, its materials, and how they are mixed.

The corpus of music theory produced within the century of Schoenberg's birth wore two faces. One represented re-stirrings of and footnotes to the century-old framework left by Rameau; the other represented attempts to replace in some way the French master's physico-mathematical models, carefully argued systems of thought and procedure as disparate as the Hegelian-based dialectics of Moritz Hauptmann (1792–1868) and the prosaic didactics of Ebenezer Prout (1835–1909). Although as a discipline music theory may not have achieved an impressive record of final answers, by the end of the century it had impressively settled in on a body of standard and provocative questions. As a discipline, it had at least risen to the sophistication of self-inquiry, especially of seeking definitions for its own major premises. One of the most astute theorists of Schoenberg's formative years, Hugo Riemann,[1] defined the field of music theory in 1898 by what it studied. In the very opening of his essay "Musical Logic," he claims that music theory must

> investigate the natural laws which consciously or unconsciously rule the creation of the art and present them in a system of logically coherent rules.[2]

The history of theoretical speculation carries the weight of some earnest wool-gathering about music's "sources" and "derivations" that are no more substantial in basis than astrology or pyramidology.[3] But despite some embarrassing pontifications, these earnest struggles by some of the ablest minds of the past to explain the dynamics of music compel our admiration. It is wise to keep in mind that the fleeting nature of the object makes its rules hard to catch. Our methods seem doomed by the very nature of the quarry; freezing music's motion destroys its essence, defying our attempts to apprehend what we value most.

THE HARMONIC SERIES AS NATURE'S SOURCE

Every historical period has its perspective, its local guidelines to problem-solving. The assumption nearest and dearest to most nineteenth-century theorists' hearts had been passed on to them mainly by Rameau: the harmonic or overtone series, which, replacing the senario of Renaissance system building, has persisted as a point of departure for theoretical speculation for over two centuries. An understanding of precisely how the harmonic series relates to pitch ordering has been the goal of a host of theorists since Rameau.

Although striking correspondences clearly exist between series components (partials) and music practice, the two have endured a rocky relationship. Over the past half-century, speculation on their exact bearing have run the gamut from Paul Hindemith's reaffirmation of the series' primacy to all music[4] to Milton Babbitt's haughty dismissal of what he refers to as "the overtone follies."[5] Clearly, this small but conspicuous corner of musical thought has not yet been swept clean; the very best of intentions have not yet managed to crack the code, even though the data have been carefully sifted many times.

The series played a decisive role in the way Schoenberg thought about music, especially as it related to his conception of music's evolutionary development of pitch content and pitch relationships. Let us begin by recalling some crucial evidence about this persistently fascinating aspect of aural experience.

Its most significant characteristic is its ubiquity. Human ears rarely hear an isolated sound for which the harmonic series is not present.[6] And this sweeping claim embraces more sounds than we normally deal with as "musical," from our vacuum cleaner's drive to the pre-takeoff whine of an airliner's auxiliary power unit. Hundreds of its manifestations discretely surround our waking hours, usually without our slightest awareness. It is the very shape of sound. Our aural experience yields for us a compound as a simple unity; we *hear* a cast of a multitude as a timbral singularity. Our awareness of the single focal point is a product more of perceptual habit than of inaccurate or incomplete audition. We generalize our experience, usually fixing on the series' fundamental partial, even if it is not physically present in the signal. For instance, given a tone consisting of the sinusoidal components G3, D4, G4, B4, and D5, we instead "hear" G2.

The actual pattern formed by the partials has, over the centuries, remained equally impressive. Expressible as a set of ratios, this commanding mathematical potential provided a powerful temptation for speculation for eighteenth-century rationalists. It was these two elegant potentials, the measurable presence of the series "in nature" and its partials' progression by natural numbers that so endeared it to all who, following the renown of Newton, hoped to explain the mechanics of music. It was not a matter to be passed off lightly.

We shall return for a more critical look at the harmonic series in Chapter 10, after we have reviewed Schoenberg's ideas and the role the series played in some of them. An appreciation for the series' full complement shall be added there, emphasizing the inseparability of intervallic quality from the collection of partials *as total pattern*.

SCHOENBERG'S RATIONALE

Schoenberg probably devoted more hours of his life to contemplating the relation of musical tones to one another than to articulating his hypotheses in composing.[7] First came his monumental *Harmonielehre* in 1911, only a dozen years after his compositional success with *Verklärte Nacht*, some nine years after his initial orchestral work *Pelleas und Melisande*. Hailed by disciples as a refreshing masterpiece in a field of stifling aridity, this book is still regarded by many musicians as a testament to its author's unique grasp of musical properties and how their organization can be accounted for.

Most of his formative theoretical knowledge was learned from his earliest teachers at the *Realschule* in Vienna, although these formal studies were certainly preceded by exchanges with early mentors such as the violinist Oskar Adler and his only acknowledged composition teacher, Alexander Zemlinsky (who became his brother-in-law upon Schoenberg's first marriage, in 1901).

These sources naturally led him to a perspective of musical structure as conservative as his political outlook. Indeed, his explanations for the origins, nature, and interlockings of musical properties were derived from ideas one could find in the respected texts of his heritage, those of Johann August Dürnberger (*Elementarlehrbuch der Harmonik und Generalbass-lehre*, 1841), Simon Sechter (*Generalbass-schule*, 1830 and *Die Grundsätze der Musikalischen Komposition*, 1853–54), Hugo Riemann (*Handbuch der Harmonielehre*, 1887, among others), Hermann Helmholtz

(Part II of his *Lehre von Tonempfindungen,* 1863), or August Halm (*Harmonielehre,* 1902). As Robert Wason has claimed, a large share of Schoenberg's tradition, and especially Sechter's fundamental bass tradition, came to him through his acquaintance with Anton Bruckner's lectures at the Vienna conservatory (which Schoenberg perhaps came upon secondhand, since he did not study with Bruckner).[8] His implicit debts went largely unacknowledged. His disdain for Riemann (and most of the German tradition) is well known, but his Austrian predecessors did not fare much better. As late as 1950, we find him saying, in an essay on Bach, that

> today's musical education is not always benefited by the tradition of the great line of Viennese teachers and theorists—the line of Porpora, Fux, Albrechtsberger, Sechter, Bruckner and Schenker.[9]

Surprisingly, Schoenberg's first exposition of the nature of music, his *Harmonielehre,* does nothing to herald Schoenbergian things to come. Not only does his serial future remain without intimation, but nothing is said directly about the free atonality that had begun to emerge in his compositions during the previous five years. Consistent with his lifelong insistence that Bach, Mozart, Beethoven, and Brahms marked the true path to musical enlightenment, his harmony book quarries much of the same conceptual lode worked by most other authors in that market, from Rameau's *Traité* of 1722 through the *Harmonielehre* of Schenker's *Neue Musicalische Theorien und Fantasien* of 1906.

For all of these theorists a simple encompassing equation prevailed: Music = Harmony. And this especially held for the kind of harmony that could be induced, by hook or crook, from the harmonic series through selective choice, whether by acoustical "demonstration," invocation of the historic senario, or by turning to numerology. Thus books dealing exclusively with the subject of chords and chord connections were revered as the exhaustive barings of music's bones, except for the processes of voice leading better accounted for by the rules of counterpoint. Except for the figured bass tradition, strong in Vienna, most eighteenth-century theorists were convinced that counterpoint also derived wholly from harmonic principles. Harmony, as it were, became implicitly known as a sufficient basis for the totality of music's structure; and, with tangential exceptions, Schoenberg's theory of harmony was not different, either in basic outlook or in expectation.

Surprise awaits one who reads Schoenberg's 1911 accounting of the origin and nature of the major scale from natural causes, an explanation at least a century old and to this day far from credible. Its essential message was that the major scale and the minor scale are *derived* from the controlling triads of the key, I, V, and IV. We can further marvel at the hegemony of harmony when he observes that

> it will surely benefit us here . . . to derive the nature of chord connections strictly from the nature of the chords themselves, putting aside rhythmic, melodic and other considerations.[10]

In this Schoenberg perpetuates the most damaging error of traditional theory-making by viewing a collection of tones, here the chord, as if it has perceptual meaning outside of time. This split of the musical substance into two realms predictably colors every conclusion he reaches, whether about church modes, consonance-dissonance, non-harmonic tones, or even the apprehension of a pitch collection (like a twelve-note series) as a tonal *Gestalt*.

SCHOENBERG AND THE HARMONIC SERIES

Of course, an experiential fact as ineluctable as the harmonic series could not be ignored. Schoenberg recognized in that incomparable matrix the same musical significance remarked upon by just about every writer since Father Mersenne (who discovered it as acoustical fact) and Rameau (who first used it to divulge the secrets of harmony). Unfortunately, he also perpetuates the same non sequiturs, attributing to the series more procreative and sustaining powers than it can bear.

Rather than behold and apply the series as holistic pattern, as the fixed totality of relations it is, he follows his predecessors' footsteps down an inviting but blind alley: the series is made a tonal ladder of separable intervals, a collection of individual rungs whose dismantling into parts becomes a model for pitch organization. The perfect fifth, for example, is assumed to possess certain harmonic properties exclusive of its membership within the series. With those forerunners he fails to recognize the central point: the series is an irreducible pattern, its full and indissoluble complement a potential guiding paradigm, much as converging lines in vision can provide the vanishing point of linear perspective. If one line is removed from a compound of lines, it loses the property of *convergence*; it may even be unable to support the same point of convergence projected by the compound. Similarly, a pitch interval derives its vectorial meaning, its potential "rootedness," from the compound which is the harmonic series. Each interval can have tonal meaning only as the considered part of a larger context. We shall discuss this property in greater depth in Chapter 10.

There are echoes of Rameau's lingering voice, especially from the *Génération Harmonique* of 1737, each time Schoenberg tells us that tones lower in the series contribute more, the more remote contribute less. So he reaffirms that the lower intervals of the series represent, or provide music with, the most influential tonal relationships. The perfect fifth is the first, after the replicative octave; it furnishes the central girder of Schoenberg's tonal system, the dominant above tonic. And so far, so good. But then, perhaps yielding to the temptation of the fictional *über-unter* mirror symmetry[11] that became the nemesis of late nineteenth-century German music theory, he niftily displaces from the series this undergirding interval of the fifth, transposing it to below the central tone to provide the system's subdominant.[12] In this he contradicts the very system he employs as his tonal basis, just as Schenker had done six years earlier (and Rameau almost two centuries earlier). Each interval—as here in the case of the perfect fifth—is regarded as an isolable relationship, possessing powers separate from its harmonic archetype. See Example 7.

EXAMPLE 7. Schoenberg's derivation of the tonal system from the *Überklang-Unterklang* structure.

In this Schoenberg engages explanatory resources learned from his venerable predecessors when he observes that,

> by using C as a midpoint, then its situation in the key of C major can be described by reference to two forces, one which pulls downward, toward F, the other upward, toward G.[13]

He repeats these gravitational metaphors as self-evident fact, even though most other theorists (including Hugo Riemann) had previously abandoned all hope of finding empirical confirmation of such "pulls," especially downward, in nature's mother lode.

And thus the point of departure taken in *Harmonielehre* for showing music's basis in the haven of empiricism was hardly new; it was the same shaky foundation that had supported a multitude of eighteenth- and nineteenth-century sins. Any attempt to reveal the pitch organization of music as "generated by" or as "derived from" the harmonic series by using isolated intervals as building blocks was foredoomed.[14] Like those of his contemporaries and predecessors, Schoenberg's tone-collecting trip up through the partials discovered only that Mother Nature was not quite so bountifully obliging as first imagined, leaving "artistry" responsible for some of music's more elemental treasures (like minor harmony, the subdominant relationship, the minor scale).

Nevertheless, there are sufficient bounties to be discovered in the series of partials to keep Schoenberg busy. Exercising the will to "derive from nature what nature provides," he describes the historical development of the major and minor scales as the reduction of *natural* relations to *manageable* ones.

> It is necessary to use in the course of a piece only those sounds (*Klange*) and successions of sounds . . . whose relations to the fundamental tone of the key, to the tonic of the piece, can be grasped without difficulty.[15]

And, of course, his phrase "grasped without difficulty" indirectly refers to intervals whose ranking locations lie low in the harmonic series.

There is even more to discover, for the series provides a guide to consonance and dissonance. As Schoenberg observes, "consonances are the sounds closer to the fundamental, dissonances those farther away . . . their comprehensibility is graduated accordingly, since the nearer ones are easier to comprehend than those farther off."[16] Or, we might say in other words (more explicitly Pythagorean in tone) that the simpler numerical ratios represent more consonant intervals, complex ratios more dissonant.[17] But we soon find with Schoenberg (as with Schenker before him) that art and artist once more must enter a scene nature doesn't tread. For instance,

> The minor mode is thus purely synthetic, a product of art, and attempts to represent it as something given in nature are pointless.[18]

And we are left wondering if perhaps that underfifth, the IV, might not also be a bit on the synthetic side, seeing that it too cannot readily be found in the series.

These flights of theoretical fancy remind us that Schoenberg's views of the musical basis are no more (and certainly no less) defensible than the poetic verbosities, the flights of arithmetic symbolism, the slanted empiricism that marred some of the most confident pronouncements of his era and before. Indeed, Schoenberg's explanation of music's tonal basis offers nothing that was not recoverable from the treatises of the Leipzig and Vienna academics of his time and just before—the theorists and "aestheticians" he so openly disclaimed. None of his output reveals the conservative thinker more vividly than these revelations of music's presumed sources in the fabric of nature. In this he was every bit a man of his own time, albeit a monumentally gifted one. This rare blend led novelist Thomas Mann to indict the *Harmonielehre* as an "extraordinary mixture of pious tradition and revolution."[19]

There is nothing inherently wrong about absorbing the ideas of one's times. Far from it. But it is important to acknowledge that although Schoenberg's intuitive *understanding* of the dynamics of music may have been exceedingly perceptive, his grasp of their structural wherewithal, qua unified system, was as weakened by half truths and non sequiturs as those of his contemporaries.[20] Our disappointment in his limited originality and insight as a theorist lies less in the substance of his errors than in the obstinacy and allure of his message. His first principles formed a shaky basis for his subsequent conclusions, conclusions passed on to posterity with the confidence of a biblical prophet.

A BLINKERED VIEW OF THE MUSIC OF HISTORY

Although he frequently refers to the musical tradition and to the continuing artistic chain of which his own labors formed a major link, Schoenberg's knowledge of the music of history, even of pre-eighteenth-century German music, was severely limited. It is hard not to conclude from his musical comments and from the repertoire he draws upon for illustrations that his acquaintance did not extend much beyond what had been composed between 1700 and 1900, and the first century of that period was furnished for him mainly with music by Bach and Mozart.

This limitation was mitigated somewhat when, after 1918, he enlarged his frame of reference by learning some of the music of peers from other countries, Debussy, Ravel, De Falla, Prokofiev, Stravinsky, et al., whose works were performed in the concerts he organized as the *Verein für musikalische Privataufführungen*. But throughout his career the examples he turned to for explaining technical details are drawn from the Bach-Haydn-Mozart-Beethoven-Schubert-Schumann-Brahms orbit. So when he speaks of wishing to preserve the glorious tradition of German leadership in the larger world, no immense span of human history is at stake.

It is unlikely that he knew music composed by some of Bach's forerunners, even those of Germanic ties, and especially not foreigners such as Monteverdi, Machaut, Lassus, Morley, Landini, or any of those illustrious composers' contemporaries.[21] This narrow perspective of precedents was maintained by an uncharacteristically closed mind, one sometimes encountered in persons who in all other aspects of life are open and free minded, curious to a fault to confront the unknown. Pianist Glenn Gould once observed that Schoenberg "had little interest in music prior to the time of Bach, was suspicious (and possibly a bit envious) of such musicologically astute colleagues as Krenek and Webern," adding as well that he "regarded medieval modes as 'a primeval error of the human spirit.' "[22]

Such an insular approach to music could scarcely fail to leave its mark on one's way of thinking about compositional techniques and resources, mainly because of the confined sampling of structural alternatives known for dealing with any problem. For a person of the twentieth century, it was too limited to support the kinds of encompassing declarations and predictions about music that Schoenberg made. Biographer Malcolm MacDonald regrets this confining base of understanding by noting that in his conceptions Schoenberg was even indifferent to the merits of those who developed the same tradition in a different style (such as Kurt Weill, who for him was a musical nobody).[23]

THE HARMONIC BIAS

It is critical to remember that tonality for Schoenberg was inextricably associated with such ideas as key system, major and minor scales, and what the twentieth century has come to enshrine as "functional harmony."[24] This latter concept is especially important, for Schoenberg speaks repeatedly of tonality as a product of scale degrees or of chord movement. He further refers, over the years, to non-chordal music (such as chant) as devoid of tonality.

In *Harmonielehre* he observes that "melodically the key is represented by the scale, harmonically by the diatonic chords,"[25] although just 124 pages earlier he has told us that the scale is itself *derived* from the principal chords of a key, the I, IV, and V triumvirate. Schoenberg's alleged derivation, like all such explications of the tonal system, harbors a singular major flaw: it employs the term it defines in its definition.

To say that "the C major scale is derived from the principal chords (I, IV, V) of C major" is, to say the least, tautological.

But the scales and harmonic system of functional chords are only representatives or resource prototypes rather than the actuality of tonal dynamics which exist in real music; they are not that which is prior to and causal of tonality. Schoenberg only hints on occasion at what conditions prevail in "harmonic music" to produce the inequity of pitch focus that is tonality, and these few hints are wholly circumscribed by harmonic (i.e., chordal) considerations. Here again he followed the lead of nineteenth-century theorists, who in turn were reiterating Rameau's premise that the harmonic triad, as posited by nature in the senario, is the singular source of musical order.

For Schoenberg, tonality is represented most unequivocally by the tonic triad, whose focal role is confirmed by the counterbalancing of its subdominant and dominant chords. All other chords are entities of lesser or greater harmonic strength, but their roles are not as determining, not as inexpendable or irreplaceable as the beautifully poised trio of I, IV, V. And those three chords constitute the pitch firmament, as received opinion would have it. Let us observe for the moment only that exclusively harmonic properties (which here means combinations of chords) are operative in this definition of musical controls.

MELODY AS AN AGENT OF TONALITY

The complete hierarchy of harmonic givens, branching out from the tonic chord, dominated Schoenberg's thinking about tonality. Although he made occasional passing remarks about how melody might support a chord succession in creating his scheme of pitch focus, he must have felt no need to describe just how melodic contour or the play of rhythmic accents within a passage can join with chords (or act as confirming or denying agents of chords) to co-embody joint structure. Since, as he made clear, "every tone tends to become tonic, every triad tends to become a tonic triad,"[26] one major task for the composer is to ensure the crucial balance between chords that will maintain an intended tonic without the encroachment by another tonic, producing an unintended modulation.

At one point in *Harmonielehre* Schoenberg even observes that melody alone, when it directly outlines an appropriate chord, can project a tonality without support from the chords of an accompaniment.[27] But the implication of this discussion (and of the melodic examples used in support) is that the power of the harmonic triad, as tonic, exerts the exclusive force, even in these melodic instances. That "non-harmonic" figurations (bearing no evident chordal associations) might play a role in the pitch focus of tonality seems never to have occurred to him. Curiously, the *process* by which a tonic chord acquires its unique status (and thus the related designations of subdominant and dominant as well) is never discussed. It is merely postulated, ex cathedra.

TONAL, TONALITY; ATONAL, ATONALITY

Although dispensing with tonality was just one aspect of the structural renovation Schoenberg sought, it was the most broadly embracing musical property to feel his unique touch. It became by far the most discussed technical aspect of modern music from 1910 until well past the half-century. The adjective we all use to describe most of his music, *atonal*,[28] became for some critics more a word of aesthetic condemnation than of structural description. Schoenberg himself despised it, his objections based mostly on linguistic grounds.

But *tonal* was itself an unfortunate term, since it literally (as Schoenberg was quick to remind us) denoted nothing more than possession of the quality tone. Jargon of the music community nonetheless had supplied it to represent the attribute of pitch focus with all of the ancillary qualities that follow from it. Some theorists have conjectured that the word *tonicality* would have been a better descriptive, although as Rudolph Reti once remarked, it may have been rejected early in order to steer clear of the tongue-twister *atonicality*.[29] As a result, Schoenberg and posterity were stuck with *tonal* and *tonality, atonal* and *atonality*.

Schoenberg preferred to avoid emphasizing such matters, at least as they pertained to his own compositions. He thus typically managed to skirt such linguistic peeves, as in this bit of historical reminiscing from 1926:

> The leap from a method of composition that emphasized key to mine was very swift and sudden. For a long time to come, the listener's ear must still be prepared before he finds dissonant sounds a matter of course and can comprehend the processes based on them.[30]

TONALITY AS FORM DELINEATION

That Schoenberg may not have fully comprehended tonality's nature, causes, and history is further thrown into relief by observing what he regarded as its role in music, what function he thought it performed when it was a determining agent. In his view it was a condition tailormade for west European art music of the common practice period, a conception readily and understandably held by anyone whose purview was circumscribed by the masterworks of the German Baroque and Viennese Classicism. Tonality in his opinion was not a "gift of nature," nor was its presence essential for the achievement of structural clarity or musical meaning. Indeed, tonality was for him a consciously imposed musical element whose day had passed; its capital function lay in providing formal unity to the large parts of an ongoing musical texture. The "true reason for the marked development of tonality," he said, was "to make what happens easily comprehensible. *Tonality is not an end in itself, but a means to an end.*"[31] And in this context "making what happens easily comprehensible" refers to the demarcation of formal parts.

Although they may be widely separated in time, the succession of formal parts can be held together, bound as related, by tonality. And tonality also, Schoenberg adds, provides an articulating function, one of separation as well as joining together:

> Just as important is its other, the articulating function, by means of which parts that previously were unified by a different application of the same means are limited and separated. . . . I perceive in both of these functions, the co-joining and the unifying of the one hand, and on the other the articulating, separating and characterizing, the main accomplishment of tonality.[32]

In elaborating on this forming function he speaks of how it might operate in the apprehension of a large form:

> The listener with a schooled musical ear will recognize the reprise of the theme through the return of the original key; he will also feel that as long as foreign keys are present, the main theme is less likely to recur, but rather secondary themes and developments.[33]

And then a full decade after his formulation of the serial method, he moves to the ultimate point of his description of tonality's function:

> It is evident that abandoning tonality can be contemplated only if other satisfactory means for coherence and articulation present themselves.[34]

In other words, all would be well in the music-sans-tonality world if "all the parts unfold clearly and characteristically in related significance and function."[35]

Schoenberg went to great lengths in a number of his essays to emphasize this displacement of tonality's form-giving role by other musical properties. He does this without speaking of rhythm's stake in affecting tonality or about any of the kinds of purely melodic (and thus time-bound) processes that might contribute to that end. His conclusion was that the ultimate replacement for tonality lay in the motivic and thematic domains, these regarded by him as the irreducibles of meaningful music. In his judgment they alone could satisfy the unifying and the separating functions tonality had fulfilled during the preceding two hundred years.

It is interesting as well as informative that in 1911 Schoenberg soothed doubtful people's fears of potential musical chaos with the assurance that,

> if the laws issuing from tonality, the laws of the autocrat, were rescinded, its erstwhile domain would not thereby necessarily sink into chaos but would automatically, following its own dictates, make for itself laws consistent with its nature.[36]

But in his 1922 revision of this comforting passage (around the same time he was composing Opera 23, 24, and 25), he adds a more suggestive prophecy: "Anarchy would not ensue, but rather a new form of order."[37] And he was, of course, ready to prescribe the nature of this new order.

NOTES

All quotations from *Harmonielehre* will be cited first from the Carter translation, accompanied parenthetically by page locations in the 1922 German edition.

1. Schoenberg sometimes referred to the great historian-theorist with mischievous mock-formality as "Mr. Riemann," at times adding that his theories were "built on air."

2. Translated by William Michelson, in *Hugo Riemann's Theory of Harmony and History of Music, Book III*, 185. It compares surprisingly well with a more recent definition of Lerdahl and Jackendoff (*A Generative Theory of Music*, 1) which, as might be expected, leans more heavily on the role of the listener: "A formal description of the musical intuitions of a listener who is experienced in a musical idiom."

3. A crowning example is Moritz Hauptmann's *Die Natur der Harmonik und Metrik*, whose first, and painfully forced, principle is the Hegelian dialectical triad. Hauptmann's application of the thesis-antithesis-synthesis triangulation should be required reading for all aspiring music theorists.

4. Hindemith, *The Craft of Musical Composition*, I.

5. Babbitt, "The Structure and Function of Music Theory," 19.

6. Any illustration of *the* harmonic series is necessarily generalized if musical notation of pitch is expected to be precise. Vibrating materials are quite different in makeup, and thus their variances ensure slight differences in the series that a particular material will produce. Overtones will vary in relative intensities and sometimes partials (including the fundamental) will be absent.

7. This speculation is made especially plausible because of Schoenberg's phenomenal speed in composing.

8. Wason, *Viennese Harmonic Theory from Albrechtsberger to Schenker and Schoenberg*.

9. *Style and Idea*, 532, n. 2.

10. *Theory of Harmony*, 8 (1922, 9).

11. The most thoroughgoing champion of this notion of balance between *above* and *below* was Riemann. His *Überklangs* and *Unterklangs*, quaint as they seem today, still indirectly influence the way some people think about our harmonic system, especially in the doctrine of the subdominant as "balance" for the dominant. Clearly, however, degree functions possess no *above* and *below*, since they are pitch-class functions.

12. Readers interested in the details of music theory's history may nonetheless enjoy knowing that "finding" the subdominant's nature-endowed source provided one of the most unrewarding, yet over-booked, expeditions of theoretical speculation, 1750–1950.

13. *Theory of Harmony*, 8 (1922, 9).

14. See also the discussion of derivational pitfalls in this volume, pp. 139–142.

15. *Theory of Harmony*, 27 (1922, 28). Schoenberg's cultural blinders are at no point more evident than when he informs us how lucky we Westerners were to have discovered the major scale in the series rather than some other potential, such as the inferior patterns "discovered there respectively by the Arabs, the Chinese, the Japanese, and Gypsies" (*Theory of Harmony*, 25). To my knowledge this is the only reference he made to the musics of other cultures.

16. *Style and Idea*, 260.

17. For nineteenth-century theorists, influenced by the "scientific" aura of quantification as well as swayed by number mysticism descended from Pythagoras, the ratio 3:2 was further confirmation of that interval's very special role in the series. For Pythagorean purposes it was the first conjunction that, like male and female, joined opposites, and thus was uniquely endowed. I have never been able to find out which member of the ratio was regarded as male, which as female.

18. *Style and Idea,* 260. See also *Theory of Harmony,* 20.

19. As reported by biographer Stuckenschmidt, 461.

20. We must emphasize that Schoenberg's weaknesses as a systematic theorist did not reduce his insights into the structural wherewithal of the music he knew best, Bach through Brahms. His explanations of this music remain incomparably revealing today.

21. Otto Friedrich tells of an attempt by Krenek to tell Schoenberg about the glories of some thirteenth-century motets, only to be rebuffed by a demoralizing disinterest (Friedrich, *Glenn Gould,* 190).

22. *The Glenn Gould Reader,* 144. It may or may not be accidental that Adrian Leverkuhn, Thomas Mann's Faustus, was similarly narrow in outlook, confined to an interest in and understanding of German music.

23. MacDonald, *Schoenberg,* 59.

24. An expression derived mainly from Riemann, it was meant to convey that chords are organized to interact in certain categorical ways. Riemann was the principal modern exponent of the idea that there are only three harmonic functions, Tonic, Dominant, and Subdominant, and the related notion of "root by supposition."

25. P. 129. Note a curious and critical slip here—at least a sin of omission—in that whatever are to be designated as "the scale" and as "the diatonic chords" are both necessarily dependent on the pre-determination of what is *the* tonic. See also *Style and Idea,* 271.

26. *Style and Idea,* 264.

27. *Theory of Harmony,* 131 (1922, 160).

28. I am aware of the tendency (Allen Forte, "Sets and Non-Sets in Schoenberg's Atonal Music" and *The Structure of Atonal Music*; Jan Maegaard, *Studien zur Entwicklung des Dodekaphonen Satzes bei Arnold Schoenberg*; and Fusako Hamao, *The Origin and Development of Schoenberg's Twelve-Tone Method*) to use *atonal* only for early non-serial works that dispensed with key. But since this usage implies what is not true—that the later serial works are therefore not atonal—this is a misleading use of words. It derives from the same misguided conception of language that would have us use the word *trichord* in referring to what in any other discipline would be known as a *triad*.

29. In *Tonality in Modern Music,* 25.

30. *Style and Idea,* 264.

31. Ibid., 259.

32. Ibid., 278.

33. Ibid.

34. Ibid., 279.

35. Ibid.

36. *Theory of Harmony,* 152 (1922, 185).

37. Ibid.

CHAPTER **5**

Scales, Modes, And Evolution

Consistent with this conviction that harmony was the sine qua non of tonality, Schoenberg maintained a provocative notion of how scales relate to musical structure and what role they play in the processes of conceiving, producing, reproducing, and hearing music. Throughout his career, from the *Harmonielehre* until essays written toward the end of his life, he was convinced of the controlling power exercised by a scale, as note collection, in shaping a piece, in establishing coherence. As we shall discuss presently, he held that a relationship of virtual identity exists between the diatonic note collection and a particular major key, an idea darkly coupled with the contradictory notion that the scale was prior to the key, that scale was a cause rather than an abstracted result.

If we accept his statements as definitive, there inheres in the collection C D E F G A B, a "C-majorishness" just as within the collection E♭ F G♭ A♭ B♭ C♭ D♭ there inheres the same identity with the key of G♭ major (and not, please note, E♭ minor).[1] In other words, the mere collection, regardless of the real-time deployment of its parts as a musical context, bears an inherent tonality-identity peculiar to that collection. He repeatedly refers to scales as if they were anterior archetypes that govern musical utterances rather than as patterned derivatives from the sonic thing itself.[2] His unacknowledged shift from effect to cause was not trivial.

Before discussing his scalar theories, and at the risk of belaboring the obvious, we should briefly note the role scales play in musical explication. Historically, (and this includes modes as well) they have been collections of notes abstracted from real passages to represent pitch content and the most basic kind of structural properties, the collection reduced by convention to an octave. A quite different kind of music— say a "remote" or "exotic" musical style—might (or might not) exhibit pitch collections quite different from those derived from more conventional music; indeed, a music's scale is one index of its tonal content. Scales are extracted from music; they are generalizations of pitch structure.

Thus we are surprised when Schoenberg speaks of them as if they are cultural archetypes discovered sui generis in nature, as though they are raw tonal fabric from which to make music.[3] He extends this conception to the chromatic scale as well.

THE EVOLUTIONARY TRAIL: MODALITY→TONALITY→PANTONALITY

The modes of chant were but an early way station in Schoenberg's conception of scalar history. Like major and minor, they were kinds of tonal prototypes, albeit of less clarity and tonal definition (in his judgment) than their later counterparts. His notion that the modal system merely plowed the ground for the major and minor crops, and his apparent indifference to the music whose content it represented, led him to neglect it as a discardable segment of music's development. For him the church modes were only a confused prologue to the temporary (1650–1900) paradise of the bicameral major and minor world. Yet these modal scales were critical to his impressionistic understanding of earlier music and to several of his own theoretical stances. Because they played a formative role in his renunciation of tonality as a primal and necessary ingredient, they are relevant to our main story.

Recall again that Schoenberg's self-imposed mission entailed the necessity and inevitability of an evolutionary process that guided music's changes in style. This dependence on predictable change as controlling process, whatever might be each of its ultimate substantive stages, led him to frame a three-fold dialectic of Modality-Tonality-Pantonality.[4] For him these represented the definitive and exclusive stages of Western music's tonal development. This dialectic held that the pitch structure of earlier music (at least from the time of the codification of Gregorian chant until the late Renaissance) was explicable by the system of modality. As this repertory grew obsolete, so we are led to believe, the modes faded away, to be replaced by their simpler progeny, major and minor scales. And to complete this evolutionary scheme, music after 1900 would be explicable by invocation of the even simpler chromatic scale, which itself, according to Schoenberg's reckoning, was traceable to the selective mergings of major and minor with the seven church modes.[5] It is a theory rich in allusions and dear to a nineteenth-century Hegelian heart. There is abundant evidence that Schoenberg was convinced of the truth of this evolutionary progression of survival of the fittest:

> The decline of the church modes is that necessary process of decay from which sprouts the new life of the major and minor. And even if our tonality is dissolving, it already contains within it the germ of the next artistic phenomenon.[6]

> If we sum up the characteristics of the church modes, we get major and minor plus a number of non-diatonic phenomena. And the way in which the non-diatonic events of the church modes were carried over to the other

modes I conceive as the process by which our present day modes [major and minor scales] crystallized out of the church modes.[7]

Schoenberg assures us that a demand for simplicity and coherence are the driving forces for this evolutionary advance, saying:

> Perhaps it is an unconscious striving for a simplicity that leads musicians here; for the replacement of major and minor with a chromatic scale is no doubt the same sort of step as the replacement of the seven church modes with merely two scales, major and minor: greater uniformity of relation-ship within an unchanged number of possible relationships.[8]

Whatever may happen in the future, we can count on the continuing march forward that is scalar evolution:

> Nothing is definitive in culture; everything is preparation for a higher stage of development, for a future which at the moment can only be imagined, conjectured. Evolution is not finished, the peak has not been crossed.[9]

Schoenberg appears to have put together this notion of historical progression with little more than a superficial understanding of what the church modes actually were, as theoretical models, what the music they represent was like, or how the former were intended to designate tonal distillations of the latter. As John Spratt tells us in his synopsis of speculative issues in the *Harmonielehre,* Schoenberg's insistence that the scalar evolution he described was a process of simplification, each subsequent stage a "notable advance" over the previous stage, was itself an oversimplification. Spratt elaborates his charge, noting that:

> the *de facto* reduction of twelve modes to two (which is discernable in Willaert, for example) was ultimately made explicit as the major-minor harmonic system. This system is neither more nor less simple than the original modal system, but it is simpler and more workable than a modal system acutely out of accord with musical practice.[10]

MODALITY AS PRE-TONAL CONFUSION

The church modes per se, as formulated by any medieval or Renaissance theorist known to me, did not contain what Schoenberg called "non-diatonic events." And furthermore, whatever may have happened in performance as deviations from desig-nated pitch (as *musica ficta*) was dealt with by explicating theory only as addenda to the classificatory system itself. The modes were fabricated by theorists in attempts to codify tonal organization as it was perceived in the music of their times. As generalizations they were not presumed to account for singers' conscious or unconscious pitch deviations.

Schoenberg seems to have preferred the idea, still harbored by some musicians today, that any mode was in reality just a segment of the major scale, that a Dorian passage, for example, could most appropriately be imaged as lying within the supertonic octave of major. This flawed view may have stemmed from his belief that the modes were really without organizational basis, that, unlike major or minor scales, they were not "derivable" as tonic-dominant-subdominant hierarchies from a harmonic base. The modes suffered, in his judgment, the damaging absence of discernible hierarchy; they lacked a centralizing pitch. He refers to this deficiency in the *Harmonielehre* when he observes that in the modes "the effect of a fundamental tone was felt, but since no one knew which one it was, all of them were tried."[11]

Apparently he was unaware that two of the essential steps in mode identification—and the two most elemental steps—demand the discovery in a melody of two properties: *ambitus* (or pitch boundaries) and *finalis* (or principal note), the latter's principality confirmed most often by its appearance as the melody's final note. These two characteristics are at the very basis of modality—at least they were for Odo of Cluny, around 935, when he defined modes and how they are determined. As he observed,[12] the mode of a melody is classed "according to its final." And, he continues, "unless you know the final you cannot know where the melody ought to begin or how far it ought to ascend and descend."

And as another respected theorist some five hundred years later makes clear and emphatic, a mode is considerably more than a mere note collection. Delineation of the melodic range (which this theorist calls *species* rather than *ambitus*) and recognition of the principal note (here called *finalis*) are first steps in making meaningful statements about a mode. Pietro Aron tells us that "the cognition of species is essential and therefore necessary."[13] And further, in order not to slight the final's role in this nomenclature of species, Aron adds that the foregoing attention to high-low boundaries in no way reduces its significance. He continues by saying that it is not

> an objection that we are for the most part accustomed to base our cognition of music on the finalis, for . . . this has been for the sake of readier understanding, inasmuch as those things that are at the end are customarily more closely observed than those that are at the beginning and in the middle.[14]

And in this Aron is alluding to a characteristic that is as true of contemporary pop music as of the plainchant of his time: a tune usually ends with its tonic.

Renaissance musicians found principal pitches in their melodies easier to identify than Schoenberg realized. And it is reasonable to believe that their auditory perceptions were equally adept. Pietro Aron's remarks were in no way unique. Only hyperbole could lead one to claim that the concept of tonic (meaning most important structural pitch or hierarchical nucleus) was irrelevant for modal music because "no one knew which one it was." Schoenberg's cavalier attention to structural implications projected by the modal system is especially disturbing when coming from one who draws emphatic conclusions such as "We must concede that the church modes do not at all conform to the law of tonality."[15]

A CONFLICTING READING OF THE MODES

Schoenberg's notion of scales as controlling paradigms is evident in another strange way. In this it is part of an idea that actually contradicts his earlier contention that a mode harbors no distinguishable tonic function. While in *Harmonielehre* he claimed that modes lacked the tonic phenomenon, he later reports a quite different problem: how each mode projects *two* tonics simultaneously, and in a curious way:

> These [church modes] reveal a remarkable phenomenon: the key of the underlying tonal series of which they are composed is different from *the key in which the piece really exists.*[16]

This strange statement denies the very essence of what a church mode—in fact, what any real scale—is supposed to signify. Even more startling, in it Schoenberg once again attributes to a note collection, such as D E F G A B C, an a priori tonality that derives solely from that collection's members. In this case it is the seven natural notes, so its group identity, in Schoenberg's taxonomy, is "Key of C major." We can only speculate about the cause of this bizarre condition: perhaps it is that the natural notes constitute—are isomorphic with—*that* key system. In Schoenberg's conception the two are, incredibly, one and the same.

THE MAJOR SCALE AS MODAL ARCHETYPE

Schoenberg's condescending attitude toward modes made a comforting, if odd, corollary to his notion of scales as prototypes. But his perspective ruled out the most elemental meaning of a mode: that a singular collection of pitches, by the way it is deployed in time as melody, can project any one of its members (and only one at a time) as resolutional pivot for the set. Each mode is thereby stamped with a slightly different matrix of feeling for each different combination of intervals (as they bear on the central pitch, or final).

This is the kernel of meaning behind the distinction made, to take just one example, between authentic Dorian and plagal Mixolydian; both have the same *ambitus* and notes, but each projects a different tonal context because of different finals. As Zarlino explained this shifting of identical internal parts to make different pitch resources, each ordering is separate; each is of a different "constitution" that arises from its unique deployment of intervals.[17] Even as early in the history of modal theory as Boethius the distinctive distributions of intervals within the octave were recognized as characterizing. "This was the whole purpose of the scheme," as Harold Powers tells us in his monumental *New Grove* survey of all things modal.[18]

The most baffling of all in Schoenberg's speculations is the claim of bitonality. The hypothetical music fragment he holds in question (see above) contains the natural notes with D as final, and with a range of an octave, d–d'. The melody's modal designation would thus be "authentic Dorian," and Schoenberg presumably agrees with that. But he adds the unprecedented claim that the *melody* is in a different key from the key of its underlying scale.

> If, for example, a piece is written in the Doric mode on D, the tones of which it is composed are those of C major. But in this mode the tones D, E, F, G, A, B, C should be related in the melody to the fundamental D, and all endings, all semi-cadences and all else that expresses the key should refer to this D. Naturally these tones which are fixed in their intervals, with the leading tones E–F and B–C, are without a doubt in the key of C major tonality.[19]

An additional clue to this critical misunderstanding resides in his last sentence. He refers there to the note conjunctions B–C and E–F as "leading tones," which are "without doubt in the C major tonality." And although we cannot but agree that they are leading tones in that key (allowing a semitonal relationship to be so-designated, even if not in a 7–8 position), the fact is that they are also "leading tones" in the scales of G major and F major. Schoenberg's misstep lies in what a dedicated Gestaltist would consider a confusion of attributes of parts for the whole. These particular half steps *belong* no more to the C major scale than they belong to the Japanese *ritsu* scale based on D. Schoenberg's curious juxtaposition of experiential reality (D Dorian) with postulated theoretical prototype (C major) bespeaks of the kinds of non sequiturs that undermine his discussions of scale systems and tonality.

THE EVOLUTIONARY SAGA WIDENS: CHROMATICISM

While Schoenberg proposed two contradictory explanations for the role of a tonic in the modes, he proposes no less than three sources of "origin" or "derivation" for the chromatic scale. Perhaps he conceived of all three as cooperatives in culture's drive from modality to pantonality.

One of these three need not be dealt with at any length here. Attributed to acoustic "fact," it consists merely of his recognition that one can "find" the replica of chromatics in the higher partials of the harmonic series, which in Schoenberg's metaphor resided in nature as a ladder, upon which the improving auditory skills of humanity led to ever more enriching discoveries. As we increase our powers of concentration and precision in hearing, we move up the ladder, as it were, from intervals of the senario into the semitonal regions (regardless of how one prefers to spell them) of 10:11:12:13:14. We shall deal with the other two at greater length, as two related explanations drawn from a single cause.

CHROMATICISM: OPTIONAL SOURCE NO. 2

In a late section of *Harmonielehre* Schoenberg discovers how the appearance of non-diatonic chords in a key can lead to the evolution of new scale prototypes, new collections which themselves then bear form-giving potential. "It is evident," he remarks, "that chords remote from the key, appearing in large numbers, will favor the establishment of a new conceptual unit (*Auffassungseinheit*): the chromatic scale."[20] As a consequence of this consistent overloading of the diatonic circuit, he explains that:

> the tonality could thus be demolished . . . if a rupture does . . . occur, the consequence is not necessarily disintegration and formlessness. For the chromatic scale is a form too. It too has a formal principle, a different one from the major or minor scale, a simpler and more uniform principle.[21]

So this assumption of formative powers for discovered or evolved (or merely invented) archetypes carries over for Schoenberg to the chromatic scale, which he conceived to be the latest product of a simplifying evolution. The path led first through the church modes, then to major and minor scales, finally yielding to the chromatic scale.[22]

CHROMATICISM: OPTIONAL SOURCE NO. 3

He speaks explicitly of chords "remote from the key" in presenting the previous source (Option No. 2) within his theory of *Auffassungseinheit*. But I see no good reason for ruling it out as a part of another explanation, one that suggests an additive development with melodic processes. In earlier pages of *Harmonielehre* he argues that nineteenth-century chromaticism was produced by composer's artful (and will-ful) overlay of the older modal system (complete with its possible alterations of *musica ficta*) on to the major and minor textures, rather like a master carpenter's veneering of one wood with another of more comely surface. For him, *musica ficta* yielded "useful chromatic pitches" whose most valuable function was to herald the coming world of major-minor.

For instance, he explains that applying "normal" alterations to Dorian mode can add C♯ and B♭ to the composer's arsenal of notes. In other words, Dorian mode, because of common improprieties of pitch production, yields two "foreign notes," which in turn become, by some unexplained proprietary right of association, the inclusive property of that mode. And thus one may speak of the chord A C♯ E in the key of C major as a "borrowed chord" from its "Dorian second scale degree." But these notational branchings are no more than strained accountings of internal parts, as empty as the claim that the word *culpable* is "derived from" (and thereby of direct kinship to) the words *elaborate* and *pulchritude,* which "supply" its alphabetic content.

Following this evolutionary bent and his major-minor bias, Schoenberg seems to have regarded singers' introduction of false notes into performance as proof of music's teleological urge toward the greater tonal simplicity he claimed for the key system that, by the late seventeenth century, would dominate music. And it is those later evolutionary simplifications of pitch resources that profit, in his opinion, from the indiscretions visited upon the modes. As he explains it:

> Should our major and minor actually contain the entire harmonic wealth of the church modes, then we must include these characteristics in a manner consistent with their sense. It becomes possible thereby to use in a major key all the non-diatonic tones and chords that appeared in the seven church modes, which were constructed on the seven diatonic tones of our major scale.[23]

We need not attempt to unravel the historical, the logical, the musical, or the ontological bog this paragraph presents. The chromatic scale is without question a unique pitch collection in its own right, but Schoenberg's explanation of its "derivation" is one of those explanatory apologia left largely unchallenged because it combines the surface appearance of historical succession with ostensible empirical confirmation. But it is a classic instance of muddled concepts, reordered history, and shaky inference. It is a model of what neurologist Richard Bergland had in mind when he spoke, in *The Fabric of Mind,* of *mismemes,* meaning mistaken ideas passed down in history as unchallenged fact, often because of the respect felt for their authors.

SUMMARY

Whether Schoenberg's assessment of pre-*Aufklärung* pitch structuring was in whole or in part accurate, or even useful as theoretical model, is a question best left for the moment to the reader's judgment. Perhaps we can agree that his explanations were largely derivative, on occasion incongruent with experience, sometimes inconsistent internally; they often were drawn from an insecure knowledge of the most relevant considerations.

It is not easy to square Schoenberg's reliance on the tattered remnants of Rameau's harmonic theories, as they had been mulled through by several generations, with the empiricism claimed for him or with the identification with twentieth-century scientific outlook attributed to him. Noting the deterministic and metaphysical surface of his ideas, Benjamin Boretz and Edward Cone nonetheless find that he "behaved theoretically, as he behaved compositionally, in a truly empiricism spirit."[24] But I find little to support that claim. In *Harmonielehre* his skepticism about rational principles bursts forth on occasion, as when he observes that "it matters little whether one's initial hypothesis is 'correct' or not, for in the long run both the true and the false hypothesis will be proven inadequate."[25]

His approach to answering questions of perceptual identity contrasted sharply with the empirical attitude of the Gestalt psychologists of his time. They *hypothesized* that certain shapes might be experienced as equivalent under certain circumstances, holding out, however, that such hypotheses must be confirmed or disconfirmed by experiment. Schoenberg on the other hand confidently declared identities by fiat. In the essay "Composition with Twelve Tones," for example, he announces the preservation of row identity under the operations of inversion, retrogression, and retrograde inversion, telling us that our minds always recognize relationships of parts,

> regardless of their direction, regardless of the way in which a mirror might show the mutual relations, *which remain a given quality.*[26]

But regardless what his epistemic assumptions may have been, an empirical spirit by itself has not proved, over the centuries, to be sufficient cause for a maximum yield of truth. Prominent figures of unimpeachable inductive-deductive credentials have erred remarkably in sizing up the external world.

Schoenberg was sure that tonality had outworn its utility. He based this on strongly felt and closely reasoned ideas, some without empirical confirmation. They were that (1) tonality's musical function was of recent origins, certainly post-modal; (2) its perceptual usefulness was derived from the functioning of major and minor triads as harmonic anchors; (3) its pitch content was the product of an evolution that replaced church modes by their improvements, major and minor scales, which by now had evolved into the chromatic scale; (4) tonality's chief role—delineating formal sections—was replaceable by other musical properties of cohesion and articulation; and (5) its necessity had already been denied by the chromatic indulgences of Schoenberg's most illustrious predecessors, especially Liszt and Wagner.

Although Schoenberg thought he had persuasive evidence that the last of these might be true, the other four were less than unassailable. In fact, one of our goals will be to show that his limited knowledge of music in history led him to infer from his own musical milieu some untenable conclusions. His certainty that musical evolution dictated taking a drastic stylistic fork off the chromatic road appears to have been groundless. But even if true, his complex deductions from that premise—about where music had been and where it must now go—rested on a collection of uniquely personal conclusions.

NOTES

1. Schoenberg curiously overlooks how he rules out, by omission, the minor sets, presumably because only the major is "given by nature." This notion of inherent priority for one diatonic set does not fare well in contemporary empirical studies. Helen Brown ("The Interplay of Set Content and Temporal Context in a Functional Theory of Tonality Perception") found temporal order in control. She concludes (p. 242) that it was not pitch sets which guided perception but "the manner in which their intervallic relationships were exploited temporally."

2. Compare Hindemith's view ("Methods of Music Theory," 25) that scales are no more than the "sterilized derivative of melody."

3. No doubt, music can be and on occasion is composed *from* scales, so to speak. But such a process is not a necessary one, nor was it even a customary departure for the creative process until the advent of serial composition, and even there it is used to yield only a pre-compositional ordering of pitch-classes.

4. Schoenberg preferred *pantonal* to describe what others insisted on called *atonal, atonical,* or *tonicless.*

5. Elsewhere he discovers additional members of the chromatic scale in the harmonic series, up through the 13th partial (*Style and Idea,* 272). Contradictory or dual attributions of origin of this kind are not peculiar to Schoenberg; by the end of his career Rameau had formulated three different explanations for minor harmony.

6. *Theory of Harmony,* 97 (1922, 118).

7. Ibid., 427 (1922, 299).

8. Ibid., 247 (1922, 299).

9. Ibid., 97 (1922, 118).

10. In "The Speculative Content of Schoenberg's *Harmonielehre,*" 247.

11. *Theory of Harmony,* 25 (1922, 22).

12. *Enchiridion Musices,* 113.

13. Aron, *Trattato,* in Strunk, *Readings in Music History,* 208.

14. Ibid.

15. *Style and Idea,* 276. Schoenberg's opinions of the possession of tonality by traditional British hymns are not known to me, but this same matter was broached obliquely by the incomparable Donald Tovey. In *A Musician Speaks,* 24, he slyly confides:

> I believe it is still held by some teachers that students who are allowed to write strict counterpoint in the Church modes are thereby undermining their grasp of classical tonality. If a sense of classical tonality is to be represented by the harmonic style of our unrevised *Hymns Ancient and Modern,* it is difficult to see how any of the laxity of Palestrina's tonality could make a student's style worse.

16. *Style and Idea,* 276. My italics.

17. Zarlino, *On the Modes,* 11–12.

18. *The New Grove,* 12, 378. Also see R. P. Winnington-Ingram, *Mode in Ancient Greek Music,* 2.

19. Schoenberg, *Style and Idea,* 276.

20. *Theory of Harmony,* 247 (1922, 299).

21. Ibid.

22. The chromatic scale remains, however, as the generalized reservoir, as the major scale is for thousands of melodies, both noble and slight. We might presume that this generative potential could yield any microtonal scale as well, since its reach is theoretically infinite. A theory even more intriguing

(and as manifestly implausible) can be found in Joseph Yasser, *A Theory of Evolving Tonality.*

23. *Theory of Harmony,* 175 (1922, 215).

24. Boretz and Cone, *Perspectives on Contemporary Music Theory,* 8.

25. P. 16.

26. *Style and Idea,* 223. I doubt that empirical research could support Schoenberg's suggestion in this essay that Beethoven's *contoural* inversions of the *Muss es sein?* motif of Opus 135 are analogous to the inversions (*non-contoural*) of a dodecaphonic row. What we have learned so far about the preservation of identity via such transformations, even in patterns within a clear tonal context, dampens one's expectations. For example, see Dowling, "Recognition of Melodic Transformations: Inversion, Retrograde, and Retrograde Inversion"; Dowling and Fujitani, "Contours, Interval, and Pitch Recognition in Memory for Melodies"; and White, "Recognition of Distorted Melodies."

CHAPTER 6

The Emancipation of Dissonance

There is yet another way Schoenberg's conception of tonality, with its dependence on major and minor chords and chord successions, had a bearing on his perspective of musical evolution. It has to do with harmonic sonance, which we know more conventionally by its polar manifestations consonance and dissonance.

The "simpler" (in a generalized Pythagorean sense) consonant intervals, he correctly reasoned, were more conducive to tonal stability, a condition antagonized by the more "complex," more dissonant intervals. Again, his conceptions, like his perceptions, were strongly influenced by his interpretation of the harmonic series as a progressive ladder of values. In this interpretation was embedded a metaphysic of intervals, a conception whose principles were as specious as its history was august.

The Pythagorean Tradition

Traceable through Ptolemy and Boethius to Pythagoreanism, this interpretation's most powerful pre-modern advocate was Johannes Kepler, who helped pass it on to the modern world. Kepler's harmonic speculations were complemented by geometrical "proofs," much the same kind of fanciful cosmic ruminations one finds enlisted in the first century by Aristides Quintilianus. In his inimitable way, for example, Kepler came to the conclusion that the major third was concordant because its geometrical form, pentagon enclosed by circle, could be constructed by using nothing more than the classical geometers tools of compass and rule. It represented the ratios of 1:5 and 4:5; see Example 8. Figures so constructible by compass and rule, as is the septagon (1:7 and 6:7), possess relationships that yield discords. According to Kepler they suffer a fate worse than mere unattractiveness: they are unknowable (*inscibilis*), unspeakable (*inefabilis*), and—as if things weren't already bad enough—nonexistent (*non-entia*).[1] But octaves, fifths, and fourths, like the major third, are all renderable in their geometric analogues, as Kepler demonstrated, using no more than compass and rule.

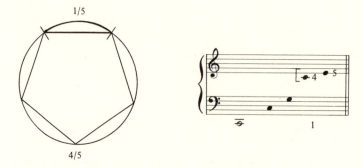

EXAMPLE 8. Kepler's proof of the major third's superior quality.

The same simpler-thus-better bias was influential in Schoenberg's harmonic theorizing. In one form or another this pre-modern manifestation of Less-is-More lurks yet today behind the hidden assumptions of many discussions of harmonic theory, especially when they touch on issues of concord and discord. Some of these biases, when exposed, are less contrived than others; most are not so colorfully enunciated as Kepler's. Few do not depend for their appeal on one's aesthetic attachment to number theory. But whatever their particular slant, they provide lame explanations for the manifestations of consonance and dissonance in music.

For the moment let us assume an evolutionary progression that conforms with Schoenberg's, that early melody (and later polyphony) was confined to tone patterns controlled by a fifth, a fourth, or even a third (the last occurring "later," by Schoenberg's timetable, as numbers 4 and 5 in the series). Then music's continuing metamorphosis, over the ensuing centuries, can be explained as a developing awareness of the ever higher (and "more complex" but "less comprehensible") partials, from the fifths and fourths of organum through the thirds and sixths of the early Renaissance to the seconds and sevenths and formalized microtones of the twentieth century. This neat picture, elegantly based on an acknowledged phenomenon of our hearing and presumed to be consistent with the gradual accumulation of higher and more dissonant relationships in harmony, is appealing. It ties into a single sweeping perspective the kinds of empirical-historical interactions that compel belief in any field of inquiry. For Schoenberg it was captivating.

THE PYTHAGOREAN FLAW

These flights of discovery through the extensions of the harmonic series produce more pseudo-science than productive theory, more weavings of poetic images and invocations of ancient myths than reflections of aural reality. The experiential disunity—the *dissonance, non-fusedness, roughness*—of the interval of the minor second is not a direct product of its archetypal appearance in a relatively remote position within the harmonic series (between partials 11 and 12). That overlapping (and thus conflicting) excitations of hair cells on the basilar membrane may occur when we listen to sustained dyads like seconds or sevenths or minor ninths only *confirms* the unique phenomenal separation of those intervals from fifths and thirds. It does not, and cannot, provide a sufficient cause for the totality of harmonic dissonance.

Agreement is possible about one thing: the pitch intervals traditionally classified by musicians as more dissonant can be seen to arise "higher" in the series than their "more consonant" counterparts. And to whet Pythagorean appetites further, the numerical representations of those more remote intervals form ghastly ratios compared with the simplicity of the 2:1 octave, the 3:2 fifth, or the 4:3 fourth. But this remains coincidence rather than causality. People do not hear ratios, no matter how hard their intellectual predispositions may lead them at times to try.[2]

Let us examine these matters in greater detail as they relate to the rich history of speculation about intervals, including Schoenberg's. Like most theories of this kind, hopeful claims offer enticing support for what musical people have concluded to be the relative structural merit of pitch intervals. The perfect fifth, for instance, is said to play a very special role in music. And there is no question that this is true, for Pythagoras and Kepler as well as for Schoenberg.

But nagging reality gives us pause. A perfect fifth precisely tuned in equal temperament (with the unconscionable ratio of 2.996:2.000) is as readily perceived as *consonance* to both sophisticated and unsophisticated ears, even though it misses the 3:2 ratio by about 23 cps (around 4.5%) in the middle of the piano keyboard. And the "distorted" fifth of Meantone tuning, which dominated performance in the eighteenth century (and is computed as the product of the ratio 5:1 divided by $[\frac{3}{2}]^4$) was not mistaken for a discord by the listeners of its time. As Charles Shackford reveals in his careful study of tunings preferred by professional string players,[3] longer-held intervals are closer approximations of pure intervals, but even the harmonic series' major third of 386 cents is unhesitatingly replaced in actual practice by the much larger Pythagorean third of 408 cents. The very thought of some common musical ratios may bring tears of joy to the eyes of ardent fans of simple numerical ratios (as in Just tuning), but this is yet another instance where concepts of mathematical parsimony are speciously misleading in the face of raw aural perception.[4] In the harmonic series even the minor seventh, an acknowledged "discord" in the history of musical speculation, enjoys the comparatively respectable ratio of 7:4.

The fact is that the human perceptual agency is liberally forgiving. It will unflinchingly accept an equally-tempered major third, whose "nature-given" ratio of 5:4 has been defiled beyond recognition, and, likely as not, call it beautiful. The crisp and pure facts of perception—even of trained, precise perception—are only crude approximations with the lower-higher biases derived from the harmonic series. As psychologist Diana Deutsch comments, we have known since the late nineteenth century that the most skilled musicians do not always tune the melodic octave as a precise 2:1 ratio. In actual practice (and in this even across cultures) we tend to stretch the octave a bit when tuning can be controlled,[5] which doesn't speak to well for the relation that bears between the relative simplicity of ratios and judgments of intervallic sonance.

SCHOENBERG'S CONTINUUM OF SONANCE

Schoenberg accepted neo-Newtonian natural science and neo-Pythagorean mathe-matical causality fed him by his century. Mixed with the inducement of an evolution-ary imperative, they had a powerful effect. For him distinctions between consonance and dissonance, concord and discord were only remnants of an earlier evolutionary plateau. With a few more years of the right musical exposure, right-thinking listeners (with help from right-thinking composers) could bring the musical world into align-ment with this new conception, the egalitarianism of sonance. Eventually, the eman-cipation would be ratified by the common man.

Schoenberg's American protégée Dika Newlin states his position clearly:

> Schoenberg's justification of atonality rests directly on the overtone sys-tem. For him there is no traditional division into consonances and disso-nances, since these sound combinations which we conventionally term "dissonances" result simply from the use of tones more remote in the overtone-series, and so differ in degree only, not in kind, from the familiar fifth, third, or sixth. By the same token, there can be no tone "extraneous to the harmony," for the chordal combinations produced by passing tones have as good a right to be used independently as any other harmonies.[6]

AN UNFORESEEN RESULT OF SCHOENBERG'S PROCLAMATION

Schoenberg's explanation of consonance and dissonance as mere extensions of a single continuum is a good case of explaining mushrooms by acknowledging their kinship with toadstools. By this logic since intervals we identify as *dissonant* actually reside in the same taxonomy as the intervals we call *consonant,* the two are not to be construed as categorical opposites. (And, for that matter, mushroom fanciers can relax their efforts to distinguish the poisonous from the non-poisonous.) The tradi-tional classification of dissonant and consonant must be abandoned; henceforth we must speak only of "less consonant" and/or "more dissonant," and never in the divisive and delimiting sense suggesting that the one is not of the same family as the other. As Schoenberg himself explains:

> Dissonances are nothing else than remote consonances whose analysis gives the ear more trouble on account of their remoteness [in the harmonic series] but once analysis has made them more accessible, they will have the chance of becoming consonances just like the closer overtones.[7]

And, as a corollary to his prediction that time and appropriate concepts can correct faulty perceptions, Schoenberg concluded that music freed from the bonds of tonality should not—indeed categorically could not—retain the shackles of consonance.

Since, in its bid for tonal freedom from the past, such music has moved into the stratosphere of the harmonic series, it must reflect its escape from the gravitational field by using chords made exclusively from "remote intervals." Thus music takes on the mantle of what we can best describe as a perpetual high degree of dissonance. (Or should that be "a perpetual low degree of consonance?")[8]

Chords that might allude to a condition of harmonic resolution and thereby support a potential tonic pitch class must disappear from the musical texture. And so Emancipation of the Dissonance turns out to be Expurgation of the Consonance. It is a unique and drastic application of the old pleasure-pain principle. In this instance, goes the implicit reasoning, if the pleasurable is totally removed, then the painful ceases to exist.[9]

If one accepts Schoenberg's premises, the argument is wholly reasonable. A major triad could be deceptively out of character in a work intended to be without key.[10] Of and by itself it could arrogate a role of harmonic focus, first because of its comparative structural simplicity and second because of its contextual uniqueness (if surrounded by chords made from sterner stuff). As Schoenberg describes the situation, "a tonal triad makes claims on what follows, and retrospectively, on all that has gone before."[11] In this way, he appropriately argued, an inherent contradiction can occur.

But the full consequence of this view turns out to be a loss that cannot be taken lightly, the loss of the very musical property Schoenberg is trying to rescue from obsolescence. Since a perpetual sameness of harmonic content (whether constant high consonance or constant high dissonance) negates harmonic fluctuation, far more is at stake than just major and minor triads; broader issues covering more fundamental matters are threatened.

THE RISK OF HARMONIC ENTROPY

Let us recognize what happens when a calculated and consistent level of harmonic sonance prevails. Whatever the chosen band of acceptance, ultra-consonant or ultra-dissonant, only monotony, *within the property of sonance itself*, is the consequence. This is especially true if no tonality prevails, thereby denying even a sense of tension and release made possible within a hierarchical system. Although a style like the Gagaku tradition of Japan might rely on the kind of suspended stasis generated by its Sho's persistent background chord, harmonic fluctuation has through the centuries been a staple of Western music.[12]

Even the organum developed from polyphony's tenth-century origins fought back to counteract the greatest enemy of a time—art's existence, the threat of continuous sameness, the neutrality that is total entropy. It did so by developing mixed organum, in which constant patches of like intervals did not prevail, replaced by textures of oblique movements between voice parts that could yield a variety of harmonic alignments. And in this an object lesson of history is provided by the dramatic difference between harmonic fluctuation and harmonic stasis.

EXAMPLE 9. Composite organum at the fourth (top); free organum (bottom) (Gleason and Becker, eds., *Examples of Music Before 1400,* 26).

In music of major-minor keys, in which triads played out the drama's defining roles, harmonic fluctuation was supplied in two ways: first by a pool of chords covering a broad sampling of sonance types, the second by being a party to hierarchical relationships of unequal value, in which only the tonic chord is a pole of repose. Music of Bachian harmonic style, for example, includes chords of a broad range of interval content, a rich variety of sonorities constituted by everything from open octaves to seconds and sevenths.[13] This music's recurrent ebb and flow away from and back to the chord of stability (its tonic) supplied an additional sense of mobility, another level of meaning for structure. And for listeners especially aware of pitch relationships, the key schemes of common practice period music enable one to respond to an even larger level of tonal tension, that of the movement away from and back to a single pitch-class of focus.

Even beyond exclusively chordal potentials, any interval that might not be compatible at a particular moment as a full chord member could readily occur—and be so perceived—as part of a melodic configuration, enacting the role of non-harmonic tone. The conventions controlling what kinds might occur in what contexts vary, as has been fully documented, with the musical style of the particular historic period. The music of post-Gothic Machaut provides slightly different probabilities from the music of pre-Bach Buxtehude. And the special kind of harmonic piquancy found in a work like Purcell's *Dido and Aeneas* derives from the comparatively great number of non-chord tones that occur for extended durations and are further articulated on metric accents. The point is that the music of our history reveals a wealth of interval combinations—in fact, all intervals of the chromatic gamut—as fair game, all occurring too frequently in a variety of mixes for any to be regarded as rare.

So what is the upshot of Schoenberg's emancipation proclamation? It would appear to be a distorting inhibition, an imprisoning emancipation. It tends to produce the same neutering effect Ernst Krenek described decades later in his criticism of the leveling effect produced by over-rich tonal combinations in electronic sound genera-tion. As Schoenberg's younger ally observes, "the more abundant the sound mixtures become the more they approach the neutral roar of 'white noise.' "[14]

According to Schoenberg, however, evolution found humanity inching aurally ever upward, one partial to the next, gradually absorbing, as stylistic periods rolled by, the "less comprehensible" intervals into a culture's arsenal of musical sounds. The appearance during the late nineteenth century of chords that reflected partials up around the eleventh and thirteenth (Scriabin, Debussy, et al.), proved to Schoenberg that this march was well on its way to tonal egalitarianism. Only through recognition of dissonances as norm, he decided, could the composer fulfill nature's destiny, enabling music to utilize fully the fruits of the evolutionary journey.

This second act of Schoenbergian banishment (the first having been nothing less than pitch focus itself) rent the musical fabric more extensively than initially imag-ined: it spelled the virtual loss of harmony as a structural property. If all chords in a series lacking a tonic are of the same sonance level (determined by interval content), then harmony ceases to have power as an agent of contrast; harmony has become a single-level property rather than a multi-tiered potential of meaning. Thus strings of fifths in medieval organum and strings of unvaryingly astringent chords in a Webern sonata cannot rely on harmony to affect musical form or musical engagement. Harmony is neutered. And this gives sharpened meaning to Adorno's claim that the twelve-tone technique "enchains music by liberating it."[15]

Lessons from History

Two centuries before Schoenberg, Rameau could speak of how the dominant chord more forcefully confirms the tonic chord's role when it is dissonant (as V_7) because an additional pitch has been added.[16] But describing harmony whose every unit is of identical sonance becomes an idle gesture; harmony is no longer a differentiating property. Even the most precise and thorough methods of pitch-set identification have no bearing, for they turn out to be notational nitpickings of events whose phenomenal differences, as harmony, are indiscriminable.

We are also reminded of Zarlino, who pondered this same issue of harmonic fluctuation (without calling it that) and proposed prescient opposition to Schoenberg's conclusion. In reviewing the wisdom of his predecessors he observed in 1558 that:

> The ancient musicians judged that they should admit in composition not only the consonances which they called perfect and those which they called imperfect, but dissonances also, knowing that their compositions would thus attain to greater beauty and elegance than they would without them.[17]

In Zarlino's judgment music made exclusively from consonances would be in-complete, lacking, in his words, "the greater beauty and elegance" that dissonance affords. For him, the one without the other would have spelled impoverishment of music's powers.

A DUBIOUS SOURCE IN RELATIVITY

Aside from causing the intrinsic loss to music of one of its most effective structural ingredients, one of its most potent conveyors of feeling, Schoenberg's conclusions were not derived from reliable cognitive precepts. He assumed perceptual relativity where it does not exist.

There is no argument among music theorists or composers or listeners that each interval formed from any two pitches, within and including an octave, can be lined up in a meaningful continuum that runs from "most consonant" to "most dissonant." In this respect relativity prevails: no interval type quite corresponds in sonance with any other. That which is most dissonant is especially so in relation to that which is most consonant. Compared with a major third, a major second is appreciably more dissonant; but compared with a major seventh it is less so.[18] Thus a grading of relationships, generally acceptable by persons who are at all aware of the property of sonance, can be made. In all attempts I have seen these gradings take a form something like that in Example 10, with the usual disagreements occurring about which of the thirds and sixths is more consonant, and just where in the lineup the tritone should appear.

EXAMPLE 10. Sonance grading of intervals, consonant-to-dissonant (Perle, *Serial Composition and Atonality,* 32).

SCHOENBERG CONTRADICTS HIS OWN PREMISE

But another kind of relativity, and one enjoined by Schoenberg in his argument for the emancipation of dissonance, does not operate here: the continuity in history of human response to particular pitch combinations, the apparent absence of evolutionary change from rejection to acceptance or limited consent of intervals once regarded as categorically different. My argument is not that we today perceive the contrast of dissonant and consonant intervals as Aristoxenus did. Although I feel confident that we do, it is only by circumstantial evidence, a few veiled references to such matters, and my own rather deep inferences that I have any knowledge of how Aristotle's contemporaries heard intervals. But I speak from a continuity of personal experience as, we shall see, did Schoenberg.

The renowned C–Db in the opening of Mozart's great Eb symphony, K. 543 (measure 18) remains for us *dissonant* if that word means "lack of agreement," or "discord," or "inharmoniousness," or "incongruity," or "incompatibility," or any other adjectival state whose principal meaning is lack of fusion, effect of disunity. Twentieth-century ears are not different in this respect from Wolfgang Amadeus's, or, for that matter, from those of an amateur. The captivating bite of this passage remains, like similar unions of the pleasurably "unagreeable" in music composed before or since 1788, whether in the *Viderunt* of Perotin or the *Madrigals* of George Crumb. It holds undiminished its captivating dynamic of a tension that demands resolution, even if that resolution is not forthcoming. It will continue to, so long as human hearing remains what it has been for the past several thousand years. (By *hearing* I refer to the total cognitive process as well as the purely peripheral neural aspect provided by receptor organs.)

Perhaps unaware of the ultimate contradiction it forms with his prognosis that dissonant intervals will one day greet our ears as gentle euphony, Schoenberg in another context testifies to the enduring power of the consonance-dissonance polarity he denies. He exults, and with good cause, in the inherent beauty of instances of harmonic "upset" in the music of three of his favorite composers, admitting that "what is truly new remains as new as it was on the first day." He recalls that:

> in Mozart's *Dissonance Quartet* I feel it over and over again when there is that daring contradictory entry of the first violin on A, directly after the A-flat just left by the viola. Or the bass B-natural passing against the B-sharp in Bach's C-sharp minor Prelude (Book I). Or in the expressive power of the third A-flat to C-flat, at Ortrud's lamenting cry of "Elsa." For what is truly new remains. . . .[19]

But could it have remained new if, as predicted, the evolutionary advance produced by salutary experiences eroded the blessed difference between consonance and dissonance? In 1911 it was Schoenberg's opinion that the two terms, if used as antitheses rather than as terminal ends of a single continuum, were false:

> It all simply depends on the growing ability of the analyzing ear to familiarize itself with the remote overtones, thereby expanding the conception of what is euphonious, suitable for art, so that it embraces the whole natural phenomenon.[20]

But Schoenberg cannot have it both ways. If an interval such as the minor second gradually comes to seem euphonious, essentially no less reposeful than the major third, how can its disruptive "wrongness" remain so gorgeously "right" in Mozart's Quartet?

Schoenberg's error is not an uncommon one; it lies in overestimating the influence of our concepts over our percepts.[21] This is an uncharted sea of experiential psychology that begs for study, but it is not too dimly known to deny comment. There are numerous cases of concepts' impotency in the face of perception. My own concept of cigarette smoke long ago adapted to acknowledge its life-threatening dangers; I accepted as fact that ingestion is riddled with health nuances of utmost gravity. And yet, this long-developed conceptual set has in no way altered my perception of secondhand smoke from others's cigarettes. The perception has retained its impact, its aroma of sensual delight; only my actions following those perceptions have changed.

At one point Schoenberg appears to have considered his exclusion of consonances a necessity only on an interim basis, a kind of moratorium of harmonic purification and rededication. During a self-imposed trial period, he conjectured, the modern listener would grow accustomed to dissonance as harmonic staple. Thus he tells us that this drastic measure (of unrelenting "dissonance") need not be forever; it was to be, so he speculated, only a "step for a short period, but one which I have shown to lie along the path followed by the evolution of music, through the works of our greatly revered predecessors."[22]

Some Broader Issues Implied

I would be remiss to ignore the hint of Hegelian dialectic in all this, the implicit underlying logic of the historical process Schoenberg envisioned. Through turning his back on the "traditional consonances" (by rejecting them from his harmonies and creating textures exclusively from the "traditional dissonances"), he was providing the *antithesis* to tradition's consonantal *thesis*. His imposed second stage in this process would be followed eventually by the development of a state of *synthesis*, finding sonorities of simpler constitution once again in league with the less gentle kind. Thus, emancipation will be followed by harmonious cohabitation of all the sonorities in a musical Utopia.

With this Schoenberg once again betrays entrapment by the Darwinian hypothesis—or rather a clumsily distorted version of it. His notion of humanity's development of perceptual emancipation from the condition of dissonance was another self-fulfilling prophecy; his conclusion fit a personal program for change in musical style more than it fit the grind of music's inexorable evolution. Even if Lamarckian hypotheses about acquired characteristics proved to be feasible in such areas of human experience, their working out—in the absence of an instantaneous mutation—in the timetable of this world's evolutionary crawl would have required at least several millennia. Certainly such sensory feats would seem unlikely within the fleeting cosmic moment between Jacobo da Bologna and Jacob Druckman.

The Harmonic Problem

In confirming and undergirding the purge of tonality, the conceptual forfeiting of the harmonic plane has not gone unnoticed. It is one aspect of an unsolved harmonic problem (Rochberg, Gould, Francès). Added to the reduction of perceptual correspondences that could be drawn from the kinds of building blocks formerly provided by a hierarchical harmonic vocabulary—the resultant loss of play between tension and release (dissonance-consonance, non-harmonic-harmonic)—it could but further corrode the aural experience. Loss of harmonic fluctuation[23] leaves the listener with one less path to perceptual meaning, one less range of clues for decoding the musical message.

The harmonic problem, when regarded at all as such, was never convincingly addressed by Schoenberg or by his successors. Instead, generalizations speak to us in vacuous tautologies, as in the following from Rufer[24] who is quoting Schoenberg:

> The elements of a musical idea are partly incorporated in the horizontal plane as successive sounds, and partly in the vertical plane as simultaneous sounds. The mutual relation of tones regulates the succession of intervals as well as their association into harmonies . . .[25]

So much for questions of harmonic cohesion drawn from the row. It just happens.

But the problem does not go away. It is especially important to our discussion because it is so intimately bound up with Schoenberg's emancipation of dissonance. As we shall note in greater depth and detail subsequently, empirical research in perception has not supported claims made in the past for the cohesive powers incumbent to pitch orderings by virtue of their membership in a twelve-note row. For the moment let us note that psychologist Robert Francès concluded from empirical studies that serialized pitch orderings provide no more perceptual memorability than do random collections. Addressing the harmonic facet of the same problem more directly, he also concluded that a harmonic presentation of a twelve-tone series (chords imposed from row segmentations) can be regarded as neither the equivalent nor the analogue of its melodic presentation, which is a stark and serious departure from the harmonic-melodic equivalences of tonal music. In his words,

> A dodecaphonic melody accompanied by chords dereived from its own series or from its own permutation presents the listener with inevitable non-meaning, in so far as the harmonic parameter is concerned . . . everything is unexpected; nothing is predictable, nothing can be counted on.[26]

George Rochberg, himself an apostate from the dodecaphonic persuasion, explains this gnawing absence of musical cohesion as the inability of Schoenberg's system to provide a suitable harmonic accompaniment for a melody, noting that there is no inherent reason for one set of notes to belong with another set just because both happen to occupy locations within a single collection of twelve. He observes:

> The point is that when harmonic support contradicts—has no common tones with—the melody it is obliged to project and carry, it is not the accompaniment which suffers but the melody itself.[27]

To this Rochberg adds a wistful observation of the historical record, saying that "the intuitive understanding that a given melodic line had an implied harmonic content was never questioned prior to the twentieth century."

NOTES

1. Johannes Kepler, *Harmonice Mundi,* Book V. Aristides Quintilianus favored similar demonstrations (*On Music,* Book II), and these kinds of geometrical fancies were perpetuated into the eighteenth century, notably by Giuseppe Tartini. A modern exposition of the latter is Alexandro Planchart, "A Study of the Theories of Giuseppe Tartini," especially 41–47. A thorough synopsis of Kepler's speculations from a non-musician is Arthur Koestler's arresting study of history's scientific dry-runs, *The Sleepwalkers.*

2. Attempts to rationalize precise harmonic series ratios with the hard knocks of music perception persist yet today. One of the most fascinating (and tenuous) is that of Vladimir A. Lefebvre ("The Fundamental Structures of Human Reflexion"), who postulates an "on-board" computer that controls our appraisals of all things auditory.

3. Shackford, "Some Aspects of Perception."

4. The bounds of "acceptable" interval tuning are discussed recently in Moore, Peters, and Glasberg, "Thresholds for the Detection of Inharmonicity in Complex Tones." Empirical studies of preferences for tuning intervals as categorical objects (as in Hall and Hess, "Perception of Music Interval Tuning") yield predictable conclusions: sustained intervals formed by pure tones are preferred in Just tuning, especially octaves, fifths, fourths, and major thirds (intervals that are easier to tune than remaining categories). But these conclusions can be misleading in regard to sonance judgments *in music.* Even when sustained dyads occur (and are not pure tones), our perceptions are necessarily influenced by the pitch patterns that precede and follow. Also, listeners' preferences for Just (as opposed to equal-tempered) thirds never led them to brand the latter "dissonant."

5. Deutsch, ed., *The Psychology of Music,* 193; Ward, "Subjective Musical Pitch"; and Terhardt, "*Oktavspreizung und Tonhohenverschiebung by Sinustönen.*" Burns and Ward ("Categorical Perception—Phenomenon or Epiphenomenon") concluded that a melodic pitch may be mistuned by as much as a semitone ($\pm$) and still be perceptually categorized as its neighbor.

6. *Bruckner, Mahler, Schoenberg,* 243. It is perplexing that her view (that "there is no necessary connection between the twelve-tone technique and the 'emancipation of dissonance' "), differs so markedly from William Austin's, *Music in the Twentieth Century,* 303.

7. *Theory of Harmony,* 66 (1922, 80).

8. The innovation called "dissonant counterpoint" was indirectly related to Schoenberg's preachments. Charles Seeger described it in *Modern Music* 7 (1930): "On Dissonant Counterpoint." Examples ("Every verticality must bear at least one 2nd or 7th!" the axiom seemed to be) are in Ruth Crawford's *String Quartet,* Charles Ruggles's *The Suntreader,* and in *Symphony No. 4* of Norwegian Fartein Valen (1887–1952).

9. At times we even call black "white." Thus Horace Reisberg tells us that the constant "vertical dissonances" of the "Mondestrucken" of *Pierrot Lunaire* are "stable and therefore consonant" (Wittlich, ed., *Aspects of Twentieth Century Music,* 374).

10. I would counter that stretches of convincing atonality occur in some of the pan-triadic textures of William Schuman's music (as in his *Third Symphony,* "Chorale"). And let us not forget Lowensky's coinage "triadic atonality" to explain the ultra-chromatic textures of Gesualdo et al.

11. *Style and Idea,* 263.

12. Yet even the textures of Japanese Gagaku employ ample melodic embellishments—nonharmonic tones, if you will—set against its droning heavenly chord played on the sho.

13. Attenuation of harmonic variety, especially in serial music, was benignly remarked upon by Wittlich (*Aspects of Twentieth-Century Music,* 458), observing that the "general impression of intervallic similarity" resulted from a constancy of minor seconds and major sevenths.

14. Krenek, "Schoenberg the Centenarian," 90.

15. *Philosophy of Modern Music,* 75.

16. *Treatise on Harmony,* 61 (opening paragraph of Chapter 2, Book II).

17. Zarlino, Book III, in Strunk, *Readings in Music History,* 232. Later theorists have made the same point. Hindemith in *The Craft of Musical Composition,* I, for example, urges the power of harmonic fluctuation as an integral property of structure.

18. Musical comparisons depend upon all other relevant factors (range, timbre, texture, et al.) being equal, but none of those alter the sonance factor itself. What I describe here must be understood as a unique quality of pitch intervals, to which I assign the neutral noun *sonance*. Empirical studies of this property range over the century from C. F. Malmberg in 1918 to Hutchison and Knopoff in 1978.

19. *Style and Idea,* 375.

20. *Theory of Harmony,* 21 (1922, 18).

21. See the discussion of the same problem in Chapter 11.

22. *Style and Idea,* 260.

23. Note that this term is not used here to denote the highly controlled kinds of harmonic fluctuation Hindemith discusses in *The Craft of Musical Composition.*

24. Rufer, *Composition with Twelve Tones,* 83.

25. *Style and Idea,* 220.

26. Robert Francès, *The Perception of Music,* 119.

27. *Aesthetics of Survival,* 59. Observe that George Perle takes exception to the idea that the vertical dimension of atonal music and dodecaphonic music are only a product of linear motions (*Serial Composition and Atonality,* 24). He regards this as an "evasion of the problem and, in any case an overstatement."

CHAPTER 7

Preserving Music Theory's Trinity: Scale, Chord, and Key

Hampered by a fragmented conception of modal theory's basic precepts, and probably unacquainted with the actual sounds of modal music, Schoenberg's assessment of tonality in terms of its longevity and its potential expendability bears examination. Since for him tonality was a product of post-modal chord successions, then music in which the I IV V triumvirate did not prevail (with its derivative scale) must be denied the status of tonality.

Schoenberg gives us no date around which music bearing these properties may have begun to emerge, but for him composers of tonal music initiated the compositional process by pre-selecting (consciously or unconsciously) a particular key, with its scale and chords. And this choice entailed adoption of a harmonic system rooted in the tonic triad of that major or minor key. The tonic chord then required support in real time—we are not told just how—by its dominant and subdominant to confirm its continuing reign. And finally, the melodic figures surrounding and linking these chordal motions are derived from the chosen scale, which is itself a tonal paradigm that confirms the chordally posited tonality.

An accurate history of this chordally-determined conception of tonality is perhaps beyond reconstruction. Yet it is easy to understand how Schoenberg, among others, may have found support for it from no less a figure than Helmholtz, without sufficient attention to the final clause of the great physicist's tracing (which I italicize here):

> As the independent significance of chords came to be appreciated in the fifteenth and sixteenth centuries, a feeling arose for the relationship of chords to one another and to the tonic chord, *in accordance with the same laws which had long ago unconsciously regulated the relationship of compound tones.*[1]

One of Schoenberg's prominent contemporaries, composer Ernst Krenek, expressed the essence of this chordally controlled tonality in his book of 1939, *Music Here and Now*. It is a view that lingers, the received opinion that surrounds many theories of tonality. As Krenek put it:

> Tonality is . . . a harmonic principle. . . . A tone becomes the tonic only when the central triad is built over it.[2]

This apparently benign statement is important because it harbors the crux of a distorted "harmonic" claim to tonality and, even more pertinent to our discussion, perpetuates a strange logical blunder that neutralizes all similar expressions of the condition of tonality. Krenek claims the power of a central triad but fails to tell us just *how a chord achieves centrality* in the first place. Schoenberg at least demands that a *progression* of chords unfolds a tonality, distinguishing between progression and succession with the cryptic observation that "a certain order" promotes the condition of the former.[3]

It is one thing to posit as an a priori condition a chord as tonic, much as Schoenberg divines a priori C-majorishness in the collection of seven natural notes. It is quite another to reveal how the role of tonic arises in a context as the datum of listening. This is really the nub of the matter for a theory of tonality: what dynamics prevail to make one pitch class (or the pitch class's extension, a chord) the tonic for a collection of pitches?

If Schoenberg or Krenek knew the answer to this question, each kept his secret. Before we grapple with it directly, we must test the historical validity of Schoenberg's claim that tonality was absent from music prior to a particular time and ask whether the concept of "central chord" is as vital to a theory of tonality as both he and Krenek contended.

DATING TONALITY

For Schoenberg "the church modes do not at all conform to the law of tonality,"[4] and Krenek supports him obliquely with the claim that "a tone becomes the tonic only when the central triad is built above it."[5] The two composers nonetheless seem to have disagreed a bit over just when tonality came about. Krenek, whose knowledge of early music surpassed Schoenberg's, suggested what he referred to as "the late medieval period."[6] Schoenberg opted for some time around the end of the Renaissance. He was never specific, to my knowledge.

Other writers, and especially German music historians who matured during the 1910–40 decades, leaned more toward Schoenberg's calendar, at times pointing out that the concept of tonality, like the concept of gravity, arose at the same time (Rameau's and Newton's mechanics, respectively). The terms *tonality* and *tonic* do not appear in our literature prior to the nineteenth century. And some historians, like

Manfred Bukofzer, remarked at a conjunction of tonality with the concept of gravity that suggested a curious set of causal relationships. They seemed to assume, and so they inform their readers,[7] that the *condition* of tonality therefore could have existed only after its concept had been formulated.[8] In so doing, those historians ignored the irksome consequences to which such reasoning would lead if applied to gravity. Wolfgang Köhler made clear the fallaciousness of the notion—that perceptual events could not have prevailed before their descriptions were objectified in formal discourse. It is our good fortune that he even used gravity for his example:

> Everybody knows that objects will fall if they are not supported. But, although they actually will fall to the ground, it took mankind a long time to realize that "the ground" plays an active role in the event. *Falling* is a common fact, but gravitation, a fact of functional dependence, is not directly observed.[9]

No elaborate historical-deductive process is required to show that the hard and fast marriage of tonality and functional harmony was made not in heaven but in ignorance. Historians subsequent to Bukofzer's generation have been less wary of correspondences, less prone to stress differences between repertories from widely separated times.[10] It is not true, as rumor once had it, that the musical Gothic was populated by people whose aural processes were different from ours. Today we can better comprehend the connecting tissues that make our tonal history whole as well as believable. Clearly the minds of our remote ancestors worked quite as do ours, speaking through tonal languages with their own special piquancies, yet ordered within common perceptual channels. As Richard Crocker argued in a classic statement, we are grossly misled when tentative understandings lead us to annex our musical ancestors off into stuffy little prisons. Some of our misconceptions of medieval music arose, as Crocker recognized, from a penchant for attributing alien musical bases to anything that differs markedly in style from what we are accustomed to hearing. Some music historians of our first half-century found medieval melody shapeless, its accompanying harmonies crude; and in this, Crocker notices, "the modern mind was willing to attribute philosophic brilliance but not common sense perception to the musical contemporaries of St. Thomas Aquinas."[11]

THE HARMONIC SCHISM: CHORD PROGRESSION VERSUS MELODY

Some theorists who agreed with the concept of modal-tonal standoff argued most notably by Schoenberg maintain, nonetheless, a slightly more liberal perspective. They admit at least of tonality in non-chordal textures, favoring a double accounting for tonal structure. Such reasoning usually involves what is called "harmonic tonality," suggesting that the chord-based version is somehow ultimately separable from any other kind, like "melodic tonality." Whatever its historical or perceptual shortcomings, it is at least an explanation that avoids the embarrassments that associate with a tonality-gravity conjunction. One theorist who appears to embrace this dualism, though a bit tentatively, is Carl Dahlhaus. He writes that "Harmonic tonality . . . formed the foundation of compositions from the 17th century to the early 20th."[12] But he then confides that the whole notion of a separate, chordally controlled tonality "is largely a matter not of hard factual evidence in musical sources but of interpretation and inference." The actual historical development of this harmonic tonality, he continues, "is shrouded more in conjecture than in traceable paths of change."

And then, perhaps suffering the same ontological twitch that often surfaces in discussions of tonality in history, Dahlhaus observes that it is a moot point "whether the 15th century cadence form shown [in Example 11] . . . is a dominant-tonic cadence."[13] This leaves one with a perplexing question. In what sense can one deny that this succession exemplifies every necessary ingredient of a dominant-tonic cadence—at least, if its context justifies calling it a cadence in the first place?

EXAMPLE 11. Problematic V–I cadence.

HARMONY/CHORD: AN IDENTITY PROBLEM

This disjunctive view, severing harmony from melody, like mind from body, nature from nurture, most often holds implicitly that the concept and the condition of harmony be synonymous with the concept and condition of chord,[14] forgetting, among other annoying facts, that the etymology of the word *harmony* demands no such exclusivity. Certainly the "agreement in feeling, approach, action, disposition, sympathy, and accord" one finds abundant in dictionary entries for the word, as generic noun, imposes no restrictions of simultaneity. The history of uses in the music record, prior to the current century at least, provides no support either. As Gustave Reese reminds us, early Greeks used the term *harmoniai* in the sense of *tonos*, or key system. Both Plato and Aristotle use the word most frequently as interchangeable with mode (meaning considerably more than just a collection of notes, or scale).[15] And Zarlino, nineteen centuries later,[16] confides that his contemporaries and their immediate predecessors at times used interchangeably the terms *modes, harmoniae, tropes,* and *systems.*[17]

The narrow (and unfortunate) meaning that links harmony inextricably with chords has developed and solidified in musicians' vocabularies only since the late seventeenth century. It remained entrenched in the musicological psyche as a profound truth well into the twentieth century, to be dispelled only when an acquaintance with early music became more readily achieved. The idea was a confederate of the opinion that medieval and Renaissance polyphony were neither controlled by "harmonic laws," that they answered, on the contrary, only to "purely linear" processes.[18] Benito Rivera has assured us that this misleading yet long-revered remnant of our past has been "finally rejected" by the scholarly community,[19] but even today the lingering conventional wisdom occasionally reflects the mischief of this unconscionable idea.

I do not wish to quibble over words or foolishly to bemoan the vicissitudes of linguistic change. It is only when the altered connotations and denotations of a term begin to cloud our understanding of reality that we must grow concerned. And the loss of *harmonic* in describing tones deployed in other than simultaneous configurations has led to an erosion in our comprehension of tonal kinetics. Perhaps most directly, it has been a factor in denying chordal and melodic patterns one of their most important ties.

We have noted continually that pitch focus is the central and controlling condition of tonality. Let us further observe that those who agree with Dahlhaus, Krenek, and Schoenberg, on positing the concept of *harmonic tonality,* also agree that pitch focus is crucial to it; it is embodied therein by the tonic triad, and thus ultimately by that chord's root. On the other hand, those who could not admit of a "non-harmonic" tonality—and this appears to include Krenek as well as Schoenberg (see p. 79)— have argued that music lacking chords deployed in some ordering of tonic, dominant, subdominant cannot possess pitch focus. That attribute arises as an exclusively harmonic phenomenon.

If pitch focus is, as we have argued, the irreducible condition of tonality, and if pitch focus can be shown as a property in non-chordal music from beyond the West-European cultural orbit of the past three hundred years, then it follows that tonality must be recognized as a property of far broader scope, syntactically and historically, than Schoenbergian tradition has allowed. And to anticipate subsequent discussion, the evidence of early music (let us say music produced before the seventeenth century) and the evidence of music of non-Western origins both strongly suggest that humanity has been making music within the steadying influence of pitch focus from the earliest preserved melodic relics, from the initial uses of sound as more than the expression of immediate emotional or functional cares.

TONALITY AS STAPLE

Finding music whose patterns do not explicitly and directly project a central pitch (or pitch class) as pitch nucleus is a rare exception, no matter what the music's cultural or chronological origins may be. It is furthermore rare—and this is central to our story—when prominence is not handmaiden in some simple fashion to the delineating powers inherent to the pitch-rhythm amalgam, in synchrony with an archetypal role of the harmonic series. The accessible record of ancient West-European music and of primitive musics blocks the conclusion that textures outside the Zarlino-Rameau-Riemann-Schoenberg purview somehow escaped the primacy of tonality. That record shows that they achieved coherence through allegiance to a hierarchy of tonal relationships that is uniquely and emphatically *harmonic,* even when chordless.

However eccentric the idea may seem to some, it is neither difficult nor new as it applies to perception in general. Gestaltist Köhler called the principle that makes credible this kind of harmonic monism *sensory transformation.* In one of his classic statements of what today we would usually call "grouping processes," he discussed how in a structural sense a chord is the same as the identical collection of pitches sounded in succession, observing that one "unity" is no less real than the other.[20] "We have no right," he adds, "to contradict similar observations in other cases." That this kind of harmonic coherence applies to far more than the chord successions of Bach-through-Brahms is implicit in every statement we find in the historical record in which melodic tones are characterized in hierarchical fashion, by their relatively *stable* or *neutral* or *alien* statures within a context.

In this respect a picturesque analogy from the lore of ancient India forcefully predicts the kinds of tonal dynamics later Western music theorists would write about. Although couched in the colorful metaphor of a feudal society, its meaning is clear, its message timeless. (I am indebted to Lewis Rowell, whose *Thinking about Music* brought it to my attention.)

> *The Ruler:*   the tonic as goal and ultimate stability.
> *His Generals and Ministers:*   Strong, prominent, stable tones.
> *His Vassals:*   Weak, neutral, unstable tones.
> *His Enemies:*   Foreign tones.[21]

And stability, we must urge, is ultimately a harmonic condition.

THE CONCEPT-PERCEPT ANOMALY

As we saw in Chapter 5, Schoenberg's evolutionary conception envisioned music's development in part as a progression from the crudities of limited pitch collections (the modes, various non-Western scales) to the simple but supremely rewarding state of total chromaticism. Aside from the tenuous historical view this conception poses, it also raises critical questions of perceptual processes and how they may or may not equate with our conceptualizations.

For example, a crucial difference separates the perceptual potential of major and minor scales and the chromatic scale, as we shall discuss in some detail presently. It is a difference that thwarts attempts to confer analogous powers on the latter as an evolutionary replacement for either of the former. It is not my intent to laud the "nature-given" or the "miraculous" beauties of the major or the minor scales; I find all scales equally implausible objects of veneration, equally unlikely gifts, received fullblown, from Mother Nature. I wish only to observe that inherent differences separate the chromatic gamut (which in a strict sense should not even be called a scale) from scales composed of unequal intervals.

INQUIRIES FROM PSYCHOLOGY

The question whether a twelve-note scale or a twelve-note row derived therefrom can provide an archetypal pitch function in perception arose early and rarely received the disciplined and impartial discussion it merited. Schoenberg minced no words about the role of the series in providing coherence to an extended work. In *Structural Functions of Harmony,* which he completed in 1948, Schoenberg observes (p. 194) that the harmonic progressions of dodecaphonic music are not governed by harmonic roots. They derive coherence from the set itself; "They are vertical projections of the basic set, or parts of it, and their combination is justified by its logic." In the essay "My Evolution" of 1949 he tells us that,

> every unit of a piece being a derivative of the tonal relations in a basic set
> of twelve tones, the "Grundgestalt" is coherent because of this permanent
> reference to the basic set. [22]

Then Josef Rufer, in a book originally planned as a collaborative effort with Schoenberg, confirms that effective identity relationships bear between row permutations and basic set. On those structural interdependencies he comments:

> So far as I know, no one has yet discussed the powerful effect of these
> symmetrical relations on the creation of form—those in the horizontal
> (melodic) dimension, between the original series and its retrograde and
> between inversion and retrograde inversion; and those in the vertical
> (contrapuntal) dimension, between original series and inversion and be-
> tween retrograde and retrograde inversion. But this seems to be of great, if
> not fundamental importance for musical coherence. [23]

Yet one of the first to begin filling in the empirical void that surrounds these questions, French psychologist Robert Francès, arrived at conclusions as early as 1968 that negate Schoenberg's assumptions and Rufer's enthusiastic support. [24] Francès concluded that even without the added complexities of the transformations of inversion, retrogression, retrograde inversion, serial unity lies more on the conceptual than on the perceptual level; when thwarted by melodic motion, rhythm, and the harmonic grouping of tones, it remains very difficult to hear.[25]

One facet of his study revealed subjects mistaken more often (61.2%) than not in their attempts just to identify correspondences between melodies and a parent series.

More recent opinion, similarly drawn from empirical research, offers no greater promise, suggesting instead the accuracy of Milton Babbitt's idea that music molded from permutational operations demands a different perceptual processing from music yielded by the tonal syntax of combinational methods.[26] Informative reports can be found in Deutsch, and Krumhansl, Sandell, and Sargeant.[27]

Approaching the problem through use of pitch recall strategies, as proof of pattern apprehension and association, Diana Deutsch's conclusions stress the need for phenomenal hierarchical relatedness of some form in the perception of tones:

> Sequences whose tonal structure could be parsimoniously incoded in hierarchical fashion were recalled with a high level of accuracy. Sequences that could not . . . produced substantially more errors in recall.[28]

Adding some insight about how the perceptual act occurs, she goes on to observe that,

> We encode tonal materials by inferring sequence structures and alphabets at different hierarchical levels, together with rules of combination.

Only the 1988 study of Krumhansl et al. holds a ray of hope for dodecaphonic perceptual solvency, and it is tenuous. The study cautiously concludes that the matter cannot be considered fully closed, that further research might confirm rudimental kinds of perceptual coherence of the sort claimed by Schoenberg and implied by an abundance of serialists' analyses. But even the "qualified" hope held out by the authors is tempered by their recognition that the experimental design of their study was biased in favor of positive results and that anomalous individual differences arose in subject responses.

While empirical support for Schoenberg's central thesis continues to be un-verified, one conclusion cannot be ignored: to assume the auditory invariances of dodecaphonic series, in their permutable forms, demands more optimism than appears to be warranted.

THEORISTS MULL THE QUESTION

Some writers who raise such a question impart a certain air of nervous indecision, the specter of walking fast while looking nervously back over the shoulder. But opinion runs a wide gamut, a·broad range of presumed certainty. At one extreme is Will

Ogden, who finds harmonic roots of the Rameau variety in Schoenberg's atonal music[29] (and would, we presume, find them as readily in serialized textures). At the opposite extreme is George Rochberg who has come to regard the twelve-note series as experientially impotent.[30]

In less extreme positions between these two are persons who appear to adopt an attitude of benign agnosticism, calling all the while upon colleagues for a rational approach to analysis, to claims made on behalf of dodecaphonic processes. One of these, William Benjamin, tackles the problem head-on, although implicit in his argument is the assumption that atonal sets, whether serialized or not, can give rise to structure. Pleading for explicit and ordered rules in analytical procedures, he recognizes that deductive excesses have made many analyses a priori rhapsodizing rather than musical clarification.[31] However emphatically the analytical predispositions of Serialism may deny the relevance of perceptual correspondences to pre-compositional and compositional processes, the musical transaction doggedly does (and most likely will continue to) impose some human predilections. Whether we call them "natural" or "unnatural," whether we view them as genetically "wired-in" or as contextually learned impulses, is beside the point. There is a ring of authenticity to Leonard B. Meyer's reminder that we "infer causal relationships" from the de facto chronology that is a necessary component of the musical act, whatever may have been the composer's intention or working habits.[32] As Meyer goes on to say,

> We attempt . . . to relate earlier events to later ones, discovering implications and attributing a causal order to the series of stimuli.

And Meyer's words are musical confirmation of psychologist Jerome Bruner's criticism of the old empty-vessel notion of perception. As he noted, over a quarter of a century ago,

> We know . . . that the nervous system is not the one way street we thought it was—carrying messages from the environment to the brain, there to be organized into representations of the real world. Rather, the brain has a program that is its own, and monitoring orders are sent out from the brain to the sense organs and relay stations specifying priorities for different kinds of environmental messages. Selectivity is the rule, and a nervous system . . . is as much an editorial hierarchy as it is a system for carrying signals.[33]

Regardless what may turn out to be the perceptual/cognitive endowments of the chromatic scale or of serialized pitch orderings, let us for the moment observe that it is neither experientially plausible nor historically demonstrable that (1) the church modes replaced (c. 900 A.D.) a loose, unformalized system of primitive pre-Christian pitch organization; (2) that major and minor scales rendered obsolete (c.

1650) the earlier codifications of modes; and (3) that the chromatic scale rescued music (c. 1900) from the fate of tonal exhaustion.

On the fringes of the continuing debate over the perceptual fertility of twelve-tone constructs are theorists who like Nicholas Cook confidently disown the whole notion that congruences need exist at all between concepts of musical structure and the aural experience, between concept and percept. Professing a poetic license that few musicians or psychologists would find compelling, he writes:

> There is no intrinsic need for the theorist to conceive of musical structures in the same manner that the listener perceives them.[34]

Perhaps we need add only that the adoption of Professor Cook's immaculate conception would certainly make music theory much easier.

THE CRITICAL DIFFERENCE OF ASYMMETRICAL SCALES

Church modes and major and minor scales, as distinguished from chromatic ones, are capable of projecting structural hierarchy. They embody internal parts which, when joined, possess beginnings and ends; they are by definition bounded collections.

It was Heinrich Schenker's insight that tonal structure arises from the deployment through time of a basic chord, and that the implicit structural meaning of major and minor scales is their potential for doing just that.[35] Their pitches simultaneously outline and "pass through" the chord, so to speak, which is the act of *Auskomponierung*. The differentiation of their parts, through mixtures of tones and semitones, can delineate a harmonic ground in a way the chromatic scale cannot.

The potential for closure of most of the scales singled out by our tradition (a variety of gapped scales as well as the more conventional) ensures the necessary (but not sufficient) ability of the collection to project a unique tonal hierarchy. Possessing this virtue, it can achieve the status of conceptual unit, the archetypal function Schoenberg speaks of as *Auffassungseinheit*.

Musicians have recognized this octave-scalar dependence as far back as documents report on such matters. In her study of the doctrine of Pythagoras and his reporter Nichomachus (second century A.D.), Flora R. Levin tells us that even the word used in classical documents to denote the octave relationship meant "the interval which *extends through all the notes*"[36] (my italics).

The chromatic scale is the correlate in pitch space of a time period filled by undifferentiated pulses; it is an example of a flat or single-level structure, a non-hierarchy. We can paraphrase Paracelsus' indelicate condemnation of four-sided triangles by observing that God can make an ass with three tails, but not a perceptual unit from the chromatic scale. It is incorrigibly a nominalist collection of singular elements, on its own incapable of projecting hierarchic structure. Although it is richer by five elements than the diatonic scale, it cannot match at least one perceptual potential of scales made from unequal intervals. If it is the evolutionary product of music's progress, as a cognitive archetype it was a regressive mutation.[37]

As a construct, the chromatic scale is nothing more than a useful representation of pitch resources, a listing of ingredients. It needs no contrived tale about how it evolved from anything else, whether from the harmonic series' upper partials (as Schoenberg argued) or from the accidental cohabitations of antecedent note collections (as Schoenberg also argued). Nonetheless, this notion of evolution, church modes→major/minor→chromatic scale, has become the received wisdom of twentieth-century music theory, its staying power in no small measure due to the authoritative position Schoenberg has held in such matters. Accepted widely without serious challenge, its presumed verity as historical fact only adds to the presumed credibility of Schoenberg's theory of a broader musical evolution.

HISTORICAL CONSIDERATIONS

Finally, let us consider some historical points relevant to chromaticism's checkered career. Music well before Bach's time, and certainly before the date Schoenberg seemed to have in mind for the official demise of major and minor, employed extensive chromaticism. The only barrier to its fuller incorporation into music before Bach lay not in conceptual or creative limitations. Its widespread exploitation probably would have come at least as early as the fifteenth century if true equal temperament could have been applied to voices and instruments (in addition to organ and guitar) that would ensure, without intolerable attentiveness, the maintenance of consistent and accurate pitch.

Technological limitations most likely kept widespread chromaticism from flourishing before Bach's time, although its occurrence before then was far more extensive than Schoenberg's simplified scheme suggested.[38] It is important in passing to note that a madrigal of 1551, Cypriano de Rore's *Calami Sonum Ferentes,* begins with a theme that comes close to duplicating the full chromatic complement. And Edward Lowensky's provocative study of *Tonality and Atonality in Sixteenth-Century Music* reminds us of how richly endowed with pitch resources one small pocket of the late Renaissance was.[39]

Conclusion? The obstinate evolutionary cant of modality→tonality→pantonality owed more to Schoenberg's earnest wish to fulfill the promise of the final stage than to an omnibus view of music from both of its two preceding stages. But even if the developmental procession he described had taken place with such pristine clarity, his presumption that humanity was enlightened by this knowledge was misguided. He was a victim of the Genetic Fallacy, the error of supposing that one knows the substance of a thing when its origins have been sorted out.

The evolutionary scheme was nonetheless central to Schoenberg's belief that he needed to "replace the no longer applicable principle of tonality by a new principle."[40] Regardless how the scheme fit his hopeful willing of music's future, it required an unconfirmed developmental process; it also postulated that in due time the new, the surviving (shall we say "the fittest?") pitch collection would become for music listeners an acquired auditory characteristic. It is an idea unlikely to survive. While the biological hypotheses of evolution presume a drama played out over millions of years, the fleeting time assumed within Schoenberg's scenario seems eminently implausible. His theory is a sobering example of how a premise need not be true to alter the history of an art.

NOTES

1. Helmholtz, *The Sensations of Tone*, 369.

2. *Music Here and Now*, 108.

3. *Structural Functions of Harmony*, 1.

4. *Style and Idea*, 276.

5. Krenek, loc. cit.

6. Ibid., 209. Don Randel speaks of the emergence of "triadic tonality" at a time about midway between Krenek's and Schoenberg's datings ("Emerging Triadic Tonality in the Fifteenth Century").

7. Bukofzer, *Music in the Baroque Era*, 12 and 385–386. Schoenberg's perspective corresponded well with historian Bukofzer's, who saw tonality as a slow emergent of the middle Italian Baroque, reaching full development in the late Baroque works of Provenzale (1627–1704) and Corelli (1653–1713).

8. Historical musicology suffered an excessive case of nominalism just after World War II, when its formative giants were largely the brilliant refugees from Hitler's desecrations. The times were marked by a vigilant patrolling of the tidy fence that separated "authenticated hard facts dug from contemporary sources" from "wanton interera syntheses." One spoke, in those days in certain circles, about correspondences between, say, fourteenth- and eighteenth-century musics only with the fear of losing tenure. It was a period described by Joseph Kerman (*Contemplating Music*) as "poised on the brink of the positivistic dilemma: more and more facts and less and less confidence in interpreting them."

9. Köhler, *Dynamics in Psychology*, 15.

10. Compare Hoppin's *Medieval Music* (1978) with Reese's *Music in the Middle Ages* (1940) for one contrast in perspectives.

11. Richard Crocker, "Discant, Counterpoint, and Harmony."

12. Dahlhaus, "Tonality," *The New Grove Dictionary of Music*. Rudolph Reti, *Tonality in Modern Music*, devotes lengthy discussion to *melodic tonality*, especially within pages 32–35.

13. Dahlhaus, "Tonality."

14. For a classic statement of this position see A. Tillman Merritt's entry, "Harmony," *Harvard Dictionary of Music*, 1944 ed.

15. Reese, *Music in the Middle Ages*, 44. Also see Anderson, *Ethos and Education in Greek Music*, 194.

16. Zarlino, *Istituzioni Armoniche*, 12.

17. The changing technical vocabulary in our early history is helpfully assayed by Wingell, "Anonymous XI and Questions of Terminology in Theoretical Writings of the Middle Ages and Renaissance."

18. In this respect, I find it compelling that thousands of music students each year, when directed in ear training classes to "sing a major chord," produce an acceptable response, albeit decidedly "melodic."

19. Benito Rivera, "Harmonic Theory in Musical Treatises of the Late Fifteenth and Early Sixteenth Centuries," 80.

20. *Gestalt Psychology*, 124.

21. Makund Lath, *A Study of "Dattilam" : A Treatise on the Sacred Music of Ancient India,* 233. See Leonard Ratner's *Classic Music* for a charming eighteenth-century version of a similar taxonomy (Riepel's *Grundregeln,* 1755).

22. *Style and Idea,* 91.

23. Rufer, *Composition with Twelve Tones,* 85.

24. *The Perception of Music,* 116–127.

25. Ibid.

26. Babbitt, "Twelve-Tone Invariants as Compositional Determinants," 108.

27. Deutsch, "The Processing of Structured and Unstructured Tonal Sequences"; Krumhansl et al., "The Perception of Tone Hierarchies and Mirror Forms in Twelve-Tone Serial Music."

28. "The processing of Structured and Unstructured Tonal Sequences," 381 (Summary).

29. Ogden, "How Tonality Functions in Schoenberg's Opus 11."

30. This is a dominant message in *The Aesthetics of Survival,* 1975.

31. William Benjamin, "Ideas of Order in Motivic Music," 24.

32. Meyer, "The End of the Renaissance?" 184.

33. Bruner, *On Knowing,* 2.

34. Cook, "The Perception of Large-Scale Tonal Closure," 203.

35. Schenker's monumental insight was marred by his conclusion that only major and minor triads could serve this archetypal function. And since in his judgment they could be horizontalized only in narrowly prescribed ways (limited degrees in certain descending orders as *Urlinien*), only compositions that fulfilled the prescriptions could properly be called music.

36. *The Harmonics of Nichomachus and the Pythagorean Tradition,* 81.

37. This is not a plea that "The older things are better!" or that "Major is the best of all possible . . .!" Far from it. The collection of twelve pitch classes is not on trial here; only the chromatic scale as conceptual unit—as candidate for the role of *Auffassungseinheit*—is being weighed in the perceptual balance and found wanting.

38. It would be tempting to claim some precedence even for the chromatic and enharmonic genera of the Greek tetrachordal system, but what little we know about that (other than as theoretical construct) restrains the urge.

39. Leonard B. Meyer long ago discussed the abundant chromaticism in text-anchored music of Renaissance Netherlands motets and Italian madrigals. *Emotion and Meaning in Music,* 219–221.

40. *Letters,* No. 78 (to Hauer, December 1923).

PART III:

Sorting Out the Issues

CHAPTER 8

A New Look at Some Old Ideas

Evidence in the lore of music theory, largely ignored or misunderstood, confirms that pitch focus does not depend for its projection upon the presence of chords.[1] Indeed, a tempting conclusion from the accumulations of history is that tonality *as a harmonic phenomenon* rests on more primitive foundations, foundations that operated in music long before chords became the all-powerful purveyors of harmonic structure Rameau led us to believe. A rich documentation of ancient and medieval musical practice and commentary, as well as the musical produce of other cultures, grants us a perspective that was not accessible to Schoenberg and his contemporaries. That which was accessible went largely ignored by Schoenberg.

THE DYNAMICS OF PERCEIVING

Furthermore, important work in perceptual psychology, much of it done within the very era when Schoenberg was active, is helpful in piecing together a better idea of the development of musical structures in the whole of history. Although often narrowly focused on studies of visual perception, the Gestalt movement in particular, early in the century, gave us some frameworks within which to understand how and why a collection of objects or events can, by properties inherent in their dispositions, cause one element of the collection to dominate, inclining the perceiver toward a particular meaning (or interpretation) of structure.

The classic figures devised by Edgard Rubin, who was a pioneer in studies of the shifting sands of visual experience, give us vivid illustrations of structural ambivalence; his work,[2] with that of others, shows us how the content and distribution of a collection leads us to the interpretation of one potential layout of elements rather than another, even though that cognitive distribution may be subject to radical realignments. For instance, the dark cross of Example 12b is more likely to be the first apprehended figure, while Rubin's rendering, as in Example 12a, offers two figure-ground potentials that are more equally probable, and thus form a more ambiguous structure.

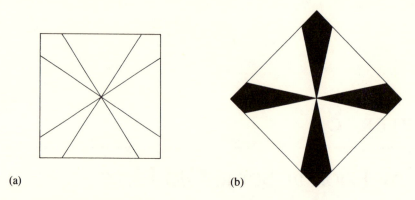

(a)   (b)

EXAMPLE 12. Figure-ground potentials. (a) more equally probable; (b) unequally probable.

A literature less well known, but more directly related to music, sheds light on how we respond to collections of points in visual or auditory space,[3] seeing or hearing them as hierarchical patterns, as objects of inherent meaning.[4]

Let us consider one instance of auditory focus, of figure-ground distribution, that can represent Gestalt findings and point in a direction helpful to our discussion. As a simple and straightforward example, imagine hearing a series of "randomized" low tones whose collective sameness is occasionally punctured by a higher pitch, an intrusion repeated in regular or irregular rhythm; see Example 13. This bare context of differentiated parts leads us to accept the higher pitched (or "separated") tonal layer as the element of concentration, as the total context's element of focus. A *pointing-to* has occurred, an auditory vector activated.[5] The result is precisely analogous to the kinds of visual examples (one pigeon separated from the flock) used by Gestaltists to make explicit how elements of visual percepts can project hierarchy.[6]

EXAMPLE 13. Figure-ground aural differentiation.

Why does the figure-ground distinction occur?

The causes seem obvious if we attend only to the surface issues of structure. The two elements (upper and lower textural layers of the auditory illustration) are starkly differentiated by pitch level, by rhythmic density and articulation, and by contour (the roller coaster bottom versus the static top). The tones separated by their pitch and rhythmic singularity thus become the point of focus, the collection's pitch locus, the passage's *tonic,* as the product of a perceptual trait that operates in our tactile and

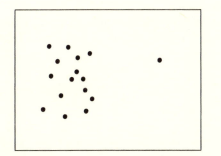

EXAMPLE 14. The one-versus-many of visual segregation.

visual fields as well. The high part is segregated out as point of focus, as foreground, by the dynamics of the context itself, not by forces of nature exclusive of the data as perceived.[7]

The important conclusion from such experiential inclinations is easy to make: perceptual forces unrelated to such things as chords operate within and shape the musical experience, sometimes separately and sometimes in conjunction with the more complex (and, in the full spectrum of history, more recent) textural factor of chords.

THE PIONEERING TAXONOMY OF OTTO ORTMANN[8]

Using an approach consonant with a Gestaltist perspective, musician Otto Ortmann once resolutely pursued this matter of how certain tones can insinuate one of their members onto our experience as focal point, as a rallying point around which all others congregate in a marvelous kind of cognitive hierarchy. In doing this he revealed some of the aspects of music which, although important for us, are easily ignored because they are as much as hidden by their simplicity and familiarity. Ortmann's researches systematized what we already knew as listeners. It is the directness, the simplicity, the utter obviousness of his conclusions that make them immediately credible, though anything but platitudinous.

Ortmann skillfully ferreted out and explained some of the latent yet wholly evident secrets of tonal interaction, with particular attention to what he called *laws of contiguity.* In doing so, he made explicit what every careful listener has learned from years of hearing tone patterns, how we instinctively and instantly stack them up against one another to "build" larger patterns from smaller tonal bits, and how these processings, these cognitive weighings, have everything to do with the structure we apprehend, the meaning we derive.[9] He found that tones become impressive by being temporal or spatial boundary tones, as first or highest, as last or lowest, or even as segregated middle within a context of highs and lows. Thus succession "a" in Example 15 contains a more dominant C than succession "b," whose pitches do not establish the same kind of tiered separation. Later empirical studies of these underlying kinds of musical dynamics have confirmed Ortmann's fundamental contentions of what conditions lead to relative pitch prominence and memorability. The work of Guilford and Hilton, Deutsch, and Brown is particularly relevant in this regard.[10]

EXAMPLE 15. Pitch emphasis through tiered segregation (Ortmann, "On the Melodic Relativity of Tones").

In describing the relative indices of first and last tones in the dynamics of pitch power brokering, Ortmann theorized that, in spite of its contextual advantage, elemental temporal matters could reduce the significance of a beginning pitch. In his words:

> Since the first tone of a melody is always the tone farthest removed from the objective presentation of other tones, its projection in consciousness is weakest. If the melody . . . exceeds the memory-span, the first tone, in spite of its original emphasis, will be last for consciousness. The last tone, on the other hand, receives a double emphasis, because to the accentuation of boundary tone is added the accentuation of greatest recency.[11]

His goal was to determine what conditions prevail to cause any one pitch to seem more important than its neighbors. He concluded his speculative study (which included empirical testing) with the simple maxim:

> The status of a tone in consciousness is not controlled by any one series, either pitch or time, but is modified by the total environment.[12]

Of greatest importance is the way Ortmann's version of melodic dynamics speaks of pitch hierarchy exclusive of chords and, in so doing, implicitly puts the burden of musical structuring on the listener, as cooperating agent with the stimulus. We shall return to this point later, but for the moment we leave the topic of melodic structuring with the observation that this matter of tonal orientation—what we are calling pitch focus—appears to run deeper than Schoenberg (and many others) imagined.

The condition of pitch focus can occur when one tone lasts longer than its neighbors, or because it is rearticulated, or because it is returned to in what we know as a neighboring-tone figure. All of these are homely instances which demonstrate how fundamental pitch focus is and what prosaic actions bring it about. These pristine shaping forces are controlled by the two inseparable musical realms, temporal order and pitch location.

I can think of no reason to assume that these elemental kinds of pitch differentiation were not present in the music of all times and cultures, at least from the day music became more than a wild cry, more than the simplest gesture of functional communication. It would be historically shortsighted to believe, as Schoenberg held, that tonality sprang forth fully developed just when the major ad minor scale (or the dominant and subdominant triads) supplanted the church modes. The "harmonic tonality" Schoenberg espoused as "the tonality" is only one stylistic manifestation of the broader condition of pitch orientation. It prevailed long before J. S. Bach conceived of a chord progression.

As a speculative issue, this subsumed harmonic tonality is especially interesting in the light of biologist Peter Medawar's description of the fate of most scientific explanations of matter. In his survey of induction he observes that:

> Sometimes theories merely fade away. . . . More often they are merely assimilated into wider theories in which they rank as special cases. The law of recapitulation and the Germ-layer Theory have not been shown to be "wrong." They have simply lost their identity and their special significance in an improved understanding of the mechanism of development. They have been trivialized.[13]

Perhaps harmonic tonality is best understood as a now-trivialized corner, in Medawar's sense, of a broader tonal explanation that works for the whole of music. And chords, along with scales and modes, turn out to be rather complicated exemplars of pitch organization, at least when compared with the more encompassing and primal aspects of perceptual processings described by Ortmann.[14]

OUTSIDE THE "COMMON PRACTICE"

Schoenberg seems to have been either unaware or uninterested in the artifacts of other cultures. Unlike Debussy, who found the Indonesian Gamelan enchanting, and unlike Picasso, who found the ritual statuary of Africa provocative and stimulating, Schoenberg was influenced rather narrowly by recent German sources. His perspective of musical structure, of the ultimate conceptual bases of his art, were similarly shaped. He most likely would have scoffed at the idea that valuable insights might be gained from knowing musics alien to his own culture. And yet it seems plausible that the music of a modern primitive society, music from people relatively untouched by the professionalization of our highly developed culture, might illuminate aspects of music rendered shadowy by centuries of development. Such music might even reflect properties and processes common to music produced by musicians of much earlier times who were within our West-European cultural precedents.

The hypothesis at least gives us an opportunity to observe first hand the musical products of our contemporaries whose cultural development in some facets of their lives is comparable to those of our ancestors. And similarly, music and concepts preserved for us from sophisticated musical systems, such as those of the Javanese *gamelan,* Japanese *Gagaku,* the *rāga* of India, also suggest a glimmer of insight into what it is in music-making that is mere local custom, what is universally obligatory.

Ethnomusicologists have probably been the greatest source of fresh insights about our art during this century. Though reared in the common-practice heritage confirmed by Schoenberg, they have not as a rule supported the notion that tonality is inseparable from major and minor scales or from the tonic-dominant-subdominant hierarchy of chords of European art music.

TONALITY IN NON-WESTERN MUSIC

Ethnomusicologists have as a rule, however, been reluctant to claim binding parallels between the musics of their concern (music at times referred to as "primitive" in a pejorative sense) and the so-called *harmonic music* and its key system of the European common-practice period. Their caution to be objective reporters has been most evident in the careful avoidance of musical descriptions that may seem filtered through perceptual misconceptions, especially misconceptions developed from hearing the music of their native milieu. So we sometimes read scrupulous disclaimers, carefully framed reminders that the melodies of Western Africa or of Aborigines of the Australian Bush or of the Japanese Imperial Court or of Shawnee Indians of Middle America must not be approached with the preconceptions of one who grew up on Wolfgang Mozart and/or Victor Herbert.

One of the founders of modern ethnomusicology, Erich von Hornbostel (1877– 1935), like the majority of his successors, was eager to avoid invoking European conceptions of harmony to understand the almost exclusively melodic objects he studied. He nonetheless felt obliged to raise the specter of harmony-related matters in discussing non-European music's structural foundations. With the maturity of one who had spent many exhausting years off the beaten track in the field studying the native musics of, among others, Indonesia, Japan, Africa, and the United States, he concluded that perfect fifths and perfect fourths, those ubiquitous girders of the modal system as well as of the music of J. S. Bach, are unparalleled structural pillars in African melody. His words have reverberated often in the discussions of his successors, especially when they speak of basic tonal organization in the music of this or that culture. As he cautiously explained in 1928, "pure melody does contain elements related to those which, in our music, have contributed to form harmony."[15]

The melodies collected by von Hornbostel in West Africa are narrow in range, rarely reaching a span of an octave. In this they resemble the unsophisticated music produced by non-professionals everywhere, the kind that demands no technological expertise and for which no formal system of musical dialectics has been framed. They are similar in structure to songs sung and danced to the world over. And von Hornbostel points out that in these songs melodically related

> fourths and fifths are more important and more frequent than octaves. . . . They are . . . used as constructive elements determining the distance between predominant notes, the compass of melodic phrases, and the rise or fall of a melody. . . . In this way they mark off the field where melody is at play.[16]

He shares with us a disarming example of this tonal framing, the same kind of pitch-bounding-in-time that can be heard in hundreds of the melodies of the repertory of Western chant, not to mention in the melodies of the folk musics of the world, in European art music, and in songs from communal repertories that serve the diverse ritual needs of humanity at large (see Example 16, for instance).[17] Like the nursery song "Mary Had a Little Lamb," *Makua* is organized in relation to a focal pitch, its tonic. Even more remarkable, both songs share the same pitch frame, functionally bounded by the perfect fifth C–G, even though their melodic patterns are geographical and cultural worlds apart. My reader may find it instructive to seek a nursery song, such as "London Bridge" or "Twinkle, Twinkle, Little Star," that *does not* exhibit the same or a similar framing action, a structural paradigm that dominates countless melodies of all times and all cultures.[18]

EXAMPLE 16. Two-part women's dancing song, *Makua* (von Hornbostel, "African Negro Music," 44).

Tonally, the usual children's songs are no less primitive than von Hornbostel's African dancing song. They certainly are no more demanding on a performer, which probably accounts for their endurance within the repertory. As these melodies make evident, the aspect of tonality that hinges on pitch focus—and this, we repeat, is the very source-meaning of tonality—is not confined to major or minor scales, nor to chords or the kinds of harmonic auras created by successions of chords. Produced by a framing action in time bounded by an octave or, in narrower melodies, fifths or fourths, or even thirds, as octave segments, this melodic tonicization is in every proper sense of the word *harmonic action*.[19] The fifth C–G that frames a West African melody or an American child's song is no less a *harmonic* event than the fifth that

separates the V and I chords in a passage composed by G. F. Handel or the ubiquitous plucks of the tanbura in a *rāga* performance. To claim otherwise dangerously
stretches the very fabric of meaning for human concepts. If taken seriously, those
concepts must be invoked indiscriminately where applicable, regardless of what
cultural or chronological or ideological trappings may form the context.

Is this an unexpected and incredible state of affairs? It need not be. In fact, this
pitch-framing action differs little from the cognitive processing that goes on in other
human domains. We know something about these from research of such persons as
Rosch,[20] and it is encouraging in light of evidence from our studies of the world's
music. Its central message is that other perceptual and cognitive processings typically
incorporate certain members of a collection as unequals to which all other members
are experienced as hierarchically related. The work of psychologist Carol Krumhansl
is equally illuminating in this respect, and it conveniently deals directly with music.[21]

Familiar Perceptions by Other Names

Modern ethnomusicologists have for the most part, as we observed earlier, shared von
Hornbostel's reticence to use the term *tonality* in discussing the music they study.
Some skirt the issue in curious ways, others simply opt to ignore the word (or at least
to delete it from their descriptive vocabularies).[22] At the same time, they often make
tactical use of the kingpin of its perceptual condition, the concept of tonic (or
"central" or "fundamental" or "organizing" or "anchoring") pitch.

The problem is confronted (without managing a reasonable solution) by one of
von Hornbostel's most eminent successors, Bruno Nettl, who goes to the heart of the
matter in his seminal book of over three decades ago, *Music in Primitive Culture*. He
explains that tonality's presence is not easily confirmed in the music of a remote style,
and not just because sophisticated Western observers have ears that filter inap-
propriately. He regretfully notes that "verification by native informants is manifestly
impossible, since they cannot verbalize on such topics." The solution has been
delayed, Nettl continues, "by the unfounded assumption that tonality was lacking in
primitive music if a Western auditor failed to sense it."[23]

But then, like many of his most circumspect colleagues, Nettl recommends a
linguistic resolution for what is a cognitive-perceptual problem. He asks that we
substitute the benign phrase *tonal organization,* which he goes on to define in the
same loosely cosmic way that tonality has been defined by just about every writer
(including Schoenberg) who has used the term since 1850: "The totality of the
relationships between all the tones in a particular piece of music."[24] And finally, he
informs us that any description of a primitive melody's tonal organization "should
indicate the tonic and show whether the tonic changes in the course of the piece
(modulation), whether other important tones function temporarily as tonic" and so
on.

All of this sounds suspiciously like the condition of tonality, regardless of what we choose to call it.

In his survey of a broad sampling of non-Western musics, *Music Cultures of the Pacific, the Near East, and Asia,* William P. Malm echoes much the same kinds of structural generalizations made by Nettl and von Hornbostel, and in somewhat the same firm yet reticent tones. He nonetheless does not hesitate to talk freely about "pitch centers," whether he is discussing the music of Australian Aborigines, natives of the Pacific Island chain, or the *lü* scale of the classical Chinese tradition. With regard to the latter he tells us that the name of the first tone of that scale, *Kung,* indicates a functional position within the total pitch collection, like the Do of the Western tradition.[25] This *Kung* function is just that, and not a symbol for a particular note or pitch; it is the tonic pitch function for an array of lesser functions. (Moving beyond that recognition to the further assertion that music represented by the *lü* scale possesses tonality would be nothing short of redundant.)

In discussing the tonal vagaries of the Indian *rāga* (which is more patterned collection than mere scale), Malm observes that although many notes of a *rāga* may be ornamented in performance, those of "the tonic and its fifth . . . are not," thereby suggesting a special place for them in the tonal scheme of things.[26] A typical hierarchy in North Indian *rāgas* favors for the function of *vadis* (or *amsa,* which is best described as the most active tone melodically) the fifth or fourth above the pitch that functions as *tonic (Sa),* as well as the tonic itself. An ancient *rāga* of India, *Rāga Takka,* illustrates this common structural condition. It is shown in Example 17 as it appears in Walter Kaufmann's classic treatise on the *rāgas* of North Indian music, with half notes representing structurally prominent pitches.

EXAMPLE 17. *Rāga Takka* (Kaufmann, *The Rāgas of North India,* 594).

Malm's pitch-centering (which Castellano, Bharucha, and Krumhansl refer to as "anchoring")[27] and Nettl's tonic-functioning describe tonal conditions apparently indistinguishable from those designated in ancient music by Curt Sachs as *centricity,*[28] which in turn is synonymous with the perihelia used as early as 1913, according to Sachs, by Robert Lach.[29] One of the melodies used by Sachs to illustrate the kind of centricity he had in mind is a striking Lapp melody collected by Werner Danckert (Example 18). Its four-note scale provides exotic contrast—dare one speak of a "Neapolitan Gb"?—for the dancing song from West Africa, *Makua* (Example 16) or for a typical Western tune. It is a convenient reminder that major and minor scales hold no corner on the tonality market.

EXAMPLE 18. Lapp melody (after Danckert) (Sachs, *The Rise of Music in the Ancient World*, 168).

These cross-cultural, trans-era evidences of widespread tonal hierarchy in melody, confirmations of the structural dependence of all manner of pitch collections on domination by a one-pitch rallying point (frequently allied with a fifth and/or fourth relationship) put to question the long-nurtured myth that tonality is the exclusive provenance of "functional harmony." As soon as a melodic pattern has confirmed its shaping through the gamut of octave or fifth or fourth (or on occasion even major third), syntactic control of a harmonic nature has emerged. "Pure melody"—whether from recent primitive cultures or from ancient high cultures or from the mouths of babes—appears not to be immune to the inequities of pitch focus. Evident surface contrasts and the desire for terminological precision need not blind us to affinities that bind ages and ethnicities together. Gravitation wields its power on the raindrop as forcefully as on the oceans.

I hold that the framing action—bounded decisively by a fifth or fourth, sometimes by a major third—found in examples of primitive melody from a variety of cultures is an incipient form of harmonic structuring. It is in essence not different from the pitch frames that channel the melodic action in modern nursery songs or melodies of the repertories of Western religious music such as chant. These linear creations, usually simpler in structure, trace through their own harmonic boundaries, which by the seventeenth and eighteenth centuries could be riveted in one stroke onto the listener's consciousness by a single chord. This I believe to be the principal message of Lewis Rowell, who (in speaking of one kind of continuity that bonds ancient with modern music) observes:

> These properties were first implemented in the melodic relationships between single tones and subsequently, in a most remarkable achievement, transferred to the more complex harmonic relationships between chords.[30]

And it is not an unbreachable gap that separates Richard Hoppin's view of the tonal conventions found in monophony of the later Middle Ages. About those he notes that

> what we are witnessing . . . is the beginning of a development that comes to full flower in the functional harmony of the eighteenth and nineteenth centuries.[31]

Testimonials of this kind help to dispel the misleading duality that has fueled our conventional wisdom for over two hundred years. They suggest that Schoenberg's narrow historical perspective flawed his appraisal of tonality as a force in history. They suggest that what have been segregated out from the historical record as *melodic tonality* (sometimes with the qualifier *modal*) and *harmonic tonality* are more usefully understood as slightly different versions of the same thing. In fact, that "central triad" championed in the harmonic tonality of Schoenberg and Krenek, which we discussed in Chapter 6, can now be seen more clearly: it becomes central precisely by virtue of the same organizational dynamics von Hornbostel and Nettl and Sachs and Malm et al. have found in primitive melody.

MELODY'S HARMONIC FRAME

Schoenberg's single direct reference in *Harmonielehre* to the linear projection of tonality (here, page 49) is indexed by a melody that redundantly outlines a major triad. But melodies are not confined, like bugle calls and the conch tunes of the Tritons, to low parts of the harmonic series. For the most part, melodies fill in the spaces "between partials," creating a more flowing stream, a potentially more expressive pattern.

Tightly restricted melodies, on the other hand—say, no more than two or three different pitches that are close together—may consist of only a single structural pitch about which the others revolve. They cannot be said to "fill in," to "move through" their self-imposed pitch frames. Bruno Nettl suggests that ditonic melodies are perhaps the oldest surviving music and that they almost always project their lower pitches as tonic.[32] Chants of tribal musics often reveal just these kinds of narrow pitch paths. Within such restricted ranges the power of tonicization commonly resides in the kinds of contextual principles first revealed by Gestaltists Wertheimer, Köhler, and Koffka, or, depending on the particular circumstances, they derive from the laws of contiguity most pointedly discussed by Ortmann and, later, Deutsch.[33] For the two melodies in Example 19 the concept of harmonic frame is not relevant. In the first, notes B and A assume principal roles as departures from the C that beings and ends the pattern and acts as their pitch fulcrum. In the second melody the lower pitch F is decidedly dependent, acting as lower neighbor to the dominating G.

(a)

(b)

EXAMPLE 19. (a) Uitito Indian song (Bose, "Der Musik der Uitito," 34); (b) Eskimo song (after Estreicher) (Sachs, *The Rise of Music in the Ancient World*, 59).

Some Gregorian melodies—the simpler, less florid kinds—are tonally similar to the semi-monotone represented by the Uitito and Eskimo examples. The setting from I Corinthians in Example 20 contains only one more pitch than the Uitito Indian melody. Perhaps both follow a general law of texted music that calls for pitch complexity in inverse ratio to informational content, as in recitative and the patter songs of Gilbert and Sullivan.

But matters change when a culture's music begins to cultivate melodies that soar in more ornate trajectories. Then a frame of more than one pitch can provide the floor and ceiling of tonal play; and this is where harmonic attraction can enter the scene, relationships known from the harmonic series providing a potential enfolding web, a neural selection model that inclines the hearer to select certain relationships as the most efficient touchstones of structure. The concentrating listener, as Paul Hindemith claimed in the *Craft of Musical Composition,* I, finds harmonic connections, over shorter or longer spans of time.[34] Harmony, and with it the condition of pitch-focus, has persisted for longer, has provided in human history for much longer, has provided a more elemental service, and denies more tenaciously its expendability, than Schoenberg could have imagined. We might amend Hindemith's proud claim to "the ear will always seek," replacing his more optimistic "the ear will always find."

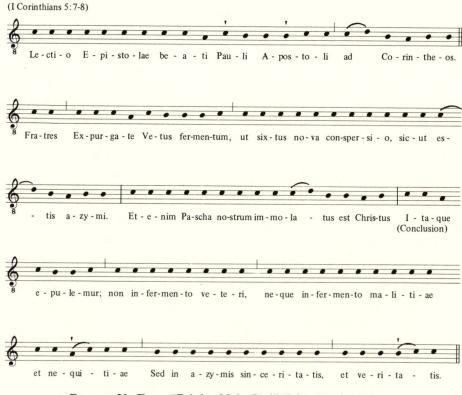

EXAMPLE 20. Chant, "Epistle of Saint Paul" (*Liber Usualis,* 778).

THE HARMONIC INCUBUS OF MODAL THEORY

Most scholars have recognized the limitations of the modal system, formalized in constraining rules as it was, for representing the pitch structure of all the music it presumably defined. In fact, it was recognition of just this slack between theory and practice that led, during the Cistercian reforms of the early twelfth century, to the alteration of some of the "incorrigible" ancient tunes to make them conform more elegantly to the theory designed to explain them.[35] But the whole of modal theory was from the beginning formulated as a grand generalization of structure, a rigorous but at times lame attempt to formalize what was experienced as tonal coherence within a single melody and as organizational continuities between one melody and another. It is remarkable, as Richard Hoppin declares, that the majority of melodies fit the new system of classification as well as they do.[36]

Modal classifications were made to provide an explanatory theory of tonal dynamics, one that could subsume, in general but revealing terms, a large body of melodies from diverse ethnic and geographic sources,[37] music that in some cases preceded by centuries the earliest attempts at classification. It is unlikely that tenth- or fifteenth-century churchgoers always heard ecclesiastical chant in ways coincident with the elaborate classificatory scheme put together to explain its tonal basis. The same conclusion can be drawn about Riemann's system of three harmonic functions and how it may bear on the way nineteenth-century listeners heard Brahms. But we do know that even after the modal system was established, its application in actual composing was often less than rigid, at other times doctrinaire. As one Renaissance scholar makes clear, in this music "irregular procedure . . . made it possible for a composition in any mode to borrow, temporarily, characteristics of other modes."[38] But to declare wholesale bankruptcy for a system because of individual variances, as Schoenberg evidently did, quite exceeds reasonable inference.

As we have noted, Schoenberg seems not to have been familiar with any actual expositions of the system he found wanting, a system hypothesized on the very premises he denied them. Nowhere does he hint that he understood hierarchical prominence for the modal *finalis* or for the channeled organization of pitches within an octave divided as fifth-fourth or fourth-fifth. His conclusions were not derived from an understanding of the modal system, but were the affirmation of what he found to be the historical consequence. That is, because of the "decline" of modality, the system must have been defective, for, after all, only the fit survive.

This was unfortunate. Recognition of the pitch framing of authentic and plagal modes was a brilliant insight in the history of music theory; segmentation of the octave into one of these two options of melodic deployment reflects a purely harmonic function, one so fundamental that it is easily ignored. This basic modal distinction exemplified by the fifth/fourth potential was denoted as early as in the ninth-century *Alia Musica,* as evidenced by the following:

The eighth trope has the same octave species [d–d'] as the first, but differs in that it has g as the preserver of its quality, while the other has d under the name of protus.[39]

Awareness of this harmonic ingredient is manifest even earlier, in the Boethian myth of music's origins in the Pythagorean tetractys of 12:9:8:6. Claiming Nichomachus as his source, Boethius tells us that music in its infancy was "composed of four strings,"[40] which I infer to be his charming metaphorical way of describing the four determining pitch elements of melody. For him the outer "strings" sound the octave, and the middle "strings" sound, each in turn, the divisions of fifth and fourth. (It is well known, as Calvin Bower reminds us, that Orpheus' lyre had seven strings, not just four.)

Some historians have resisted the conclusion we draw here, that anything like the tonic function could have been present in music before the ninth or tenth century. For instance, Bence Szabolcsi argues that the kind of pitch primacy Hucbald found in melody was quite different from ancient conceptions of a ground-note, like the Chinese *huang chung* ("yellow bell") tuning note, the *mese* of classical Greek theory, or even the pitch dynamics of early chant. In regard to the latter, he observes that "The varying endings (or *differentiae*) of antiphonal psalms show that even later chants maintained a traditional indifference to the final."[41] Speculating about the origins of this "modern" emphasis on the final-as-tonic, he appears to side with Peter Wagner's conclusion that its source was Syrian or Byzantine.[42]

But the two questions left unaddressed by Szabolcsi are crucial and, in the end, more intriguing. First, is it not reasonable to consider that this recognition he attributes to later formulation represented a development of cognitive awareness of pre-existent perceptual mores? As with gravity, are we not faced with a concept–after–percept circumstance that is common in human history? And further, when this recognition became apparent—in whatever century and culture—why did the adopted schema engage so pervasively the octave/fifth/fourth paradigms rather than others? Must we believe that the deployments sanctioned by modal theory were derived exclusively from Pythagorean number prejudices, oblivious to what theorists could hear in the music about them? Certainly there were theorists who subscribed to Guido's irreverent opinion that the treatises of Boethius were more useful to philosophers than to singers.

The matter of the final's pivotal role was not a matter of equivocation, whatever the precedents, by the tenth century. Odo of Cluny (879–942) and Guido d'Arezzo (990–1050) were emphatic in ruling that final and first note must be the same, and John Cotton (fl. 1100) was even more forceful, with his maxim "All the force of a chant is directed toward the final."

The entire ancient paraphernalia of the authentic/plagal system can be understood more reasonably as exceeding a quaint allegorical shuffling of a collection of notes into their respective Greek camps. It is in fact the revelation of how tones, by their unfolding in time, can affect their own structural perspective within the bounding octave,[43] how harmonic relatedness plays a role in melodic syntax, how tones in time add up to more than the mere sum of their parts.

The fifth relationship was emphasized in a different way by Hucbald in *De*

Harmonica. He observed that pitches a, b, c, and d enjoyed a "connective bond" with their respective modal finals d, e, f, and g, to the extent that they should occasionally be designated as suitable ending pitches for a melody. These substitutions could occur, as the illustrious theorist remarked, without "contravening . . . reason nor perception . . . and going on correctly under the same mode or trope."[44] And Guido concurs with this designation in the *Micrologus,* referring to the upper fifth as *affinal,* which for some later theorists would become known as *cofinal.*[45]

Once modal classifications had finally developed some basic uniformity and continuity of terminology (after c. 1000), an awareness of the tonal perspective rendered explicit by the system itself motivated composers to construct melodies of tighter correspondence with its precepts. Once found, the modal "genetic code" was put to work in producing predictable offspring, rendering normative the elemental principles of structure depicted by the theory. And thus historian Hoppin remarks, about compositional trends following the Cistercian reforms:

> Composers seem to have taken particular pains to make the mode of a chant obvious from its very beginning. Moreover, they quickly learned to construct a melody so that it conveyed a sense of tonal organization. This they accomplished in certain modes by stressing not only the final but also the third and fifth above.[46]

In other words, what previously had been achieved in a hit-or-miss fashion (when not outright ignored) now became rigorously achievable by intention—one of those rare glimpses of practice actually following theory.

A SUGGESTIVE ANOMALY

Before we leave this extended digression about the harmonic aspect implicit within the modal system, let us mention an additional curiosity of special relevance: as time went by, three of the modes whose designated dominants (or *reciting tones*) did not correspond with the "fifth-above-finalis" rule of the authentic forms began to disappear from use. They are shown in Example 21. The very fact that these apparently anomalous designations of reciting tones were made for all of the plagal modal forms (anomalous considering the consistent designations made for all of the authentic forms) suggests a possible confusion of perceived data during the very development of the system, a confusion which could have arisen from mistaking what was actually the perceived finalis as the dominant in each of those modes.[47] This would have created a de facto Ionian for mode 3, Aeolian for mode 4, and Ionian for mode 8 (some five centuries before their official times, of course). Glareanus was fully conscious that the vicissitudes of musical performance rendered a de facto system much less rigorous than we might wish. He was especially aware, for example, that "one rarely finds a song in the Dorian which they have not somewhere turned into the Aeolian through the synemmenon tetrachord, that is, by using B-flat. . . ."[48]

Even to suggest such defilement is heresy for some scholars who, although ready to acknowledge the modal system's incompleteness, occasional anomalies, and frequent fuzziness, nonetheless fiercely defend its sanctity. But if we ignore that such a mixup (dominant for final) may have occurred, we are left with a curious irony of more than trivial import. Each of the renegade "dominants," in the three anomalous modes cited, uncannily forms the tidiest of consonances with its respective final. The Phrygian final forms a major third (and minor sixth) with its dominant, and the Hypophrygian and Hypomixolydian finals lie a perfect fifth (or fourth) from theirs.

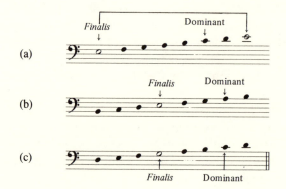

EXAMPLE 21. Dominants. (a) mode 3, Phrygian; (b) mode 4, Hypophrygian; (c) mode 8, Hypomixolydian.

This inexplicable "coincidence" seems too good to be the product of anything except the very confusion we have conjectured. Such extravagances of coincidental beauty are enough to warm the most hardened neo-Pythagorean heart.

Just this kind of classificatory equivocation is dimly suggested by one of the principal modern scholars of modal practice, the late Willi Apel, who states that the dominant, during the early days of chant history (c. 500–900), could at times be "more decisive than the finalis."[49] And as Richard Hoppin makes clear, medieval theorists were not always fastidious in reconciling their auditory perceptions with their theoretical precepts, thus confirming what puzzled enthusiasts have long suspected. The introduction of *musica ficta,* whether by B♭s, E♭s, or F♯s, or by transpositional ploys, may not destroy musical integrity, but it raises havoc with the reality of any modal classification. In the words of Hoppin, "medieval theorists did not admit these modal changes, and it is doubtful that they even recognized them."[50] So, wildly paraphrasing Bertrand Russell's provocative query about hairs-on-the-head, vis-à-vis definitions of baldness, we might wonder aloud how many B♭s can occur in a melody and its mode remain indubitably Dorian.

Finally, let us turn to an interesting reflection of early recognition that melody's pitch controls derived from an embodied pitch nucleus. It is embedded in the concept of *parallage* that prevailed in the Byzantine liturgy. According to this concept, a singer must destroy in the listener's mind the lingering structural residue of the mode from a previous melody before another melody in a different mode can be made comprehensible. For Egon Wellesz this concept proved that Byzantine composers, who knew only monophonic music and had no training in the theory of harmonic changes, "saw the same process in modulation as we do."[51] And we have every right to suspect that a causal relationship bears between the earlier and later musical events and the conceptual abstractions created to explain them.

Wellesz echoes the remarks of the nineteenth-century Byzantine scholar Chrysanthos of Madytos (fl. 1815–45) who, in his liturgical monument *Great Musical Theory* (1832) observed in the *echoi* of Byzantine melody "the scheme of a melody, arranged according to the practice of the expert musician, who knows which tones should be omitted, which chosen, on which one should begin and on which one should end." A particular mode, Wellesz concludes, is thus more than a mere string of notes. It is instead "the sum of all the formulae which constitute the quality of an Echos."[52]

PRIMITIVE MUSIC, OLD MUSIC, AND TONALITY

What does all of this rummaging around in the exotic corners of the present and in the remote past prove? It proves that the evidence favors a unitary perspective of musical mechanics, not the separative duality which underlay Schoenberg's assumption that tonality was one of history's local phenomena, not one of its structural imperatives. This does not mean that the syntactic conventions of "modal music" were in some general sense the same as those of the "major-minor music" of the eighteenth century. Far from it. It does mean, however, that both musics (and thus both "tonal systems") were subservient to the same ground rules of pitch organization, themselves a product of our perceptual habits, which transcend those differences. It indicates that the alleged duality of modality (or melodic tonality) versus tonality (or harmonic tonality), which was central to Schoenberg's evolutionary axiom, must be scrapped so that the elemental basis of both can be understood and recognized in the full geographical and ethnic breadth of its occurrences. These are ties as secure as the structural common grounds of one human language with another, regardless of the quaintness of their respective vocabularies or word orderings, regardless of how concealed (or obvious) their deep structures may be.

Describing in detail the mentation processes of remote ancestors is a foolish sport. We cannot prove nor disprove such impressive claims as "Early medieval man did not hear harmonically; he conceived only of textures as layers of melodies." Similarly unverifiable—and therefore baseless—is that "The ancients did not hear pitches (or time) as we do." In fact, we know nothing, and shall remain eternally ignorant, of such matters *except to the limited degree that plausible inferences can be made from objective data.* And when no direct statements by credible contemporary reporters about the phenomenon exist, this leaves us with only one prime bit of evidence pertaining to ancient musical perception: the record of actual music, however securely or insecurely it may be preserved for us. If that record circumstantially confirms the tonal dynamics of pitch focus, then our question, "Did tonality play an important role in music before Schoenberg thought it did?" is answered as emphatically as it ever can be.

DESCRIPTIVE EVIDENCE

Nothing in the bales of chant theory harvested by reporters through the Renaissance puts before us an unassailable correspondence between the *finalis* of former times and the *tonic* of today. We have discussed the best evidence available—of the indirect, circumstantial kinds—as indications of a harmonic presence in the relationships codified in modal theory. But we must remember that musicians from earlier high cultures were as limited as our primitive contemporaries who, as Nettl has assured us (page 100 earlier), cannot be expected to describe their musical responses in our terms. Certainly, in our attempts to confirm that we are all of the same family, we should not fault our ancestors for not anticipating what in their soundscapes would most concern us today.[53] The learning that has accumulated since 900 A.D. unquestionably guides my perceptions, provides my sensate events with different ready-made guides for understanding than previous learning would have. But learning cannot alter the substance of perception; it only vivifies, confirms, makes more readily apparent that which is perceivable. My *conceptual* framework of the earth coming between the moon and the sun (versus the moon being eaten by a dragon) influences my experience of a lunar eclipse. Yet it does not alter the spatial relationships, color content, or the relative quantities of light that characterize the structure of my *perception* of that event.

All peoples speak within the conceptual frameworks of their times, whatever the content of their perceptions. Finding Zarlino telling us that "The passage in this Josquin work is organized around the tonal center, or tonic pitch class, of G" would be like discovering a remark by Galileo to the effect that "The projectile in question fell with the force of nine Gs." Yet concluding from the absence of such statements that the conditions they describe today did not exist in the auditory experience of 1570 or in the ballistics events of 1630 is hardly defensible. Yielding to the "unchronicled-therefore-nonexistent" imperatives of historical positivism allays more personal fears than it answers public questions. To know, one makes creative leaps of inference based on credible grounds. Otherwise, as John Updike so eloquently warns,

> the nightmare of medieval nominalism is upon us again, and by a kind of
> Zeno's paradox of infinite factual subdivision the Achilles of understand-
> ing can never overtake the gargantuan tortoise of reality.[54]

THE MATTER OF PITCH HIERARCHY

On the other hand, let us observe with at least equal conviction that no direct documentary evidence proves the contrary—that tonality was any less prominent in the musical perceptions of the Golden Age Greek, the medieval Gaul or the Renaissance Italian than it is for the listener of today. Indeed, circumstantial evidence (and that constitutes but one facet of our reasoning) is wholly consonant with the position that tonality was quite as evident in ancient melody as it was in the music of the very harmonic eighteenth century.

As Gustave Reese concludes in *Music of the Middle Ages* (on the verge, it would appear, of mild desperation), the closest we may ever come to a convincing statement from an ancient writer about a tonic function occurs in a pre-Christian treatise attributed at one time to Aristotle. In the *Problems XIX,* 20, we find pseudo-Aristotle speaking of the scalar note function *thetic mese* and saying that:

> In all good music mese occurs frequently, and all good composers have frequent recourse to mese, and, if they leave it, they soon return to it, as they do to no other note. Similarly in language, if certain connecting particles are removed . . . the language is no longer Greek; . . . mese is as it were a conjunction among sounds, and more so than the other notes, because its sound occurs more often.[55]

And as Reese opines, this description refers either to a pitch functioning as a dominant (in the sense of reciting tone of the ecclesiastical modes) or as a tonic in the modern sense.

In a way, a conclusive answer to the question raised by pseudo-Aristotle's description is irrelevant, for a deeper question has been met, providing an implicit answer many writers choose to ignore. It is the question of pitch hierarchy. One cannot, in face of the claim made in *Problems XIX,* 20, hold without qualification that the notes of the Greek system's melodies were understood to operate within their contexts as equal partners, that no tonal hierarchy prevailed. The *mese* described is a busy pitch. It is a point of departure and return, a pitch more equal among equals, a pitch like that described by Nettl and Sachs and Hoppin (and every other writer who has tried to explain the dynamics of tonal play). It prevails within a context of pitches skirting around it, to return and leave and return once again.

MUSICAL EVIDENCE

If one simply ignores the unbearable weight of complexity—garbled interpretations by medieval scribes, apparent inner contradictions, uncontestable tenuousness of what can be known from classical Greek theory—then music's tonal ties with the whole of subsequent history are easier to assess merely by examining one of the few extant melodies from the pre-Christian era. The one we turn to, "Hymn to Seikilos" (see Example 22a) is perhaps the best known, for it has appeared in the prominent anthologies of early music over the past thirty years. It is one of the simplest. It dates from sometime between the second century B.C. and the first century A.D.[56] It is a brief tune, but it enjoys two sterling virtues: it is intact, and it has survived authentication. It also cuts an engagingly direct tonal path, c up to c′, with f as mediating tonic.

EXAMPLE 22. (a) Hymn to Seikolos; (b) "My Bonnie," folksong; (c) Melody in Mode I (Tillyard, *The Hymns of the Octoechus*, 111–12).

If we classified the hymn's scale content by Glarean's modal system, it would qualify as unblemished Hypomixolydian.[57] The claim that Seikilos himself might have heard it differently, with another central pitch (or none) and thus another set of tonal dynamics, entails some frail assumptions: that something of his middle ear, or his basilar membrane and cochlear mechanism, or his neural firings, or his fully developed cognitive operation somehow processed things differently from ours. And this is a far deeper conjecture, a far nimbler leap of faith than that his little tune harbors tonality with the directness and simplicity of a contemporary child's song, that F is, and was, its *Do*.

Many melodies simply defy unconditional surrender to a fifth/fourth categorization of pitch framing. Some, for example, clearly deploy within an octave frame of minor sixth/major third, as in Example 22b. Yet still others, from origins as diverse as urban American blues to the early Christian church, appear to outline a nucleus at odds with any we have emphasized as normative, projecting, nonetheless, an unmistakable allegiance to a single pitch. The ancient Byzantine melody in Example 22c illustrates one such apparent anomaly. It operates within a minor seventh, d–c' (ignoring the single brief low c that begins the final segment). But like most such melodies, the upper c of its encompassing seventh functions exclusively as part of a neighbor-tone embellishment of a, in the form b–c'–a. The melody's defining frame is its fifth, d–a. The same or a similar figuration can be heard in melodies from throughout the ages.

NOTES

1. The relatively young discipline of ethnomusicology has immeasurably improved our understanding of melody. Added to the access we have today to music of ancient times—choose your culture, choose your century—this facet of musical insight has radically altered our perspective of music as structure.

2. Especially see *Visuallen Wahrgenommene Figuren*, sections of which are reprinted in Beardslee and Wertheimer, *Readings in Perception*.

3. A recent broad resume of this literature is in Carterette and Friedman, *Handbook of Perception IX*, Part II.

4. Leonard B. Meyer's *embodied meaning* is essentially what I mean by *inherent meaning*.

5. I prefer the term *vector* to define this condition, a use consistent with that term's correct meaning of directional force. Webern's Piano Variations, II, is a complex yet engaging example of just this kind of auditory designating of a single pitch (A-440) without the trappings of major/minor implications. This somewhat over-discussed piece is still a fascinating example of pitch symmetry carried to its ultimate conclusion.

6. For example, Köhler, *Dynamics of Psychology*, Chapter 2, and *Gestalt Psychology*, Chapter 5.

7. One of the principal figures of Gestalt psychology early in the century (Köhler) called this kind of result an "original sensory fact." See *Gestalt Psychology*, 163.

8. A pianist of uncommon scientific bent, Ortmann was director of the Peabody Conservatory of Music from 1928 until 1935. He later translated the second volume of Hindemith's *Unterweisung* for Associated Music Publishers. Theorists have been largely oblivious of Ortmann's work, which was as startling for its conception, considering its time, as for its conclusions.

9. In this we repudiate the *tabula rasa* that is implicit for almost all earlier theorists, recognizing

the wisdom of Nietzsche's claim: "Everything that reaches consciousness is utterly and completely adjusted, simplified, schematized, interpreted" (*Will to Power*, ¶ 477). See also the reference to Bruner, N. 33, Chapter 7.

10. Guilford and Hilton, "Some Configurational Properties of Short Musical Melodies"; Deutsch, "Facilitation by Repetition in Recognition Memory for Tonal Pitch," and "Delayed Pitch Comparisons and the Principle of Proximity"; and Brown, "The Interplay of Set Content and Temporal Context in a Functional Theory of Tonality Perception."

11. Ortmann, "On the Melodic Relativity of Tones," 19–20.

12. Ibid., 23. Also see Johnson, "Hierarchical Clustering Schemes," for later empirical confirmation (without apparent intention) of Ortmann's conclusions.

13. Peter Medawar, *Pluto's Republic*, 90.

14. A more exhaustive discussion of Ortmann's research into these matters can be found in Thomson, *A Clarification of the Tonality Concept*.

15. Erich von Hornbostel, "African Music," 34.

16. Ibid., 34–35. Most rewarding among those reverberations of von Hornbostel's claims may be found in two recent studies. One deals with Balinese-Western perceptual comparisons (Kessler, Hansen, and Shepherd, "Tonal Schemata in the Perception of Music in Bali and in the West"), the other with tonal hierarchy in North Indian music (Castellano, Bharucha, and Krumhansl, "Tonal Hierarchies in the Music of North India"). Both conclude intervallic dominations corresponding with von Hornbostel's. In the words of the first study, "The tonal hierarchy, when it arose in response to Balinese as well as to Western contexts, exhibited essentially the same pattern for listeners from each of the cultures, suggesting that such tonal hierarchies may reflect a human cognitive universal" (164).

17. This role of fourths or fifths within (or without) an octave is especially prominent also in *rāga* performances of North India, since the invariant bourdon bass always consists of tonic octave plus the fifth (or fourth, when a particular *rāga* contains no pitch class at the fifth). See Walter Kaufmann, *The Rāgas of North India*, 3–4.

18. It is important to recall here data from studies in developmental psychology which conclude that in children's singing the tonic, its upper fifth, and its third are more accurately produced, on average, than other intervals. For example, see B. M. Teplov, *La Psychologie des aptitudes musicales*. And further, empirical studies such as those of Ritsma, "The Octave Deafness of the Human Ear" and Ritsma and Engel, "Pitch of Frequency Modulated Signals" confirm what musicians have long known from non-laboratory experience: listeners are sometimes confused over what the "real" pitch of a complex tone is, and their confusion is most often between the fundamental and its octave or its fifth complementary.

19. For a didactic presentation of this melodic framing ("the tonality frame") see Christ et al., *Materials and Structure of Music*, I, Chapter, 2, and Thomson, *Introduction to Music Reading*, Chapter 1.

20. Rosch, "Cognitive Reference Points."

21. David Butler has indicated methodological problems in the Krumhansl study ("Describing the Perception of Tonality in Music," and "Response to Carol Krumhansl"). His argument is not whether there are hierarchies of salience for pitches within a tonal field; he instead questions whether the Krumhansl studies add credible evidence of this condition.

22. One searches in vain in the indexes of many ethnomusicological studies for a *tonality* entry or even a close synonym. (*Tonal Organization* is the most common circumlocution found, when found at all.) But *tonic* and even *tonal system* occur. I hesitate to ask if the presence of a tonic without a tonality is not a bit like the squeal without the pig. (On the other hand, Bruno Nettl's *Music in Primitive Culture* mentions *tonality* several times in the text but not in its index.)

23. Nettl, *Music in Primitive Culture*, 59.

24. Ibid.

25. Malm, *Music Cultures of the Pacific, the Near East, and Asia*, 109.

26. Ibid., 71.

27. Castellano et al., "Tonal Hierarchies in the Music of North India."

28. *The Wellsprings of Music.*

29. Ibid., 168. We note in passing the affinity of recent psychologists for "anchoring tone," and the "anchoring effect." See Castellano et al., "Tonal Hierarchies," and Deutsch, "Two Issues Concerning Tonal Hierarchy."

30. Lewis Rowell, *Thinking About Music,* 235.

31. *Medieval Music,* 73.

32. Nettl, *Music in Primitive Culture,* 48.

33. Deutsch, "Facilitation by Repetition in Recognition Memory for Pitch" and "Delayed Pitch Comparisons and the Principle of Proximity."

34. Particularly relevant is Hindemith's discussion of "Degree-Progression," *The Craft of Musical Composition,* I, 183–187.

35. For example, see Hoppin, *Medieval Music,* 72.

36. In this respect it is comforting to read philosopher Karl Popper's criticism (*Conjectures and Refutations,* 34–39) of theories like psychoanalysis, which seem able to explain everything they are called upon to explain. Popper finds this facile capability disturbing.

37. Music of the Christian liturgy came from a polyglot of sources both sacred and profane.

38. Putnam Aldrich, "An Approach to the Analysis of Renaissance Music," 6–7.

39. According to Harold Powers, it was in Hucbald's *De Harmonica* (ninth century) that chant structure, modal theory, the Byzantine *Oktoechoi,* and Golden Age Greek modal theory were first synthesized, but it was in the *Alia Musica* (anonymous, ninth century also) that the term mode came to signify the particular "quality" of a *Protus, Deuterus, Tritus,* or *Tetrardus* as a unique and prominent member of a collection of pitches. See especially 379–381 of "Modes," *The New Grove Dictionary of Music and Musicians,* 12.

40. Boethius, *Fundamentals of Music,* 29–30.

41. Bence Szabolcsi, *A History of Melody,* 38.

42. Peter Wagner, *Einfuhrung in die Gregorianischen Melodien* I, 109–110 and 214.

43. A minority view regards the *finalis* and *ambitus* aspects of modal theory as separable although equally vital properties. They are quite inseparable properties; they represent, in the pitch dynamics they signify, the most informative aspect of pitch structuring passed on to us from the era of 500–1400. This single insight of interactive dependence, *finalis-ambitus,* provides the tonal linkage, the harmonic continuity, between ancient monophony and the homophony/polyphony of later Western music.

44. Powers, "Modes," 381.

45. Ibid.

46. Hoppin, *Medieval Music,* 72.

47. An interesting hint of confirmation can be seen in the Byzantine system of *echoi,* in which the final for Mode I is more often A than D, which is the more frequent final in Roman chant. See Reese, *Music in the Middle Ages,* 153.

48. Powers, "Modes," 408.

49. Apel, "Church Modes III," *Harvard Dictionary of Music* (1944 edition).

50. Hoppin, *Medieval Music,* 71.

51. Egon Wellesz, *History of Byzantine Music and Hymnography,* 310.

52. Ibid., 326.

53. Again, the Gestaltists were aware of the chasm that can separate perceptual appearance from structural reality. As Köhler expressed this problem:

Behind the apparently banal surface of the perceptual world lies unknown facts of functional dependence, but . . . it is sometimes quite as difficult to gain a clear view of these relationships as it is to solve similar tasks in the natural sciences. (*Dynamics in Psychology,* 30).

54. John Updike, *Hugging the Shore* (in his review of Peter Gay's *Art and Act*).

55. Aristotle, *Problems.* Also see Warren E. Anderson, *Ethos and Education in Greek Music,* 20–

21, for a more recent discussion of the *mese* question and some of its unsupportable answers. A slightly more emphatic, and negative, perspective is Jacques Chailly's. He insists that there is no justification for attributing a tonic function of any kind to a Greek mode ("Le Mythe des modes grecs," 162).

56. Discovered in 1883 on a burial slab in Asia Minor, the song was intended as an epitaph for Seikilos' wife, Euterpe.

57. Gustav Reese categorized this melody as Phrygian (within the Aristoxenian Greek system), ignoring all internal evidence that projects a central role for F. Or perhaps he merely rejected the opinion of early medieval theorists that a tune could end on its fifth.

CHAPTER 9

The Pitch-Rhythm-Harmony Mix

Schoenberg was certainly aware of the interdependence of pitch and rhythm and of the harmonic influence imposed by chords. He made passing remarks in *Harmonie-lehre* and in later essays that make clear his estimation of their potential either for mutual support or, in the case of non-conformity, for contradiction. But he seems never to have bothered much with their causal interdependencies, never seems to have grasped just how each can independently or in the service of the others manifest predictable structure.

He speaks of the influence melody had on the development of harmony in the early days of polyphonic music (a reference left vague), and how "in many ways each was actually determined by the other."[1] And in later pages of the same book he takes a defensive stand against those who claim—and many still do—that the chords of early polyphony came about solely through the accidents of melodic play.[2] Some fifteen years later he mentions "the laws that result from the combination of time and sound; namely, those governing the working of our minds."[3] Through knowing more about the laws, he continues, we would be in a better position to understand how, "in the small amount of time granted us by the flow of events, we can recognize the figures, grasp the way they hang together, and comprehend their meaning." It is our loss that he did not pursue with greater diligence this remarkable opening for answering some of those vexing questions which his nineteenth-century predecessors had left over-grown with weedy rhetoric. But at no time did he grub more deeply into this soil of musical hanging together, at no time did he turn up proposals which could explain this time-tone interaction. He seems never to have concluded from this detected mutual dependence of sound properties that something more complicated than standardized note collections might lie at the bottom of tonality. My argument that more elemental interactions were at stake demands a brief digression here into speculative theory.

ULTIMATE CAUSES

Simply stated, how we hear patterns of sound and what we make of them is our ultimate question. It is also one of the most fascinating questions of music, in part because it has for so long been answered in only fragmentary jousts with piecemeal elements. Rhythm can be studied in all of its complexities, in isolation. Melody can be discussed as pitch scaffolds, as if its tones are propelled through a timeless void. And harmony can assume an all-enveloping atemporal role, for which such cognitive matters as the articulation of past-present-future exert no constraints. But dealt with separately, each cannot but fail to answer our questions about how structure transpires.

One basic theoretical position contends that as we ingest bunches of tones (simultaneous or successive), we sort them into meaning according to rules imposed wholly by cultural associations, rules ultimately as arbitrary as those of stud poker, rules whose powers rest solely and exclusively with the particular population, large or small, that has adopted them. Usually projected as a "programmed from birth" ethnocentricity, it is a view attached to populations from vast to singular and maintained in varied degrees of rigidity and inclusiveness, with boundaries extending from the super-rational pluralism of the late anthropologist Alan Merriam and of composer Milton Babbitt to the mysticism of composer-raconteur John Cage. The more radical adherents to this position generally regard the suggestion of genetic imprints or of humanity-wide traits (whether acquired through nature or nurture) with a disdain normally reserved for the political opposition.[4]

This "make up the rules as we go" view has its unique temptations. It follows from a relativism that is rich in fantasizing potentials. It allows me to believe that my version of a tonal Euclid is as worthy as yours, so long as it is internally consistent, and that it need possess with your equally-valid version no common inductive basis, no shared deductive process.

But the accumulated evidence of modern biology and psychology render such a view indefensible as a base for musical explanations. Confronted head-on, it becomes tentative in the face of global similarities, untenable in the presence of evident bonds that tie together contrastive cultures and remote eras. Indeed, its simplicity is its sole virtue, for the rich picture pieced together today of humanity's musical past reveals, as we have seen, too many traces of inherent structural similarities which suggest corresponding perceptual bonds. The flimsy premises of total cultural relativism cannot pass for profundity, much less for the truth. Only in conjunction with predetermined matrices of tonal meaning can the habits-through-nurturing perspective answer questions about music's structure. We side forcefully with psychologist Floyd Allport whose conviction it was that "structures are neither random, endlessly varied, inexplicable, nor amenable only to quantitative laws." With him we hold that "there is such a thing as unique structural law *sui generis*."[5]

Like languages, musics share deep structural consistencies that defy the separations of centuries and the borders of ethnicity. So we concur that "the principle of tonality, in one version or another, has been the chief agent of coherence throughout the history of music."[6] We recognize the evidence we hear and see, and it compels us to agree that "*tonality* is applicable not just to the 'tonal period' . . . but through earlier modality and more recent freer tonal applications as well."[7] Our understanding of the old music we hear, and the reasoning we apply to theories forged on its behalf, convinces us of the wisdom that tonality is "one of the most striking phenomena of music," especially by its presence, throughout music's evolution, "in non-Western cultures, in Gregorian chant, and in harmonized music—practically every piece giving preference to one tone (the tonic) making this the tonal center to which all other tones are related."[8]

One explanation for the richness of human knowledge—the complexity and abstractness of the perceived musical surface—that makes music the enduring pastime it is, is offered by Jackendoff and Lerdahl. In their estimation we have no choice in some perceptual matters.

> Many aspects of the [musical] grammar are simply the only (or easiest) ways that one's mental abilities make available for organizing a musical signal . . . much . . . is given by the human genetic inheritance.[9]

In sharp contradiction of Schoenberg, we cannot accept his first premise: that tonality was no more than a by-product of two and one-half centuries of artful chord arranging. Nor can we accept his second, and related, premise that as a property it had become obsolete and expendable, used up like any other limited commodity, by the year 1900.

Pitch Focus in "Harmonic Tonality"

Since Schoenberg himself regarded tonality as a controlling element at least from Bach through Brahms, let us move back in time now, just far enough to see what were the causes of tonal focus in an exemplary piece from that repertory. We shall learn nothing startling, but perhaps our examination can reveal even more forcefully how that "central triad" of Krenek's tonality gets cast in its role. Let us look at how just pitch and rhythm in a simple melody confirm a particular hierarchy of tonal relationships, a harmonic whole. As we shall note later, adding the accompanimental chords which the composer attached to this melody only more tightly nails down the structure apparent in its melody alone. One could use hundreds of other passages from the 1650–1850 repertory (and beyond in either direction) and still demonstrate the same kinds of rhythm-pitch transformations into pitch hierarchies.[10] We choose for this purpose the opening of Mozart's F major Piano Sonata, K. 332 (Example 23). Our approach and our vocabulary will be severely limited to achieve a simplicity complementing the elemental nature of what we seek.

Observe first that this melody can be divided (or perhaps we should say "divides itself") as three segments, P1, P2, P3. These segments are projected most primitively through rhythm and contour. Phrase P3 overlaps with P2, its first note serving as P2's last.[11] All three segments begin with the same pitch, F. The two phrases P2 and P3 also end with it.

The octave f–f′ forms the structural limits, top and bottom as well as beginning

and end, of the melody. (The g in measure three and the e just before the final f are
fleeting, and they fall on unaccented beats, so they are not comparable to highs and
lows that occur in more providential locations.)

EXAMPLE 23. Mozart, K. 332, first twelve measures.

In its phrase-bounding function, the pitch f occurs on a metric accent (first beat)
four times; its duration is comparatively longer (thus an agogic accent) in three of
those four instances.

SUMMARY: PITCH STRUCTURE IN THE MOZART MELODY

The rhythmic life of the line is dominated by the note F:

    a. as pitch boundaries for the total pattern (high/low, first/last);
    b. as time boundaries for interior patterns (phrases);
    c. as a pitch of agogic and metric accent;
    d. as 25 percent of total consumed time in the melody's twelve measures.

How blushingly humble, these claims to pitch fame.[12] Yet they represent just
the kinds of fundamental but concealed patterning that shapes music. Add to these
evidences of contextual prominence (and thus temporally controlled) the strong
harmonic bearings projected by the up-down sweep, such as

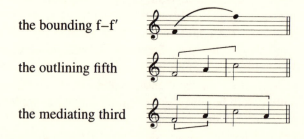

the bounding f–f′

the outlining fifth

the mediating third

and there is no wonder left that tonality was a paramount factor in the music of the
Bach-Brahms period.

    A conventional explanation (and one consistent with what little Schoenberg said
about melody) would have it that the outlining of the F-major chord in this melody

posits its tonal structure, its key. And to a certain extent, fair enough. But let us note that the presence of the arpeggiated F-major triad is in one sense beside the point; it is not the *triadic presence* that determines the focus projected. Observe that every A of this melody could be replaced with the pitch B and, in spite of dramatically altering aesthetic value, do no violence to the melody's centering on pitch-class F as tonic. We could even remove all C's and this condition of F-ness would not be violated. The melody's F-ness arises from temporal causes. The F A C triadic paradigm is mere harmonic icing on the melodic cake. The oft-repeated definer "triadic tonality" exceeds the demands for accuracy in such matters.

EXAMPLE 24. Mozart's theme revised to eliminate mediant pitches.

Before we leave this revealing example we must add to our rhythmic-tonal description some attention to the way the fifth f–c is projected within the first three sounds. Then observe the climactic f′ of measure five, how it confirms through its metric and phrase accentuation the rightness of our earlier interpretation (in the heat of listening) that the f–c relation was the vertical control for the first phrase. This gives us even clearer insight into the rhythm-pitch-harmony bearing of this music and how it is formed in perception. The accumulation of F-ness by the end of measure seven is unequivocal.[13] The "equilibration" of complex sound input, to use the verb favored by psychologist Robert Francès,[14] has produced a sound-structure.

Let us grant immediately that not all melodies, not even all of those of the historical milieu illustrated, so aptly fulfill these kinds of pitch-rhythm interlockings to create such unequivocal consolidations. On the other hand, one could as well exhibit volumes of melodies from the communal repertories, from the folk songs of the ages, from the pop classics of recent history, and representatives from the most ancient of song—pitch collections even more insistent in their exploitation of the same kinds of organizational complementarity.

One might ask at this point, however, why, for instance, the F octave or the f–c fifth of Mozart's tune achieve the status of shaping agents rather than, say, the B♭–g of measure three, or the a–d of measure five. Is it because, as Hindemith claimed, a hierarchy of intervals prevails and the fifth, f–c, is the strongest, the most capable of drawing all others within its harmonic orbit?

The answer is both simpler and more complicated than implied by Hindemith's claim—simpler because the endowment of F-ness derives most directly here from rhythmic causes, as we have observed. And the answer's more complicated facet lies in the realization that only the *potential* of framing status lies squarely within the pitch shape conveyed by the fifth/fourth mediated octave of the harmonic series. It provides a path of least resistance, a cognitive template that is operative only when temporal equivocation trips it in. Schoenberg was right in this respect; the intervals low in the series exert more power than those found higher. But those "simpler" intervals do not, Napoleon-like, crown themselves. Their *potential* can be *realized* only through their conveyance by other musical properties, most notably by rhythm.

THE HARMONIC SERIES AS COGNITIVE ARCHETYPE

In spite of the checkered past of the harmonic series, as we outlined it in Chapter 5, music scholars yet seem to agree that it is a gift of nature unparalleled in any other sensory mode. With equal conviction they reasonably see it as the veritable nemesis of theoretical tinkering, a source of embarrassment for just about every music theorist since Mersenne discovered it in the seventeenth century. Its subsequent life has been a dizzying series of intellectual ups and downs, a mercurial reputation unequaled by any other phenomenon of the natural world. Its potential for mathematical speculations of arcane elegance has led many a seeker of musical holy grails astray; its convenience as an explanatory cog in the machinery of acoustics has contributed such patently impotent "physical" theories of harmonic dynamics (like Rameau's and two hundred years later, Hindemith's) that mere mortals tremble to invoke its name, much less its reality, in the service of musical explication.[15]

But it seems certain that the harmonic series plays a primal role in our conversion of the auditory signal into musical meaning. Contemporary attempts to sort out psychoacoustic fact from fiction have only resurrected the conviction that musical meaning is in part wrested from very basic perceptual cues. So let us risk failure once more to see if we cannot make headway in understanding better how the series is directly relevant to the musical perception and the relationship it bears to the condition of tonality.

Returning to our earlier remarks about the series (especially in Chapter 4), hearing a musical tone is not usually an experience of an isolated point in auditory space, not a lonely sonic particle without inherent shape. Rare is the experience (and rare *ever was* the experience)[16] of a tone devoid of its accompanying partials. That we go through life unaware that we are bombarded by aural grapeshot rather than by solitary bullets alters nothing of the persisting wound: our perception of pitch complexes follows a relatively predictable and uniform format. A sound possesses shape. It is a shape largely determined by the harmonic series, and this shape functions as a paradigm of auditory reference whenever tones are heard, *as a template of cognitive structuring*.

On hearing a single tone or a multitude of tones, we expectantly seek an organizational modus vivendi; we expect to materialize a way of relating tone to context, a way of deriving meaning. We seek and we expect structure. Our expectations are often fulfilled, in that structure is inherent to the substance of our perception, and it is eminently consistent with the conditions of "good shape" which we seek. The general specifications of this expectation-fulfillment scenario were stated over a half-century ago by Köhler:

> It is precisely the original segregation of circumscribed wholes which makes it possible for the sensory world to appear so utterly imbued with meaning to the adult; for, in its gradual entrance into the sensory field, meaning follows the lines drawn by natural organization; it usually enters into segregated wholes.[17]

The immediate perceptual archetype for pitch available to us is the "perspective" that squares with the shape of the harmonic series, the shape known to us from birth. Presented with a single pitch, our path of least resistance matches external stimulus to internalized whole.[18] I suspect that psychoacoustician Ernst Terhardt is close to the truth when he proposes that the human auditory ability to process Gestalt tonal attributes provides a music basis, an ability perhaps developed as early as speech. As he speculates,[19]

> By repeatedly processing *speech,* the auditory system acquires—among other *Gestalt* laws—knowledge of the specific pitch relations which exist between the lower six to eight harmonics of complex tones. These pitch intervals become *familiar* to the 'central processor' of the auditory system and, moreover, convey 'virtual tonal meanings,' i.e., certain subharmonic bass notes. This way, these intervals become the so-called musical intervals.

And any interval from the series—more readily those potentially audible (and thus in the lower regions) are pressed into service in this way as pitch perspective,[20] as formative templates for tonal utterances in time.

As we have seen, melodies of the world often share an astonishing cross-cultural trait: their pitches commonly operate, when medium permits the range, within the bounding fences of the octave.[21] In melody of simpler pitch resources a perfect fifth or fourth provides the same kind of enclosing paradigm. Even when the octave prevails, it will often be segregated into a fifth/fourth disposition, a lingering fact of pitch organization that was as true for the fifth century as for the fifteenth or the twentieth. It is this harmonic envelope that supports meaning; we might even echo Descartes' charming way of putting it, when in his *Compendium* he remarks that the modes (which reflect this harmonic power) have the "ability to prevent tones of a melody from wandering in all directions."[22]

Now, any one of these intervals, most prominently the octave, fifth, or fourth, *when its tones are conformally projected by rhythm,* can trigger the formation of a field of tonality. This is a product of human interpretation of audible messages, an act of cognitive intervention. It is the invocation of a path of least resistance. It is the adoption of a *harmonic* perspective supplied preformed for our use by the very shape of the series and adaptable to the immediacy of tonal perception.[23]

In the face of these claims, consider once again, as in Example 25, that normal fixed tone, for our purposes a low C. Recall three simple but overriding features of this geometrically expanding web of tone. First, there are twice as many Cs (partials 1, 2, 4, 8, etc.) as any other pitch class.[24] Second, although there are fewer partials at the bottom, they tend to be of greater intensity (which our notation conceals). And last, the increasing abundance of successively higher partials corresponds with their growing closeness, so that the "space" between partials 7 and 8, for example, is less than that between 1–2 or 5–6.

EXAMPLE 25. Harmonic series, through eighth partial.

Let us draw some elementary conclusions from these reminders. First, the series (or what the German language renders more accurately as *Klang*) is decidedly bottom-heavy; more energy is channeled into fewer of its lower parts. This Topsy-the-Clown condition constitutes a perceptual vector, a "pointing force" whose locus resides in the lowest partial (and its octave replicas as well).[25] The tonality of the series converges toward this pitch class; it is an aural "vanishing point" shaped from the total pitch perspective of the series. Visual experiences of converging lines, overlapping surfaces, brightness of hue, sharpness of detail, and relative object sizes have by early childhood stamped into us the structural inferences we make of the vanishing point of depth perception (inferences which research has shown can be falsely imposed on us in special circumstances).[26] The experience from birth of the tonal shape—the *hierarchical shape*—projected in the harmonic series leads to a powerful part of the structural inferences of harmonic roots,[27] the tonic pitches of audition.

The identity and stability of the whole series is rooted in this fundamental, whose partials vector "toward it." We can as well call it the *tonic pitch* of the series. In fact, we can appropriately call it the root of the series, for each of these terms, *fundamental, tonic,* and *root,* has the same meaning in this context. This lowest partial (and its octave multiples) is not the root just because it is the loudest (although it often is). As a matter of fact, in many of the tones we hear, the fundamental frequency is not actually present in the signal; it is impressed upon our consciousness by the pattern of the partials which are present. More significantly, the fundamental possesses this superior contextual role because the bottom-heavy shape of the series channels focus into it. Pattern of the whole is the critical issue; physical dominance is not.[28]

Without the whole, separated parts—such as the lower intervals segregated by Schoenberg—are without contextual reference. And it is the whole that serves as a shaping matrix for our tonal perceptions, what we carry with us to our every musical encounter. Auditory processing that yields conditions of coherence, including that of tonal hierarchy, demands transient memory storage that enables the listener to synthesize briefly retained images before they have been lost in favor of more current input. Called *iconic memory* by psychologist Ulrich Neisser,[29] this is the same kind of storage capability outlined for visual perception in the empirical studies made by Sperling[30] and Averbach and Coriell.[31] It is a condition uninformed by physical presences of relative strengths like the combination tones of Hindemith and Helmholtz or the "virtual tones" of Terhardt[32] and Parncutt.[33] It is a processing that employs pattern alone in invoking hierarchy.

The Role of Learning in the Tonality Experience

While the term *root* usually refers to the pitch focus of a single chord or very brief melodic figure, the condition of tonality embraces a larger tonal pattern. In this respect it is the correlate in extended time of the more local event of rootedness.

The fragility of this condition, tonality, as we mentioned in our opening discussion of this book, arises at any moment from the possibility that subsequent events may contradict it, may replace it with another hierarchical set. The first of a series of tonal events leads us to project—to "image"—an anticipated tonal context in which it plays a role. The nature of that initial projection is to a degree determined by the expectations we bring with us, our personal repertoires of style-probabilities accumulated from all the music we have heard. We are motivated in this by an inherent will to make sense of the external world. As Howard Margolis explains this motivation:

> The brain has a bias favoring seeing something rather than nothing, so it tends to jump to a pattern that makes sense of a situation. Hence, even if there is no pattern objectively there, it tries to impute one.[34]

And Margolis reasonably calls this anticipatory action "cognitive jumping."

Let us clarify this cognitive act, as it relates to music, with a single example that can be seminal. Suppose that the chord in Example 26 sounds. Hearing it, what do I, as engaged listener, "jump" to as an anticipated tonal context? How do I project this chord as a part of an anticipated larger harmonic field? (We assume that this act occurs without one's conscious control.) Answers to these questions depend in part on the experiential sets I bring with me, which one I find most appropriate to apply.

EXAMPLE 26. Initial sound of a longer message.

Let us say that I am seated in a theater. Its stage bears an eighteenth-century scenic set, and the chord in question is sounded by a harpsichord. I fix into cognitive readiness a context that is consistent with what is for me a well-established paradigm:

Recitativo! Probably V⁷-Soon-to-be-Resolved-to-Tonic.

Of course, non-conforming or even contradictory melodic, harmonic, rhythmic, or timbral influences may come along, informing me that my hasty extrapolation must be modified or even replaced. But for the moment, this postulated cognitive path is "in place," it is my best probability inference from my collection of past paradigms. It is my first line of defense against perceptual chaos.

Now let us imagine a quite different circumstance. The room is a smoke-filled urban bar. A blues singer strums the same G^7 chord on his guitar, clearly the first chord of many. My new tonal set is indexed to the total message, so the chord enacts a new role within my extrapolated tonal fix. My sonic repertory now leads me to project it as a tonic; it is my concomitant expectation that just four pulses later will bring another chord, a C^7, thus fulfilling both the second bar of a twelve-bar blues progression and proof of the astuteness of my instantaneous projection.

Thus a single chord has triggered two different tonalities (and their respective tonic functions) because my expectations led me to impose different sets of constraints of perception on the raw data. My knowledge (or ignorance) of style has guided the meaning I derive from hearing the single chord.

The Holistic View Related to Past Explanations

For the moment, notice that our claim for the series resembles (but differs crucially from) the numerical ratio-dominated residues of Pythagoreanism and from Schoenberg's acoustical ladder. Numbers, as such, and simplicities or complexities of ratios, and stronger or weaker first or second order resultant tones have only peripheral relevance to the cognitive application of the harmonic series as tonal paradigm. It is not far fetched at this point to recall the last of Augustine's *numeri,* or sound principles, enunciated in the sixth book of his *De Musica,* where he attempts to explain the complex ontology of musical sounds, from their physical initiation (*numeri sonantes*) to their human apprehension. And this final one, the sixth, called *numeri iudiciales,* suggests an incipient recognition of just what we are talking about, an a priori template of auditory processing.

> The human sense of hearing has the faculty to construct the relationship of sounds (that is of intervals) even before the sound actually exists. Otherwise we would not be pleased with good singing and hurt by faulty sounds.

And later:

> The intellect does three things at once; the intellect expects, perceives, and remembers.

Kathi Meyer-Baer regarded this tracing by Augustine of the musical signal as "the first attempt at a method of musical psychology or phenomenology."[35]

Schoenberg's perspective of 1911, like that of Helmholtz earlier in 1863, and Hindemith later in 1937, assumed the separation of each interval from its containing series, its capacity to act individually (with self-possessed root) as a tonal paradigm exclusive of containing context. Consonance/Dissonance became confused with concepts of structural foundations. For Schoenberg, the fifth (as we are told in *Harmonielehre*) occurs first in the series; it divides the tonal spectrum by marking off the dominant (above) and the subdominant (below) a pre-ordained tonic. The fifth's unique position in the series, after the duplicative octave, with its containment of the series' fundamental, makes it eminently adaptive to this basic delineating function. My own scheme claims only that a well-defined audible shape, the harmonic series, encroaches upon our cognitive acts. Its singular unity-in-complexity is transferred by the listener as organizing schema to extended as well as to brief tonal statements; it becomes the microcosm whose pattern helps to shape the musical macrocosm. By simple association, our cognitive will imposes the archetypal pattern on to orderings of tones, which usually are themselves conveniently pre-arranged in ways consistent with the cognitive model. This, after all, is the nature of the cooperative venture between composer and listener.

All of this, let us hasten to reconfirm, occurs within the inequitable jockeyings of tones in time, the rhythms which ultimately control the vectorial dynamics of an auditory experience. Theorists who have laboriously mapped out explanatory models of music's pitch basis "from nature," Rameau through Hindemith and Schoenberg, have flawed their elaborate schemes by anchoring them in a timeless sea. Clearly, relative deployments of tones in time have as much to do with the perceived auditory image as do pitch relationships. The tonal template of the harmonic series, which is a latent cognitive accompaniment to our every listening experience, cannot fulfill its potential without confirmations from the flow of multiple accentual levels which carry along its participating pitches.

Although necessarily long in the telling, this scheme need not suggest for the perceptual event a drawn-out scanning process through N potential archetypes to find that which is best suited to the occasion. On the contrary, it is clearly a cognitive act of immediacy whose "solution" is grasped along with recognition of the challenge.[36] As P. C. Wason[37] and David Rummelhart[38] have independently yet mutually concluded: "Understanding the problem and solving it are merely the same things." Or, paraphrasing Gilbert Ryle, "the composer is leading and the listener is following, but their paths are the same; execution and understanding are products of the same experiential tricks."

NOTES

1. *Theory of Harmony*, 26–27 (1922, 27).
2. Ibid., 312 (1922, 376). See also my reference to Rivera, Chapter 7, n. 19.

3. *Style and Idea,* 259.

4. This perspective is shared by Andrew Mead, "The State of Research in Twelve-Tone and Atonal Theory."

5. Floyd Allport, *Theories of Perception and the Concept of Structure,* 622.

6. Rowell, *Thinking of Music,* 234.

7. Berry, *Structural Functions in Music,* 27.

8. Apel, "Tonality."

9. *A Generative Theory of Music,* 281.

10. We could squander thousands of words to describe adequately how a tonal hierarchy is brought about in this brief excerpt. Full explanations of simple musical events tend to expand exponentially as measure is added to measure; but our immediate goal here is to show only basic aspects of tonal-rhythmic interdependency, verbal economy our secondary goal.

11. This interpretation becomes less reasonable when the melody is heard in full texture, with its imitative line in the bass of measures 5–7. This "disruption" also urges a three-phrase structure, but each phrase consisting of four-measure segments.

12. A similar accounting of the same processing can be found in my discussion of Basic Melody in *Materials and Structure of Music* I (3rd. ed.), 93–106.

13. In the language of perceptual psychology, *event* tone becomes an *ongoing* to join with other same-level events to become a more encompassing event, melody or chord, depending upon the deployment of elements in time. A classic exposition is Allport's *Theories of Perception,* 634–643. It is comforting to notice the compatibility of Allport's generic explanation with Leonard B. Meyer's discussion of musical hierarchies in *Explaining Music,* 89–91.

14. Robert Francès, *The Perception of Music,* 86–87.

15. With the possible exception of Ernst Terhardt's psychoacoustical model (1972 and subsequently), recent theories of harmonic rootedness suffer the same dependence on a conception of raw physical reinforcement. They are hypothesized from assumptions similar to the difference tone theory of Hindemith, which he probably picked up from Helmholtz. Even Richard Parncutt's attempts to improve and to apply Terhardt's ideas to music smack of a reversion to this deadend of "objective strengths," of pitch loci determined by sheer congregations of sound level pressures. See Plomp's synopsis of recent theories in *Aspects of Tone Sensation,* 111–142.

16. We exceed self-imposed bounds of inferential propriety here, but it seems reasonable that even Cro-Magnon listeners carried the series in the baggage of their hearing.

17. Köhler, *Gestalt Psychology,* 82.

18. Thus the claim made often by astute musicians including Schoenberg and Sessions that a solitary tone heard exclusive of prepared context has imposed on it the role of tonic (subject to subsequent revision, of course). I have found this to be a reliable generalization, although I must confess having caught myself, Cartesian-like, in the act of imaging other matrices (such as $\hat{5}$ or $\hat{3}$ or even $\hat{7}$). This probably cannot pass muster as one of Köhler's "original sensory facts." See the discussion of the role of learning in this extrapolation process, 125.

19. Terhardt, "Pitch, Consonance, and Harmony," 1066. And as Terhardt acknowledges ("The Concept of Musical Consonance: A Link Between Music and Psychoacoustics," 285–286), Helmholtz anticipated answers to some of these questions by attributing the origin of music's "harmonic laws"— those of *Klangwerwandtschaft*—to the learning process that accompanies our perception of tones as varied timbres.

20. Most often, the lowest four to six partials of a complex tone are potentially hearable, although faint and thus demanding of exceptional focus. This depends largely, of course, on the sound's source, its relatively steady state, etc. Even this small number is reduced as the fundamental rises in pitch and/or reduces in intensity. (See Plomp, "The Ear as Frequency Analyzer" and Deutsch, "Delayed Pitch Comparisons and the Principle of Proximity.")

21. Thus Boethius, *Fundamentals of Music,* 153, tells us that "From the consonance of the diapason arise what are called 'modes.' "

22. Descartes, *Compendium*, 51.

23. One of the strongest empirical demonstrations of intervallic rootedness (and the fickle nature of that condition) can be found in the Leon R. Smith study of 1967. Although virtually ignored by the scholarly community, this novel series of experiments suggests a predictable hierarchy of interval values in terms of vectoral power that may reside in one of an interval's pitches. Smith concludes that "a rational order of interval values, whatever its affecting agency, is in operational force in the perception and cognition of tonal successions." The principal thrust of his inquiry is to show the relative strength of a particular interval, embedded periodically in an otherwise randomized pitch series, to project a sense of pulse.

24. Or we might add with Terhardt ("*Zur Tonhöhenwahrnehmung von Klangen* I and II"), that all the fundamental C dominates as *virtual pitch*, especially since it lies below 700 Hz and carries a full complement of harmonic partials.

25. We would mislead if we suggested that any tone's series will contain the same properties in the same relative proportions. Some instruments produce sounds lacking some partials, others produce complex tones with one (or more) excessively intense partial(s), and still others produce maverick partials that are shockingly "out of tune" with our ideal model. These comments are intended as generalizations rather than as wholly and precisely true for all instances.

26. For examples see Ittelson and Kilpatrick, "Experiments in Perception," in Beardslee and Wertheimer, eds., *Readings in Perception*, 432–444.

27. Let us not jump to the conclusion that here is revealed a full explanation for what since Rameau has been called "chord root," although I am confident that the harmonic shape of the archetypal harmonic series is relevant.

28. See note 15 above.

29. *Cognitive Psychology*.

30. Sperling, "The Information Available in Brief Visual Presentations."

31. Averbach and Coriell, "Short Term Memory in Vision."

32. Terhardt, see note 24 above.

33. Richard Parncutt, "Revision of Terhardt's Psychoacoustical Model of the Root(s) of a Musical Chord."

34. Margolis, *Patterns, Thinking, and Cognition*, 38.

35. Meyer-Baer, "Psychologic and Ontologic Ideas in Augustine's *De Musica*," 223. My discussion here is indebted to Ms. Meyer-Baer's distillation of Augustine's ideas.

36. It seems reasonable to hypothesize with Margolis (*Patterns, Thinking and Cognition*, 39) that the mind does not work in such a way that many competing patterns are entertained in the single process.

37. In "Realism and Rationality in the Selection Task."

38. In "Schemata."

PART IV

Putting Together What Belongs Together

CHAPTER 10

The Harmonic Series as Pitch Archetype

THE ARGUMENTS OF TRADITION

As we suggested earlier, claims that the harmonic series provides some demonstrable resource for the musical experience, beyond merely determining timbre, have not gone uncontested. Like the claims to which they respond, the disclaimers are as various in quality as they are numerous in kind. They can be summarized most readily in three basic arguments: (1) Historical Inconsistency, (2) Inadequacy as Source, and (3) Unequal Dualism. Although the role of harmonic paradigm I have enunciated here differs in critical ways from Schoenberg's, it too invokes the harmonic series as aural model, so it might appear to be the automatic victim of the same arguments I have leveled at his explanations. For this reason the overly trod ground of this topic justifies some review of the objections found in conventional discourse of the past fifty years.

The first argument pertains to music's stylistic evolution, which in one respect appears to have run counter to the consonance-dissonance values said to inhere, as interval hierarchy, in the harmonic series. The second argument questions the series' adequacy for deriving a scale from the harmonic partials—pentatonic, heptatonic, or chromatic[1]—which produces credible results. And the third argument hinges on recognition that the series is incapable of accounting for the major-minor dualism (equality of modes) that has prevailed in musical practice. Since the second and third arguments are related, we shall deal with them as one, as The Argument From Inadequate Source. But first to history.

THE ARGUMENT FROM HISTORICAL INCONSISTENCY

The criticism made by Jackendoff and Lerdahl of the harmonic series as an experiential model opens by echoing this old argument. Summarizing it neatly and objectively, they recognize that the fourth seems to have come along in history as a consonance before the third (parallel organum before gymel), thus confirming the hierarchy contained within the series. But this early concurrence was nonetheless subverted by subsequent musical developments. As they observe:

> Not long after the introduction of the major third as a consonance [and this would refer only to theorists' recognition] a fourth between the bass and another part came to be treated as dissonant, requiring resolution.[2]

In other words, treatment in actual music of the fourth as a dissonance resolvable to a third, when couched between bass and an upper voice, casts doubt on the alleged superiority or relative consonance claimed in theory. If the fourth is so special, in its eminent 4:3 location, why must it "resolve" to the third, whose inferior location is 5:4?

But this long-respected disclaimer is as specious as the original claim it attacks. It replaces a consonance-dissonance judgment by one based on stylistic preference and melodic-rhythmic expectations. It ignores the kinds of definitional transformations endured over the ages by the consonance-dissonance concept. James Tenney[3] has convincingly outlined the slight shift in meaning that occurred, beginning in the late thirteenth century, when prevailing considerations of harmonic affinity, not unlike the nineteenth-century fusion concept of Carl Stumpf (*Tonverschmelzung*), was joined by an operational definition aroused by awakening considerations for contrapuntal relationships. This added concern for conditions of voice against voice (recognized by Tenney as the third of five stages in the history of consonance-dissonance taxonomies) became conceptual overlay to the way people had evaluated harmonic dyads, in terms of sonance, since the advent of polyphony.

Let us recognize that the harmonic perfect fourth had become syntactically insecure by the time root position major and minor triads had become referential sonorities. Thus, in Renaissance polyphony the fourth rarely occurs between bass and upper voice as an interval of harmonic stability; its presence usually entails a justifying melodic figure—4–3 suspension, passing tone, or neighbor tone—that obviates its projection of harmonic security. This contextual control persisted through the later eighteenth and the nineteenth centuries (and even beyond, in almost all music compounded from the same harmonic staples), when tertial chords reigned supreme. Even dyads of the fifth occur in Renaissance textures only as sonorities of privilege, marking off, for example, the finality of cadences in those instances where full major triads do not. (The minor triad also was not fully accepted as a terminating chord until well into the Baroque period, again a matter of syntactic preference rather than of harmonic stability.)

Then let us observe that stylistic aversion does not of itself equate with *harmonic sonance,* whose phenomenal conditions entail degrees of non-fusion/fusion, roughness/smoothness,[4] conditions that are separable from the more encompassing judgments of instability/stability. Should future theorists infer that the absence of major and minor triads in the later works of Schoenberg and Webern is proof that those sonorities were more dissonant for twentieth-century ears than, say, a triad consisting of major seventh and tritone (Schoenberg's favorite chord)? Such a conclusion would make as much sense as deciding that the absence of "stable" harmonic fourths in Palestrina and Lassus proves their dissonance.

But syntactic rejection does not fully explain the "dissonant 4th," which lived on into the eighteenth and nineteenth centuries embodied within its outgrowth, the so-called "dissonant $^6_4$" chord. This was the sonority that led one of Schoenberg's principal influences, Bruckner, to declare that it possessed a "double nature." Although the fourth and the sixth separately were in themselves consonances, Bruckner explained that "when the fourth and sixth sound together, the fourth no longer sounds consonant."[5] In the cadential $^6_4$ we can observe a compelling phenomenological factor that contributes to this false attribution, a cause that has nothing to do with harmonic content. It is a cause bound up in rhythm.

Phrase Rhythms and the Dissonant $^6_4$ Chord

Claims for the dissonant fourth often turn for their proof to the controversial (is it I$^6_4$ or is it V?) cadential chord of common practice style. Similar to Bruckner's "bad chemistry" argument, one accounting, from a respected German text that preceded Schoenberg's by only four years, insisted that it is the "*context* in which they occur that imposes an interpretation upon our ear, according to which they appear essentially as dissonant."[6]

EXAMPLE 27. Mozart, K. 333, III, first eight measures.

We turn now to appropriate models to illustrate and study the phenomenon anew. The final movement of the Mozart K. 333 *Piano Sonata* (see Example 27) opens with a typical eight-measure period, punctuated by a half-cadence at its middle. The $^6_4$ chord on beat one of measure four is followed by the V that finishes off the phrase. The tonic begins phrase two (measure 5), which is a melodic and harmonic variant of its antecedent, its cadence a typical I_4^6–V–I turn-around that begins here in the last half of measure 7. Let us focus for the moment on the $_4^6$ chord in measure 7. Tradition tells us to regard it as dissonant; its "urge to resolution" to the chord that follows (V here) is said to justify that interpretation. Even more cogent for us is that the fourth (F–B♭) of the outer voices is said to constitute a "dissonant fourth," whose resolution occurs with the "more consonant" major third (F–A), contrary to the favored status of the perfect fourth. And this contradiction is seen as capping evidence that the harmonic series cannot be trusted as a paradigm of intervallic values. Practice, through the ages, proves it to be an inconsistent guide.

But this is no proof at all. It mixes oranges with apples, confusing consonance-dissonance with other musical properties.

CONTROLLING RHYTHMIC AND MELODIC FACTORS

Viewed as a projection in time—as a *sound vector*—Mozart's two-phrase pattern cuts the following form:

             Open   Closed

Melodic contour, rhythm, and chord succession concur in this sectioning according to Haydn-Mozart-Beethoven norms. The initial 2 + 2 pattern *could* have ended with tonic, although the harmony of measure three does not, in the style, make this outcome likely. (At cadences tonic chords are preceded by V, not ii$_6$ or IV.) But regardless, what happens next nullifies such an eventuality; a typical dominant marks off the half-cadence.

Now, by the time we are well into the second phrase, a *phrase-set* has been projected for us. (Much as the blues singer's first eight-bar phrase predicts shapes for the next two phrases, as we discussed earlier.) This phrase-set leads us to expect that the second phrase will reach its terminating downbeat on the tonic chord, *but not in measure seven*. Why not? Because the rhythmic thrust of what has preceded—let us call it *Our Inferred Rut of Periodicity*—demands that closure begin on the thesis of measure eight, parallel with closure in measure four (as well as sub-phrase closures at each two-measure unit). So regardless of what chord turns up in measure seven, it will be the prepared victim of a relentless Gestalt, one whose dimensions were set in measures 1–2 and 3–4, then reconfirmed in 5–6; it *points* to beat one of measure eight as its goal. Stylistic consistency (confirmed here by the rhythmic dynamics of local conditions) dictates *Closure* here and not before.

And so both of the $_4^6$ chords in this passage harbor rumblings of discontent, but not because of their *phenomenal dissonance*—at least, not in the *fusion* sense of harmonic sonance that underlay notions of consonance from the fourteenth century or not in the *roughness* sense described and defined by Helmholtz. Instead, two other factors control this condition. The first is the melodic implication of the chord's $\hat{5}$, as bass; it is not the most propitious for closure in this or in any style. Only $\hat{1}$ can fully perform that role in the foundation part. And second, phrase rhythms deny both chords the projection of arrival.

Simple confirmation of this conclusion comes when we substitute a different measure four for Mozart's. Observe in our reconstruction of Example 28 that the "dissonant $^6_4$" is replaced by a chord of unimpeachable harmonic purity: root position tonic. And yet in this same location, even without the offending fourth between bass and upper voice, a similar irresoluteness is projected. The vaunted dissonant fourth turns out to have been just another phantom in music theory's archive. Harmonic grammar (termination on tonic) and phrase grammar (anacrusis to projected terminating beat) turn out to be incongruent. The $^6_4$ chord is not dissonant: it is rhythmically premature, syntactically weak in projecting closure.[7]

EXAMPLE 28. Reconstruction of Mozart's phrase.

Beethoven's Opus 2 No. 1 illustrates the same principle. Notice how the first phrases of the Minuet establish a phrase-set of $\overline{2 + 2}$ units whose initial terminating goal is the downbeat of measure four. And thus the accumulated paradigms of phrases one and two urge us to expect phrase three (mm. 9–12) to continue the cycle, to end in measure twelve.

It is tempting in this age of style consciousness to beg the question: "Convention, *in the style,* makes the $^6_4$ chord dissonant." But this is lame excuse rather than clarifying explication. We certainly agree with a supportive role for stylistic convention in this matter, urging, however, that the condition of dissonance not be mistaken for what it is not.

Other properties can overcome this power of the phrase-set. In the opening of Norman Dello Joio's *Piano Sonata No. 3* (shown in Example 29) a durational paradigm of 𝅘𝅥 𝅘𝅥 𝅘𝅥 is set and reconfirmed twice. But the cadential fourth in measure five is as terminal as its very consonant nature allows, because texture (thematic imitation) and melodic contour (step-progression d c b a in measures three–four) lead us past the vectoral urge for caesura on beat three of measure four. Here neither syntactic preference nor phrase-set projects harmonic inappropriateness.

EXAMPLE 29. Norman Dello Joio, Piano Sonata No. 3, I, initial phrase. Copyright © 1948 by Carl Fischer, Inc. Reprinted by permission.

THE ARGUMENT FROM INADEQUATE SOURCE

This second disclaimer finds fault because the harmonic series cannot live up to claims that it is an initiating source for chords and scales, that it is a kind of Platonic storehouse of melodic and harmonic prototypes, that the *harmonia perfetta,* humanity's "chord of nature," is comfortably ensconced within the senario, partials 1 through 6. Theorists from the Renaissance through Schenker and Schoenberg have not failed to remark upon this spectacular presence. And, so goes the claim, scales are latent presences (vertically) in the series as well. Leonard Bernstein[8] even finds the pentatonic scale of children's chanting songs within partials 4:5:6:7 (fudging slightly on the tuning of what he calls a "sort-of-A"); see Example 30. Example 31 illustrates a more conventional discovery. It claims that the fifth, providing as it does the first non-duplicative pitch relation in the series, can yield the tones of the scale by superposition, even if the subdominant can never be produced (except by the magic of inversion).[9]

EXAMPLE 30. Bernstein's pentatonic scale from nature (*The Unanswered Question*, 26–27).

EXAMPLE 31. Scale generation from stacked fifths.

Derived perhaps with Pythagorean tuning in mind, this method was particularly important in establishing as a norm the three-function harmonic system touted by Riemann, mainly because it sports the overfifth/underfifth symmetry that for some theorists has been so impressive.

Another approach, similar to Schoenberg's (see discussion above, p. 45), begins with the fifth above and below a postulated tonic, but the triads on those roots provide the notes of the scale, as in Example 32.

EXAMPLE 32. Major scale derived from I, IV, V as over- and under-fifths.

A RESPONSE TO DISSENT

Once the arguments have been filed and reviewed, we must concur with the critics. All of the claims for the Series as Progenitor suffer from one or another unacceptable flaw. Counterarguments have followed much the same form as the following:

1. Major and minor triads are chords of equal importance in the music we know best. They are equally consonant, and they function as co-significant elements in their respective musical contexts. They form a basic harmonic duality of the Western musical system, yet one (major) is synonymous with the senario of the harmonic series, partials 1 through 6, while the other cannot be found at all, unless one is willing (and some have been) to call partials 10:12:15 nature's prototype.

But this is not a reasonable account of these two chords' equal harmonic values. If the series were our singular source of pitch hierarchy, as claimed, it would provide equally august character references for both.

2. Much the same can be said for the way scales have been "derived" from the series. Who today would concur (with Schenker and Schoenberg) that the major scale is a product of the series' fifth (3:2) used as a replicated unit to produce tonal offspring? And what has actually been revealed by showing that five overfifths and one underfifth produce notes corresponding to the major scale? It is a doubtful business. The subdominant in such a scheme must be induced, sidestepping in the process the source itself. (Schenker invokes his magic number Five as a limit to overfifths, claiming, much as did Schoenberg, that artistic insight motivates the subdominant relation.)[10] And further, even if the major scale is in some meaningful way contained as prototype by the series, where is its minor counterpart? Where, as a partial, is minor's minor third? And where its submediant? If it is said to derive from the thirteenth partial, then where is the major scale's submediant, whose pitch is slightly higher?

Indeed, these objections make the Harmonic Series as Progenitor appear disappointingly infertile. But the counterarguments are in a way as irrelevant as are their targets. The real problem exists at a prior state of discourse, which is where the whole fatuous business of seeking "sources of derivation" begins. These kinds of arguments about natural sources became common barter once Rameau began (in his *Génération*

Harmonique, 1737) trying to show how the whole musical tapestry could be woven from the harmonic series. It was Schoenberg's pitiable lot to inherit the very notion that music's secrets resided in pre-human paradigms, that the conventional scales and chords and whatever there is of music's substance receive special approbation by virtue of this pre-human pool of auditory resources.

THE OLD NON-PROBLEM OF MINOR HARMONY

But there remains a question that has bewildered music theorists for the past four centuries, one that readers may want answered directly rather than obliquely. It is "the question of minor harmony" (and of the interval of the minor third), whose inauspicious presence in the harmonic series seems to defy rational explanation, denying the origins of advantage of major harmony, whose 4:5:6 location is so commanding.

As suggested above and elsewhere (p. 142), this is actually a non-question, a question that should never have been asked in the first place. Even the exemplary 4:5:6 ratio within the senario provides no birthright for major triads (or major thirds), thereby sanctioning their *musical* legitimacy. In all such "justifications," cart has been put before horse. The real modeling potential inherent to the harmonic series is its phenomenal shape, whose vectoral force, in perception, leads only to the fundamental of the series. And this force is operative, if at all, only as reference for relationships low in the series, especially that which divides octaves for us into fifth/fourth distributions.

Even though the minor third may project a serviceable root pattern (and I am reluctant to agree that it does), that root potential is a pitch class uncontained in the original interval. A melodic or chordal pattern bounded solely by it, and thus lacking a structural fifth or fourth as framing potential, will be ambiguous unless other properties mitigate. At least three possibilities are latent in the minor third. If a prominent tonic is projected it will be a product of the contiguities discussed by the Gestaltists and by Otto Ortmann (Example 33). But if the pattern's ambitus (struc-

EXAMPLE 33. Ambiguous pattern, three potential tonics.

turally explicit range) extends to a fourth or to a fifth, a clearer hierarchy is available, and it will be forceful if contextual distribution and rhythm provide support, as in Example 34. (Obviously, preceding sounds also can affect the root/tonic images.) And yet, as in any pattern, context and rhythm can easily throw the focus toward either pitch of the minor third, bypassing the paradigmatic model provided by the series, as Example 35 shows.

EXAMPLE 34. Unambiguous Frames. (a) fourth; (b) fifth.

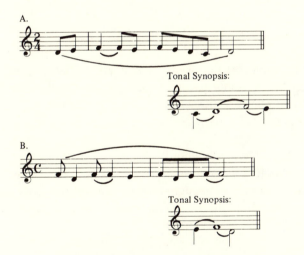

EXAMPLE 35. Same pitches, different tonics.

The universal children's chant shown in Example 36, whose ambitus is a minor third, provides an excellent case in point. I can remember as a child singing it, usually

EXAMPLE 36. Universal child's taunting song.

taunting a playmate with a text specially fitted for the occasion. And I recall vividly my tonal imagery for the pattern, certain (to the extent certainty can be trusted over a half-century later) that it was imaged by me around an "absentee tonic," (Example 37).[11] This is consistent with the 6:5 paradigm offered by the series (whose root would be the 1:2:4 partial pitch class), as well as with the root theories of Hindemith and Terhardt.[12]

EXAMPLE 37. Image with phantom tonic.

This melody could be (and may very well be, for many of its universal singers/hearers) imaged with focus on its lowest pitch (an incipient E minor) or even on its G (because of the two metric accents, articulations one and five). And thus it goes, with tonality and harmonic roots, when the fifth/fourth paradigm is not laid out explicitly. If focus is nonetheless present, its causes are rhythmic or formal or even dynamic.

So Where Do Chords and Melodies Come From?

Schoenberg's conviction that the origin of major and minor scales and their tonal system resided in forced applications of the harmonic triad severely inhibited his perspective of structural properties and processes. Motivated by the deductive habits of the theoretical tradition he knew best (and covertly respected), it was a misguided effort.

The fact is that scales, like chords and intervals, come directly from people opening their mouths to sing or from exciting air columns or plucking strings or setting off electrical currents in vacuum tubes or transistors. Once these human acts have produced a collection of discriminable sounds, *then* the perceptual machinery is in a position to seek controls, to ferret out from its available cognitive unconscious some rudimentary guides of organization. It is at this point when the harmonic series can be plugged into the perceptual process as archetype. Scales and chords come from the creative volition of human action. That they may show correspondences with pre-existent models says nothing about origins, about cause and effect.

In this sense it is instructive to go back to one of our wisest ancestors, Hermann Helmholtz, to recall a conclusion he drew about just these matters, a remark either misconstrued or overlooked by too many of his successors. In the wake of the many arguments he had heard (and had himself made) about the harmonic series as the *source* of pitch materials, he concluded that no cause-effect relationship need be sought. Instead, he suggests that "the construction of scales and of harmonic tissue is a product of artistic invention."[13]

Notes

1. Schoenberg's "derivation" of the chromatic scale from the harmonic series is discussed in Chapter 5.

2. Lerdahl and Jackendoff, *A Generative Theory of Music*, 231.

3. James Tenney, *A History of Consonance and Dissonance*.

4. Tenney, Ibid., 95–98, appropriately separates the *fusion* judgment (Stumpf, Consonance-Dissonance Concept No. 4) from the *roughness* judgment (Helmholtz, Consonance-Dissonance Concept No. 5). Also note Terhardt's conclusion, "Pitch, Consonance, and Harmony," 1068, that the condition of sonic roughness does not by itself "provide a satisfactory explanation of the ear's particular sense of musical intervals."

5. Anton Bruckner, in *Vorlesungen Uber Harmonie und Kontrapunkt und der UniversitatWien*, 150–151, as reported by Wason, *Viennese Harmonic Theory From Albrechtsberger to Schenker and Schoenberg*.

6. Rudolph Louis and Ludwig Thuille, *Harmonielehre*, 29.

7. Learned stylistic constraints unquestionably enter into this scenario as supporting influences, but rhythmic periodicity or emphasis sets the scene.

8. Leonard Bernstein, *The Unanswered Question*, 26–27.

9. Schenker, for example, in the harmony volume, *Theorien und Phantasien*, I, 42.

10. Although neither man gives credit, it is hard to believe that both were not influenced by Riemann's *Überklang-Unterklang* divinations.

11. Curt Sachs shows melodic variants of this same pitch collection whose tonics I am inclined to designate as the lowest pitch. One variant is from a Mancusi Indian song after von Hornbostel, the other the German chant-song *Laterne, Laterne*. Most Western peoples have heard numerous variants of the same collection, but sometimes with the middle pitch acting as final and, I presume, as tonic (Sachs, *The Wellsprings of Music*, 40).

12. We reemphasize, however, the exclusively physical conception of these theories of harmonic roots. And further, our designation of the absent pitch class as root is wholly consistent with out pattern hypothesis and in no way perpetuates the old "root by supposition" idea of tertial harmonic theory.

13. Helmholtz, *On the Sensations of Tone*, 365. Jackendoff and Lerdahl seem not to have taken off from this statement, which they nonetheless quote, to the reach obvious conclusion which I emphasize here.

Modal Concepts, Phrase Vectors, and the Harmonic Frame

It must have been a growing awareness of underlying contextual circumstances, which anew we call *harmonic,* that led to the postulation of the two generic scale types, the authentic and the plagal, by virtue of the optional fifth/fourth deployment within the octave. Even Hucbald directly refers to the special quality of the fifth above the finalis when he allows that those two tones are "linked by a sort of connective bond." And Guido's *Micrologus,* a century later, recognizes the same strong affiliation, emphasizing the fifth as the *affinalis.*[1] It is a "connective bond" and "strong affiliation" whose special nature continues to pervade the literature of empirical studies in psychoacoustics even nine centuries after Guido. And thus Ernst Terhardt observes that:

> The "true" pitch of a complex tone (i.e., the pitch corresponding to the fundamental frequency) is sometimes confused with another pitch which usually differs by an octave–or fifth–interval from the "true" pitch.[2]

The fifth/fourth deployment integral to the modes is the same intervallic paradigm that lies as partials 2:3:4 in the harmonic series. Its 2:3 relation is the same primal unit that von Hornbostel found "marking off" the melodic fields of his African melodies. It is the same that provides the linear-harmonic template for the Mozart melody of Example 23 and for "Mary Had a Little Lamb." Those common tonal bonds between diverse repertories are not there because we have loaded our explicative dice; on the contrary, it is difficult to find music in which they *do not* prevail. They are harder to ignore than to discover.

A Conflicting View

We hasten to add, nonetheless, that the perspective we have outlined, joining harmony and mode, melody and chord, is not universally shared by music historians and theorists. Some scholars find any conjunction of the ecclesiastical modes (or the Greek Greater Perfect System or the Byzantine Echoi, or Indian *rāgas* as well, and the music they represent) with what I have delineated here as the harmonic incubus as misguided, as misrepresentation of history.

One of the most respected critics of the kind of theory I have proposed is Leo Treitler. Since his perspective is representative and uncommonly articulate, we shall attend to his objections, as we interpret them. They derive from the conviction that the final state of the modal system's evolution represents the complete and precise information obtainable from plainsong, secular song, and polyphony based on modal principles. Professor Treitler holds that claiming tonality for this music ignores the inescapable fact that the structural norms enunciated through modal practice are "fully developed specimens of a related, but quite different, system."[3] And thus, for him, finding tonality even in early two-part madrigals is a case of mistaking, as he puts it, the caterpillar for the butterfly it becomes. (He nonetheless finds the term *tonic* useful in describing the cadences of chant, as we find in his discussion of the syntax of medieval music.)[4]

In clinching his argument, Treitler turns to a slippery (yet hardly unique) argument; it is the kind of speculative wishful thinking we decried earlier, whose very nature places it comfortably, and innocuously, beyond validation (or invalidation). "It seems clear," he writes, "that the responses to musical sounds have changed through the history of the species." And he amplifies this sweeping generalization in an extended footnote,[5] in which (following E. H. Gombrich's lead) he hypothesizes that an accommodating perceptual evolution follows in the footsteps of the revolutionary creations of truly great artists. Cognition, in other words, adapts to sensory input as modified in the heat of creation. It is an idea Schoenberg would have accepted at once. In Treitler's opinion:

> While it is certain that during the Medieval Ages the octave—considered as an interval—was heard as we hear it today, it is also clear from medieval melody that our doctrine of octave equivalence was not in effect (i.e. two members of a pitch class could not have been heard to share the same function). Similarly, it was through Rameau's teaching that we learned to hear inverted triads, functioning as versions of their root positions.[6]

Having read these remarks many times, I must confess that I still wonder if the author really meant what he says; I can find no clue in all of medieval melody to support his first claim. Professor Treitler knows medieval melody and modal theory far more thoroughly than most scholars. For him to ignore the unparalleled attention paid by theorists to octave boundaries as unique definers of modal species (terminal pitches and their authentic and plagal divisions), not to mention additionally ignoring the organizational significance of ambitus as it relates to actual music, seems to load the dice by omission. Even to say on the one hand that the octave "was heard then as we hear it today," then to deny in the next breath that the relationship's most startling aural aspect (members of same pitch class heard as same function), strikes me as self-contradictory.

From the contemporary empirical side, we can observe that research with human and animal subjects confirms that the duplicative effect of the two pitches of an octave is a perceptual given, one of the primitives of the way we respond to pitch.[7] And for cogent historical comfort we can turn once again to early spokesman pseudo-Aristotle, whose wonderment over this marvelous pitch relationship included the following musing:

> Why does the low note contain the sound of the high note? Is it because the low note is heavier? It is like an obtuse angle whereas the high note is like an acute angle.[8]

Professor Treitler's second allegation, that our knowledge of Rameau's fundamental bass has altered post-eighteenth-century perceptions of chords, strikes me as more casual sophistry than reasoned judgment. Such a view confuses explication with the event explicated. It would have us believe that we see the fall of an apple differently since Newton formulated his conceptual revelation of gravitational forces. But a few years' struggling to teach freshmen musicians to "hear the root" of first-inversion minor triads can deflate the optimism of such claims, concepts altering percepts. How one reflects on chords and how one verbalizes about them will unquestionably bear the accumulated dents of past conceptualizations, but that is quite a different matter. As Wolfgang Köhler reminded us, gravitation is not a direct observation. Nor is harmonic inversion—equally "a fact of functional dependence"—directly observed. History makes a clumsy ally for Treitler's claim, for harmonic inversion as an idea tied to audition can be traced back at least to Gafori, 1496.[9]

Idle speculations about how current aural responses differ from ancient aside, we have sufficient biological, neural, and psychological background to believe that those ancient ears were as sharp as contemporary models. And (with Richard Crocker) it seems a reasonable bet that cognitive powers then were as keen, keen enough, at least, to conclude that pitch finals in some melodies lay within their ambital interiors, reversing with the octave the fifth/fourth distribution. This bedrock difference, imputed to music by those who put stock in the cogency of modal theory, is another indication that harmonic forces prevailed then as in more recent tunes of our repertory. It is hard to imagine how the fundamental pitch orientation—the pitch schema—of the *Hymn to Seikilos,* Example 22, is different from that of Example 38.

It is important at this point for readers to recall that the notes of the Hypolydian mode are identical with those of the authentic Ionian, which was officially added to the modal roster by Glareanus.[10] But let us belabor one rudimentary but crucial point:

one of these (authentic Ionian) carries a different central tone, or final. And within this humble yet radical difference lies the most revealing insight about pitch dynamics in melodies and in the modal schemes theorists evolved to explain their raw materials.

EXAMPLE 38. Hypolydian hymn tune, "Amazing Grace" (nineteenth century).

THE RHYTHMIC-HARMONIC UNION

Few discussions of early melody recognize harmonic content.[11] Writers who do discuss such things are suspected of naivete at worst, ignorance at best. Since chords did not exist in any form—as conventional wisdom holds—therefore harmony too was necessarily absent. Discussions that do hint darkly of such properties in mere melody usually stop far short of our speculations. But our explanations of these melodic projections of harmonic paradigms, as absorbed by us from the harmonic series, is at best only half of the story of tonality. Pitch does not operate in a timeless void: as the Mozart F-major melody makes evident, rhythm plays a necessary associative role in all of these artful machinations. It is this elemental fusion of temporal signification with spatial hierarchy that previous theories (Schoenberg's among them) have shortsightedly neglected. Meticulous explanations of harmony, if artificially severed from its rhythmic dimension, can yield no better than tentative versions of structure.

The most obvious rudimentary ways rhythm governs the embodiment of tonal inequality can be enumerated directly and simply; we observed them summarily in our analysis of the Mozart tune (page 119) and in Ortmann's explanations of pitch signification (page 95). When applied to a particular pitch they render it—other properties being at least neutral—contextually prominent. As generalized laws of tonal signification they can be stated as the products of:

Longer duration (including immediate rearticulation);
Locus of returning note pattern (pitch returned to);
Accented (dynamic stress, metric accent);
Terminal location (first or last within isolable context);
Textural (or even timbral) isolation (segregated from other pitch strata as above, below or in the middle).

What we speak of here are nothing more than melodic recertification of the Gestalt laws of contiguity.

Broader Rhythmic Causes of Pitch Signification

Before we leave this topic of tone-time inseparability, let us touch upon yet another basic way rhythm has of confirming the kind of pitch inequality that is the basis of a tonal hierarchy. It is of larger temporal dimension albeit still within the domain of rhythm, still indicative of how the deployment of tones in time affects structural meanings of pitch configurations. It is precisely the kind of consideration unexamined by Schoenberg, yet one that can be related to music of all ages.

In his provocative book *Tonality in Western Culture,* Richard Norton describes this aspect in early monophony as *linguistic preformation.* It is a defining process, a way of tonal conditions projecting, by linguistic closural and non-closural states, those polar opposites so relevant to tonality. Professor Norton traces this word-tone fusion to some of the simplest music of our Western heritage, with the claim that its relatively ancient process was contributive, if not singularly causal, to the early reinforcement of tonality.

He notes that in early Jewish and Christian chant grammatical and tonal configurations were conceived as the two faces of a single coin. In this conception, he argues, there was a unified set of events thrusting forward in time, a sense of whole large pattern (in the creative consciousness) that preceded the occurrence of its parts.[12] And through this associative merging of tone and text, the way was paved in medieval liturgical song for the autonomous musical phrase and the various compound forms that developed subsequently from it.[13]

Straightforward two-part forms prevailed in liturgical recitations of the psalms, forms in which the second part of the psalm verse completes, or complements, the first. A typical example is

The Lord is my shepherd: I shall not want.

Within this binary conjunction of ideation, a pattern repeated thousands of times through the ages, resides reinforcement (if not actual cause, as well) of an *Open-Closed* succession, an unfolding of parts whose elemental nature is that of *Expectation-Fulfillment, Tension-Release.* Within this scheme, as Norton explains it,

> the beginning set of tones was felt to be a state of activity and incompleteness merely because the hearer of the text knew that the text was not yet finished; and the text continued to its grammatical close and was musically finalized by tonal motion toward a predictable conclusion.[14]

Thus two distinct parts prevail within the psalm tone verse, this conducing a musical gesture of corresponding paired parts: ———OPEN : ———CLOSED. "There is," as he observes, "a *coming to* the chief recitation tone and a *going away* from it, and it is here that we can properly isolate an early tonal function of sonic motion as directed by the internal aesthetic of the phrase. . . ."[15] Like the associational reinforcements glamorized by Dr. Pavlov's dog (bell sound + food sight = salivation), the listener's musical equations are jointly loaded by word and pitch predispositions: linguistic coupling + pitch coupling = Closure. And—or so the idea goes—just as the dog soon responds to the bell (pitch pattern) without seeing the food (word phrases), the musical condition of closure can be conveyed without its linguistic prop. A stylistic constraint has been learned.

An even more compelling syntactical correspondence, between prosody and pitch structure in early melody, has been discussed by Leo Treitler. Noting that alternative feminine and masculine prose endings of medieval chant are, in notable instances, fitted respectively with non-tonic and tonic cadential pitches, he regards such conscious rhythm-pitch orderings as

> certainly the single most important resource derived by the composers of this time to effect what appears to have been so important to them . . . a unified and directed musical entity.[16]

Using an example composed by Adam of St. Victor (twelfth century), he shows how each phrase projects its particular pentachordal or tetrachordal "location" within the pitch gamut, a passage that elegantly confirms our reiterated conviction that this harmonic *division* of pitch ambitus was paramount to modal doctrine, as he illustrates in Example 39 here.

EXAMPLE 39. Treitler's example of gestural unity, from E. Misset and D. Aubry, *Les Proses d'Adam de Saint-Victor* (Treitler, "Musical Syntax in the Middle Ages: Background to an Aesthetic Problem").

These simplest explanations of musical forming, in which time and tone are united in mutually complementary singularities from linguistic convention, could be found in subsequent centuries in every example of what textbooks began to call antecedent-consequent couplings. An unmistakable kinship with these forms of learned associations can be heard in the typical American twelve-bar blues. Here is the same kind of anticipatory projection, a cognitively fused whole that shelters transient parts within the expectation of completion. An impromptu version tells the story.

> *A* (Open)
> Goin' downtown tomorrow, get these feet some bran' new shoes;
> *A* (Open)
> I'm goin' downtown tomorrow, get my ole feet some bran' new shoes;
> *B* (Closed)
> Can't walk on forever, with these ole weary-steppin' blues.

Now the jazz singer or player who does not know and cannot readily and fully anticipate the exacting projections in time of this three-part series lacks the sufficient cognitive equipment for creating a convincing version of the blues. Its Open-Open-Closed thrust (and the extensions in time of its respective parts) is as important and as defining of "The Blues" as are meter, chord progression, verbal sentiment, rhyme scheme, or tonal underlay.

SUMMARY

In closing this long digression pertaining to tonality's primitive basis in the pitch-rhythm mix of experience, let us make a number of firm summary observations from these last two chapters. Let us first confirm that melody of all ages—regardless of how elaborate or simple, how exotic or commonplace, how uniquely depictive of a culture, or how colorful or banal its character—has unfolded through a pitch-framing action if its ambitus made that possible. Through the harmonic series as cognitive referent, otherwise neutral collections of pitch are provided with hierarchical fields of reference, and are, in short, infused with the most rudimentary potential of bearing embodied meaning.[17] The simpler and more direct the melody, the more tenaciously it hammers away on the pitches that provide the frame itself, endowing them with functional roles within the context.

In this sense harmony is no less a significant ingredient of melody—by which we mean, generally, melody of all times—than music in which chords play a defining role, the kind of music Schoenberg and Krenek regarded as tonal because it contained the "central triad." Indeed, the tonic chord of any music can have ascended to that status in part because the same temporal determinants that produce a tonic in melody exert a modifying power in the harmonic relationships borne by chords.

So far as I can determine, any statement describing the conditions that establish "harmonic tonality" can be made with equal force and verity for "melodic tonality," which leads me to the conclusion that they operate according to the same dynamic principles. That they are, in fact, one and the same.

When music turns up—and it does in some non-Western cultures as it does in contemporary society—that seems to invalidate our claim of the harmonic series as cognitive template,[18] then one must seek mitigating circumstances: arrested development, religious or tribal taboos or predilections, extramusical meanings that can explain the motivation of these irregularities. Such musics are rare enough in this world to qualify as eccentric, as conflictive with the conventions of human perception.

NOTES

1. Powers, "Modes," 381. Constant over the centuries, the 5th/4th distinction is paramount. Other factors (melodic motion, cadence types, points of limitation, etc.), although seen as crucial by some Renaissance and Baroque theorists, were not so constant.

2. Terhardt, "Pitch, Consonance, and Harmony." Also see Ritsma, "The Octave Deafness of the Human Ear" and Ritsma and Engel, "Pitch of Frequency Modulated Signals."

3. Treitler, "Musical Analysis in an Historical Context," 83.

4. Treitler, "Musical Syntax in the Middle Ages: Background to an Acoustical Problem."

5. Treitler, "Musical Analysis in an Historical Context," 78.

6. Ibid.

7. Empirical perceptual studies on the octave effect cover a wide range: Baird, "Memory for Absolute Pitch" (1917); Humphries, "Generalization as a Function of Method of Reinforcement" (1939); Bachem, "A Note on Neu's Review of the Literature on Absolute Pitch" (1954); and Deutsch and Boulanger, "Octave Equivalence and the Immediate Recall of Pitch Sequences" (1984). For many readers the most rewarding might be Chapter 9, of Deutsch, ed., *Psychology of Music.*

8. *Problems*, I, XIX, 13. Boethius expresses a similar assessment in *Fundamentals of Music*, 169.

9. Benito Rivera, "Harmonic Theory in Musical Treatises of the Fifteenth and Early Sixteenth Centuries," 93. As we have recalled, pre-modern theorists who explained melody via modal archetypes dwelt on how *diapente* and *diatessaron* split the *diapason*. And thus we find Zarlino in the mid-sixteenth century siding with Boethius of the fifth century that "the modes arise from the combination of the consonances" (*Istutizione*, 35; Boethius, *Fundamentals*, 30–31). Many later theorists were merely parroting their esteemed ancestors, but of crucial importance to us is the residue meaning, which is the very recognition of this basic deployment option within the octave.

10. So-called Aeolian is actually a name belatedly applied to the *de facto* modes produced when the B♭ of *musica ficta* altered the Dorian mode (also the isomorph of what later would be called, of course, the natural minor scale). That the scale of "Amazing Grace" (Example 38) is pentatonic alters not at all its characterizing fourth/fifth deployment within the c–c′ octave.

11. Hindemith's discussion in *The Craft of Musical Composition*, I, is a notable exception.

12. Norton, *Tonality in the Music of Western Culture*, 70.

13. Norton (ibid.) suggests exclusively textual causes in song, but we cannot dismiss the role bodily gesture may have played to produce (or to reinforce) the same musical expectations.

14. Ibid., 145.

15. Ibid., 144.

16. Treitler, "Musical Syntax in the Middle Ages," 81.

17. Keeping in mind Morris Cohen's defining statement (*A Preface to Logic*, 47) that "anything acquires meaning if it is connected with, or indicates, or refers to, something beyond itself."

18. *Template* may be too inflexible to describe this aspect of our perceptual processing. The more adaptable, yet far from "mushy"—*image schema*, as it is described by philosopher Mark Johnson, may provide a more accurate conception. (Johnson, *The Body in the Mind*, Chapter 5, "How Schemata Constrain Meaning, Understanding, and Rationality.") Also pertinent is Ulrich Neisser's discussion of schemata in *Cognition and Reality*, 52–75.

PART V:

The Compounded Error and Its Legacy

CHAPTER 12

Alleged Harbingers of the Atonal

In his decision that music must achieve total chromaticism, and with it emancipated dissonance, Schoenberg overlooked a vital aspect of the very music that reputedly led to his epochal quest for radical change. Now that we have seen the tenuousness of his theoretical stance, ideas derived largely from specious nineteenth-century sources, we need to turn over one last stone. We must round out our study by looking into the actual musical basis from which his argument sprang. We must ask what indicators are truly there, in the repertory, to support the claim that tonality was at the end of its evolutionary road, "dethroned in practice if not in theory," as Schoenberg put it in 1941.[1]

Writers who repeat claims about growing harmonic complexity and the loosening grasp of tonality toward the end of the nineteenth century ignore the potentially one-sided and distorting perspective they pass on to the unwary reader.[2] For this reason we must recall one cardinal fact about the music most often cited as leading to the very brink of tonal collapse: with rare exceptions it is program music.[3] Seldom does extraordinary tonal ambiguity take departure without some kind of extra-musical image as shaping impetus. Program music and heavy chromaticism were co-regnant forces between 1850 and 1900, leading us to raise some critical questions that have been asked too seldom.

Let us assume for the moment that Schoenberg's appraisal of tonality's role was accurate in every perceptual and methodological aspect. Let us even draw with him the same conclusion, that other musical properties can replace tonality. Then let us ask: Was the historical motivating force for discarding tonality what it has been made out to be? In other words, did the state of art music around 1905 make its displacement necessary and, from an evolutionary standpoint, inevitable?

No one seems to doubt that music with text or with textual allusions was one of the vital forces in music well past the turn of the century; it remains today a favorite part of the concert repertory. Can causal relation be drawn between programmatic popularity and the flurry of chromaticism, with its attendant tonal ambivalence, in music of late Romanticism? And further, to what degree were some of the musical monuments of the era typical of the tonal character developed by art music? Indeed, are some of the masterpieces themselves documentary of the raging chromaticism they have been claimed to be? And if they are, are they emblems of monumental change or are they only exemplary but random mutations?

These are probing questions. They merit more than casually reflective answers. Perhaps answers lie somewhere between a categorical Yes and an emphatic No. But as our storehouse of musical artifacts grows and our acquaintance with the past increases, evidence mounts that some answers have been too pat, too readily yielding to a fashionable but false sense of evolutionary determinism, as it has been passed on to us by its champions. In many instances the same answers were provided by those who had vested interests in a particular interpretation of history, and especially in the continuing solvency of the Schoenbergian legacy.[4]

Certainly there is no evidence that even a major portion of the music produced by composers of the late nineteenth century, composers whom posterity has deemed "enduring," was any more heavily laden with chromaticism or with chords based on "remote intervals" than was the music of Beethoven or, depending upon the way one might classify non-chord tones, even in the music of Gesualdo or Monteverdi or J. S. Bach. Passages within development sections of late Mozart symphonies are quite as ambiguity ridden, in respect to key, as passages in *Tristan*.

As a matter of fact, a bit of objective rummaging through the repertory of the ages, as we suggested earlier, can turn up an abundance of tonal equivocation, many of them composed well before 1850. If any of these is a part of an untexted, non-programmatic work, its tonal fluidity usually enacts a particular delineating function within the total form, a function preceded and followed by what is tonally solid and unequivocal. In a Classical sonata form, for example, such a function could be the thrust toward recapitulation, where the composer dramatically focuses by rapid modulatory play on the act of formal return, just prior to thematic arrival. There are abundant pre-nineteenth-century examples of roaming key, providing a vehicle for composerly bravura (as in Bach's *Chromatic Fantasia*) or soul-wrenching tension (in Dido's Lament of Purcell's *Dido and Aeneas*) or sheer chromatic frolics (as within the interior of Mozart's *C Minor Fantasia,* K 475), or within many of Bach's shorter keyboard works.[5]

Within the last half-century we have come to know the sixth book of Don Carlo Gesualdo's *Madrigali* (1585) as a museum of bizarre chromaticism; it was the rampant tonal fluidity in several of these quirky masterpieces that led historian Edward Lowinsky to coin the terms "floating tonality" and "triadic atonality."[6] The cultural movement of which Gesualdo was a part, the avant-garde choralists of late Renaissance Italy including Banchieri, Rore, Vicentino, and at times even Lasso, flaunted chromaticism as one of its more obvious stylistic traits.

Such passages of extraordinary tonal indecisiveness as these, from whatever historical period they come, usually share one of two common features: they are all inextricably bound up in some kind of dramatic gesture (even when within the framework of "absolute" music), of pointing beyond the sonic moment itself. Other-

wise they are intended to allude to wholly extramusical matters. They signal relationships with other contexts, whether morphological or ideational.

In view of the frequent linkages between chromaticism and extramusical idea, it
is instructive to take a quizzical backward glance, just to notable music of the half-
century prior to 1900, to ask: Is it true that art music of that period bears unmistakable
signs of chromatic saturation? Had it, by the end of the era, reached a point of tonal
non-return? Do even the works of Liszt, Wagner, and Richard Strauss accurately and
definitively reflect the tonal development of their times, confirming a true evolution
of musical values and techniques, to the degree Schoenberg represented them? And
finally, are innuendoes of chromatic saturation true even for their music, those usual
first exhibits for the atonal prosecution?

FAUST, *TRISTAN*, AND *ZARATHUSTRA* REVISITED

Early in this chronicle we mentioned Wagner's *Tristan und Isolde* as one of the
declared precursors of atonality.[7] Most writers mention *Tristan* in this context,
especially its Prelude.[8] Let us note in passing that the entire opera would by all means
be difficult to describe as non-referential, as representative of the musical objectivity
and embodied meaning touted by aesthetician Eduard Hanslick.

We also mentioned Liszt's *Faust Symphony*. Unquestionably, it is an acceptable
representative of nineteenth-century skill in the play of chromatic melody and harmony. It is also symptomatic of its composer's passion to produce music of the future
(*Zukunftsmusik*), which for him entailed a marriage of music and philosophical idea.
But we should add, anticipating subsequent discussion, that it does not in its entirety
live up to its advance billing for loose tonality bordering on the atonal.

Also mentioned was Strauss's *Also Sprach Zarathustra*. Like most of that
master's works, it too is music consciously conceived as depicting an extramusical
idea. With an opening that projects one of the most confining tonic triads in history
(music immortalized, as they say in Hollywood, by film and television), it is hard to
regard it as music fleeing the compound of tonality. In fact, the whole of *Zarathustra*,
as will be seen presently, can scarcely be classified as exceedingly chromatic, much
less as tonally revolutionary.

Measure-for-measure, *Tristan* is the most chromatic of the three. But a comparison of total output of the three composers would probably yield a different winner.
In that race it was the older man, Liszt, who was at the cutting edge of nineteenth-
century chromaticism. His enduring penchant for the chromatic led Schoenberg to
recognize in him

> one of those who started the battle against tonality, both through themes
> which point to no absolutely definite tonal centre, and through many
> harmonic details whose musical exploitation has been looked after by his
> successors.[9]

Most important for our present understanding is to what extent and in what details all three of these compositions fulfill their reputations as agents of tonality's demise, as proof of the next evolutionary cycle's requisite dimensions. Our goal is singular and modest. We wish only to confirm that chromaticism (and any attendant tonal disequilibrium) is in these works a direct function of programmatic intent, so our analyses are as fragmentary as they are focused.

THE *FAUST SYMPHONY*

As Example 40 reveals, its quiet beginning is tonally spectacular. Forged from the prophetic linking of four successive augmented triads, it is an amazingly bravura display, for its time (1857), of atonal melody. Its sound is well calculated to leave the impression that the movement's title, "Faust," suggests ambiguity, or at least indecision, as its overriding condition. Subsequent melodies and motifs and chord successions of the first section do nothing to dispel the principal tonal thesis of this daring opening episode, in which a toehold by a tonic chord is relentlessly thwarted.

EXAMPLE 40. Liszt, *Faust Symphony*, I, main theme. Copyright © 1904 by Jos. Aibl-Verlag, renewed 1932 by C. F. Peters. Used by permission of C. F. Peters Corp.

But Liszt is not here establishing a permanent tonal posture. His opening may be consistent with, yet it is hardly representative of, the rest of this composition or of the remainder of the composer's oeuvre. Here he is tone-painting with his most facile brush: the musical characterization of Faust himself is at stake, and it demands a special kind of tonal palette. Much of the subsequent music, however, employs less striking tonal means. What follows, including the chorale finale, is often as diatonic as the key of E major can get. So it is through Liszt's first movement, except when the initial idea, the Faustian allusion, returns; chromaticism and diatonicism form inseparable programmatic links with, respectively, the opposing states of disquieting ambiguity and placid security.

The symphony's second movement, "Gretchen," suggests something more continuously placid, more confirming. Its music corresponds with that allusion, tonally secure with the key of A♭ major. Only fitful returns to the twelve-note melody of the first movement—clear allusions to its angst-ridden ideational content—suggest greater tonal fulsomeness than one might expect in a Schubert slow movement. Only relatively brief perorations, series of successive motivic jabs, each in a different key, offer reminders of the first movement's chromaticism before long stretches of tonal stability reestablish (at letter *T*) the serene flow that is the movement's essence. It ends as it began. A more substantial statement of A♭ major would be hard to find. Gretchen, as we imagine her, has been tonally personified.

EXAMPLE 41. Liszt, *Faust Symphony,* beginning of the "Gretchen" movement. Copyright © 1904 by Jos. Aibl-Verlag, renewed 1932 by C. F. Peters. Used by permission of C. F. Peters Corp.

The work's last movement, "Mephistopheles," returns in its early moments to a more tenuous hold on tonality, reminding us of the "Faust" movement. It is a dramatic *Allegro Vivace, ironico,* a sweep of motivic flourish whose chief characteristic is emphatic rhythmic pulse. But this busy rush of tones gives way on occasion to majestic patches of unadulterated major key, textures more suggestive of William Walton's most regal C-major pomp and circumstance than of raging miseries of the inferno. Indeed, the term *tonal ambiguity* has only occasional relevance in such contexts. And so it goes throughout the movement; it is chromatic abundance sharing time with diatonic parsimony, each state an apparent auditory allusion to a particular dramatic image, whether cynical ruminations about the supernatural, the chaste plaint of maiden, or the paralyzing tremblings of Lucifer. The Lisztian leitmotif is hard at work here, and the interwoven contrasts, chromatic versus diatonic, provide a critical part of the pictorializing. Liszt's sonic representations of the mysterious calamities of the underworld are tonally contrasted with the purity and verity of human fragility. Tonality, *through its very presence or absence,* assumes a programmatic function.

Is the *Faust Symphony* atonal? Well, yes and no. Tonal focus is unclear only when that condition serves the composer in his flamboyant editorializing. And when it does, chromaticism is most often sported as brief passages of kaleidoscopic keys, each an established unity unto itself following shortly on the heels of another. Like his curious pianistic experiment in atonality, the *Bagatelle sans Tonalité* (a composition lost to posterity until its rediscovery in 1956), the symphony's tonal indeterminacy, when present, arises from melodies of bountiful chromaticism accompanied by chords which, although separately like those of more conventional music, are mixed in unconventional relationships.

TRISTAN UND ISOLDE

Completed just two years after Liszt's *Faust Symphony, Tristan* long has served as the paradigm of nineteenth-century extended tonality,[10] of tonality-gone-over-the-edge. Its reputation may have been slightly exaggerated, but one need look no further for a better exemplar of chromaticism from its time. As with Liszt's symphony, our objective is not a musical analysis in any real sense; we seek only to show one facet of an immensely intricate and complicated work—how the play of chromaticism against diatonicism is used to underline histrionic content.

More than anything else, *Tristan* is about painful, languorous, tragic longing, especially the quintessential Romantic kind (which means the nineteenth-century kind) that can be redeemed only by dreadful denouement, most effectively by the death of him or her who suffers the affliction (and preferably both). It abounds with discomforting suggestions that sublime love and death are somehow compatible playmates, perhaps even necessary accomplices in grandeur. Indeed, the Buddhist notion of Nirvana as the peak state of non-desire, appropriated by Wagner via Schopenhauer, might be regarded as the *idée fixe* of his drama.

In this way *Tristan* continues a lineage from *Tannhaüser* (1845) and *The Flying Dutchman* (1843), both populated with heroic male figures whose personal salvation depends upon the sacrificial death of a female counterpart.[11] It seems to have become Wagner's personal leitmotif, his obsessive dramatic conflict, which he continued on through the Ring. It is the core of profundity to *Tristan und Isolde.*

In playing out this basic idea in *Tristan,* Wagner has fastidiously organized melodic and harmonic patterns, even tonality itself, in ways to designate and confirm the emotional content of moments within the unfolding story.[12] To a degree unsurpassed in history, music and dramatic process are bonded into one powerful alloy. In fact, they coexist here to the extent that a particular idea's appearance in the libretto can lead one reasonably to expect, within the immediate vicinity, its corresponding musical analogue. As Pierre Boulez remarks, "the dramatic myth becomes effective by means of, through, and within the musical structure."[13]

Tristan is probably the most thoroughly chromatic work composed prior to the twentieth century.[14] It is far more chromatic, measure for measure, than anything Debussy composed. It harbors more and longer moments of tonal equivocation than Stravinsky's "pathbreaking" *Petrouchka* or *Firebird,* each more than a half-century later. But *Tristan* contains something else as well, something usually ignored in the effusive testimonials to its pivotal role in music's evolution: amidst all its unsettling chromatics it contains contrasted sections of extended plain diatonicism, passages in which the listener is immersed in unequivocating pitch-focus, passages firmly entrenched in a key.

As one example—certainly not the first in the opera yet remarkably representative—extended tonal resoluteness settles in just after the beginning of Act II.[15] We focus on it because of its simple harmonic content and its naive analogical matching of music to drama. It is music of the hunt, its rhythmic rollicking dominating first as foreground, setting the scene, then later as background. Clearly a part of the storytelling, it confirms that the alleged hunting party for King Marke is in progress. Its fade to background comes when the party moves off into the distance beyond Isolde's chambers.

This musical galloping through a dominant ninth chord in B♭ major continues unabated until the chromatic rising and falling line of a brief interlude intrudes, musically preparing the anticipated tryst of Isolde and Tristan. As the hunting sounds fade, Isolde sings:[16]

> No hunting call sounds so beautiful.
> No more sounds of horns; now I can hear
> the gentle spring rippling along out there.
> (Piano-vocal score, page 90)

A master of depiction, Wagner uses diatonic (and incisively tonal) passages of this kind when the prevailing scenic or psychic image calls for it. The complexity of a rhythm, the disjunctness of a melody, or the simplicity of a harmony bears directly on what is happening on his stage. Diatonic textures, like chromatic, perform their scene-forming power over long and frequent stretches of action.

CHROMATIC-DIATONIC CONTRASTS AND THE LEITMOTIF

Tristan is the very embodiment of the leitmotif technique of Romantic music, not just as encyclopaedic sonic cues for announcing characters or identifying artifacts, but rather as auditory links with a large cast of controlling emotional states. More than any other Wagnerian creation, *Tristan und Isolde* is about inner feelings rather than public actions.

Even the Prelude represents the crowning achievement of Wagner as musical revolutionary. It is well known that the opening evocative series of harmonized sighs introduces some of the elemental melodic and chordal kernels of the whole drama. Within its first few sounds Wagner deposits motifs (Example 42) that will furnish the landscapes of the subsequent two and one-half hours of near-seamless music. Whole chords or melodic fragments later erupt whose origins in the opening chromatic expansion of lines are unmistakable. From these melodic and harmonic bits Wagner weaves a vast stock of dramatic events. Whenever they occur, they are highly chromatic and tonally ambiguous because their motivic antecedents were. And they occur routinely and often.[17]

EXAMPLE 42. Wagner, *Tristan und Isolde,* twin chromatic pitch series of the Prelude.

It would be easy (but redundant) to gild the lily of leitmotivic controls by hunting down other alignments, paired in *Tristan* with the tragic communion of its principal players. Those who have turned over every rock of the opera's three acts have come up with as many as fifty separate motifs (harmonic as well as melodic-rhythmic) that constitute its sonic bill of materials.[18] For our purposes we shall mention only one other example, important because of its directness and its prominent role throughout the drama. Mainly a two-chord conjunction as in Example 43, its blatant chromaticism consistently and continually sets the scene when Isolde (less often, Tristan) mentions death. Most often heard in its entirety, there are nonetheless statements when it is abbreviated to its first two chords, usually A♭ to A.[19]

EXAMPLE 43. Death motif, Wagner, *Tristan und Isolde.*

EXPRESSING THE INEXPRESSIBLE

We have belabored this matter of tonal content as dramatic agent only to drive home a simple but crucial point: the consuming goal of *Tristan*'s music is to tell a story with utmost effectiveness, given the inescapable limitations of staged drama and operatic conventions that can inhibit expressing the real. Music is a full participant in the dramatic process, not a mere accompaniment that loosely corresponds with a prevailing stage action. We may veritably swoon at the resonances that rise from these voices and instruments. That has not been a rare response. But from the composer's point of view the music's success lies foremost in how fully his listener absorbs the total message, feeling as well as concept, and responds to it. The particular chords or melodies or rhythms he employs at any particular moment within the unfolding drama *are not primarily determined by an embodied musical logic*. They are largely determined by the commitment to confirm sonically an emotional state, to communicate with compounded force a human feeling that prevails between cast members.

It is in this sense that *Tristan* is a tone poem in the Beethoven tradition, which was Wagner's interpretation of his largest instrumental compositions. In the music drama Wagner applies every resource of orchestral nuance and vocal tone to create the utmost reality and the most intense expression of feeling, which, after all, was the paramount goal of Romanticism.

This is basic to an understanding of much of the text-anchored music left to us from the second half of the nineteenth century. In their quest to plumb the depths of the hidden yet awesomely real nature of the human psyche and its manipulations, some late Romantics composed music whose essence is most realistically experienced not as abstract sound pattern but as the critical participant in some form of dramatic circumstance. It is music attempting to vent real feelings, feelings unexpressible by language.

SUMMARY OF THE *TRISTAN* DISCUSSION

Tristan und Isolde is loaded with tonal ambiguity, with tonal surprises, with some passages quite as devoid of pitch focus as the most calculated of Schoenberg's dodecaphonic phrases. Charles Rosen was on target when he once recognized monumentality in the way ambiguity is sometimes sustained over long spans in this opera. But that condition is not an exclusive one for the drama nor is it present because some irreversible evolutionary thrust had remarkably brought Wagner, along with some of his most sensitive European colleagues, to the brink of tonal anarchy. Only a naive and fragmented interpretation of history could accommodate such simplistic reasoning based on such slanted data.

On the contrary, *Tristan*'s chromaticism is a direct product of the composer's will to infuse uniquely his music with the toll of emotion borne by unrequited love, of a longing that in an overromanticized, ultrafantasized *Weltanschauung* could be quieted only by death. The evidence of *Tristan*—the way tonality is at times weakened to the point of virtual annulment, as a function of dramatic imagery alone—is sufficient refutation of this persistent cliché that so motivated Schoenberg and, through him, exerted a disproportionate influence on the history of Western art music.

It is instructive to recall what happens in Wagner's work after *Tristan und Isolde*. From a tonal perspective they are docile essays compared with the impetuous chromatic flexings of his earlier testimonial to ill-fated love. Listen carefully to *Die Meistersinger, Das Rheingold, Die Walküre, Siegfried, Gotterdammerung*, or *Parsifal*. Within the totality you will hear more than twenty hours of music that, for the most part, when compared with the earlier *Tristan,* is prudently diatonic. This being the case, we must ask: What happened after *Tristan* to the evolutionary thrust that would spell the bankruptcy of tonality? Did the musical development that made total chromaticism music's new silver bullet fall short of its ultimate target? Was *Tristan* a fluke? Was it merely the ultimate contribution of Wagnerian genius to the chromatic flux, a very special kind of success even he found unmatchable?

A more fruitful view, a view that explains more with less special pleading, sees *Tristan* as a peak within the development of Wagner's theatrical rhetoric and within the history of the ancient marriage of drama and music. Much of its music is enigmatically beautiful, sensuously resonant, and in large measure tonally ambiguous. In its entirety it is what Nietzsche mockingly termed "psychologically picturesque." It is all of these because that is what it took for Richard Wagner to tell the story he had in the ear of his incomparable mind.

ALSO SPRACH ZARATHUSTRA

If chromaticism truly was soaring to its evolutionary zenith, toward the end of the nineteenth century, one could expect the tone poems of Richard Strauss to contribute to its local progress. Celebrated conductor as well as composer, he was no less in touch with reigning issues of music than Schoenberg. His arena was considerably more spacious.

Schoenberg attempted to develop a friendly professional relationship with this powerful man, and he enjoyed gestures of help from him between 1902 and 1911. The two shared common geographical ties, between Germany and Austria, as well as mutual admiration for the music of Wagner. But an initial warmth sparked by the younger composer later cooled when he learned, via Mahler's wife Alma, of Strauss's low opinion of his music.[20] It is a mark of Schoenberg's admirable character that he did not let their strained friendship overrule his public admiration for Strauss's music; he readily admitted having learned from it, especially from *Salome* and *Elektra.*

Completed in 1896, *Zarathustra* is depictive music tied to a most unlikely program; it loosely follows the scheme of a visionary philosophical tract by Nietzsche, parts of which are couched in poetic form. Strauss was attracted by the philosopher's ideas in general, but especially by his early devotion (later renounced) to Wagner. His decision to transform into music the abstract images of Nietzsche's deification of the prophet-philosopher as Superman seems particularly strange since *Zarathustra* followed one of his wittiest and most compelling works, *Til Eulenspiegels lustige Streiche*. But our concern is not for the composition's ideological basis nor with its success in conveying vague messages of nihilistic idealism; our concern is rather with the degree to which the work's substance does or does not attest to the creeping annihilation of tonality.

What close study of the music reveals is that a less likely candidate for demonstrating this evolutionary premise—tonality's quickened demise—would be hard to find.[21] A strong sense of tonality dominates the work as a whole, exceptions—and these must be the source for the work's fame as tonally revolutionary—occurring in several notable sections. One of these occurs in the oft-cited fugue, "Von der Wissenschaft," which in English is usually known as "The Scientific Fugue."[22] The remainder of *Zarathustra* reveals tonality actually used as a programmatic resource in ways unanticipated by earlier composers, even Liszt.

"THE SCIENTIFIC FUGUE"

Like Liszt's *Faust*, this fugue's six-measure subject (Example 44) methodically runs through the twelve notes of the chromatic scale. Although clearly assembled from segmentation into blocks of simple harmony (C, B-minor, E-flat major, A major, D-flat major, G), its overall effect is unmistakably that of intentional atonality. Also like Liszt's theme, it is intended to convey an extramusical idea. Most who describe its meaning suggest a satiric intent, perhaps ridicule of pedantry. This makes some sense, justifying in a subtle way (in the composer's mind, perhaps) the use of an "academic" texture for conjuring up sound-analogies for the arid ingenuity of abstract science, science doggedly pursued only for its own sake. But arriving at a sure and clear idea of just what Strauss intended the fugue to convey is as problematic as deciphering precisely what Nietzsche meant by the brief analogous section of his lengthy tract.

EXAMPLE 44. Subject of Strauss, "Scientific Fugue." Copyright © 1904 by Jos. Aibl-Verlag, renewed 1932 by C. F. Peters. Reprinted by permission of C. F. Peters Corp.

Whatever this music's intended message (or even its success in depicting such erudite matters), Strauss's explicit intention was to represent specific extramusical ideas through musical sounds. The extreme chromaticism he chose for the passage did not arise from purely *musical* needs, needs engendered by a music caught in the mid-flight of a larger evolutionary process. This theme and its consequent textures, unashamedly and simplemindedly chromatic, are meant to be heard in conjunction with their extramusical motivation, to conform with their storyline, no matter how sketchy or inappropriate that may be. As such, Strauss's music acts as a medium of ideational exchange, certainly not exclusively as an aesthetic end in itself.

ATONALITY VERSUS TONALITY AS PROGRAMMATIC CUE

For Strauss, this witty essay in chromaticism indicates something quite other than the failure of tonality. In fact, the absence of resolved pitch focus here constitutes a principal part of the message; by contrast, tonality's absence is a chief means for conveying pointlessness, for suggesting the churn of clever activity for its own sake rather than for some coveted humane motive.

No other section of *Zarathustra* approaches the overrich chromaticism of the Fugue, which itself occupies no more than a few minutes within an extended work. So it seems appropriate to turn the argument upside down, to realize that *Zarathustra* in its entirety is compelling proof of the continuing solvency of tonality. The contrastive tonal ambiguities of "The Scientific Fugue" provide a primary example.

Further confirmation of this point of view is not hard to find. It is especially evident in the way tonal focus becomes an agent of allusion throughout the work. Strauss pits the transcending power of Nature (represented by the key of C major/minor) against the aspiring mind of humanity (represented by the key of B major/minor). The scene is set in the very opening of the tone poem for this play of key against key. Strauss's "Sunrise of Mankind," with only the opening of Wagner's *Das Rheingold* as competition, is surely the most dogged statement of a tonic chord in all of nineteenth-century music.[23] These are sounds ill-suited to show tonality hobbling along on its last leg, and Strauss's first allusion to the feisty human psyche is not far behind, with B as its undeniable tonic.

EXAMPLE 45. Initial motif, Strauss, *Also sprach Zarathustra.*
Copyright © 1904 by Jos. Aibl-Verlag, renewed 1932 by C. F.
Peters. Reprinted by permission of C. F. Peters Corp.

EXAMPLE 46. B-minor of Humanity, Strauss, *Also sprach Zarathustra.* Copyright © 1904 by Jos. Aibl-Verlag, renewed 1932 by C. F. Peters. Reprinted by permission of C. F. Peters Corp.

This conflict of tonics is a musical condition unachievable, let us note, without access to the primary quality of tonality. In fact, these sections provide some of the earliest instance of bi-tonality, preceding *Petrouchka*'s chord by some fifteen years. (We wonder if it is only by chance that Strauss's version incorporates a similar harmonic duality of F♯ and C.)

EXAMPLE 47. Dual harmonic allusions to Nature/Humanity, Strauss, *Also sprach Zarathustra.* Copyright © 1904 by Jos. Aibl-Verlag, renewed 1932 by C. F. Peters. Reprinted by permission of C. F. Peters Corp.

And true to Nietzsche's philosophical message, the C-ness of Nature overcomes Humanity's B-ness in the end: it is hard to escape the language of a music appreciation text when describing these clearly histrionic actions.

EXAMPLE 48. Ending passage, Strauss, *Also sprach Zarathustra.* Copyright © 1904 by Jos. Aibl-Verlag, renewed 1932 by C. F. Peters. Reprinted by permission of C. F. Peters Corp.

Long stretches of music in this composition are unmistakably tied to a single tonality. For one example, the section subtitled "Von Freuden und Leidenschaften" ("Of Joys and Passion") cuts a clear swathe through C minor.[24] There are passages in which one key immediately follows another, sometimes in such successions that tonality is momentarily toppled. But they take turns with stretches of unequivocal pitch focus, music of inescapable key. The tonal directness and simplicity of the section entitled "das Grablied," illustrated in Example 49, is symptomatic. Is it chromatic? Slightly. Tonally weak? Hardly. Its projection of B minor persists.

EXAMPLE 49. "Das Grableid," Strauss, *Also sprach Zarathustra.*
Copyright © 1904 by Jos. Aibl-Verlag, renewed 1932 by C. F. Peters.
Reprinted by permission of C. F. Peters Corp.

When a high volume of chromaticism in *Zarathustra* threatens to usurp a strong tonal allegiance, it does so only for the sake of contrast, and then as a programmatic function. Tonally indecisive passages derive their ideational functions largely from being placed in stark relief with passages of the opposite condition. Were it not for the poignant programmatic vacillation toward the end between what we have called Humanity's B-ness and Nature's C-ness, the whole thing would dissolve in a quiet B major glory, unrivaled in its tonal decisiveness by the most redundant of Rossini final cadences.

Our conclusion must be that Strauss's music makes a poor argument for tonality's growing impotence. Indeed, in *Zarathustra* he exploits tonality in new ways to achieve kinds of musical coherence peculiarly suited to his programmatic needs.

TWO NOTABLE MAVERICKS: REGER AND SCRIABIN

Several other composers between the time of Wagner's innovations and Schoenberg's full break with tonality did things a bit differently. They incorporated the kinds of elements we have associated here with dramatic allusion, yet in music that was not explicitly programmatic. (They composed openly programmatic works also.) Especially noteworthy among those who did are Max Reger and Alexandre Scriabin. (I do not include Debussy here because his music was with few exceptions less chromatic, less tonally venturesome, than Reger's and Scriabin's.) Although both composers were born at about the same time as Schoenberg (1873 and 1872, respectively), musicians usually see their places in history more as closing shadows of late Romanticism than as pioneers of the twentieth century.[25]

Calling to mind almost anything composed by either man will make clear that they were radically different in musical approach and aesthetic outlook. The streams of modulating harmonies of Reger and the atmospheric mysticism of Scriabin excel as proof that full content of the twelve chromatic pitches was being used intensively, in some quarters, to press the bounds of tonality, not always in the same way and not always in putting across an explicit extramusical storyline.

A preponderance of organist Reger's music is cast in the molds of his more "classical" Germanic predecessors, in the formal architectonic procedures inherited by Schoenberg as well.[26] Formal titles like Sinfonietta, Variations, Fugue, Sonata, Sextette, Quartet, and Passacaglia line his oeuvre as suggestive links with the Hanslick-Brahms "objective" side of the aesthetic fence. As a whole, these works are just as chromatic, just as tonally unstable (or stable, as the case may be) as those he composed in support of an external idea, usually more suggestive than rigorously programmatic, works such as the *Symphonic Prologue to a Tragedy,* Opus 128. But from the perspective of a century later, Reger's chromaticism smacks of academic tour de force more than of pitch complexity in search of heightened communication of non-musical things. It is not uncommon to find passages in which modulatory action seems to be motivated by the joy of parading an astounding compositional technique rather than by purely musical considerations.[27] Whatever his interior motivations may have been, some of his textures, even like Wagner's, justified the repeated plaint that music had absorbed about as much tonal fluidity as it could take on and still float.[28]

Scriabin's case is remarkably similar while being drastically different. There is nothing academic about his music; in intent and in effect it is music preoccupied with the will to project strong feeling, to express uncommon things. Even his imposing *Études* for piano, clear benefactors of the vast legacies of Chopin and Liszt, are compelling examples of a surface objectivity that camouflages an interior of high feeling. Technical studies well calculated to exhibit superior pianism, they also encompass such a broad latitude of expressive gestures—harmonic, rhythmic, textural, dynamic—that listeners are inclined to conjure up their own personal programs of meaning.

Some of Scriabin's last works reveal his search for a technical mandate that could effectively harness the threatening tonal chaos of the chromatic scale. Whether a listener might be equal to the kinds of theosophic interdependencies and analogies he harbored in his harmonic intricacies is beside the point: that some kind of extramusical urge is conveyed is the unavoidable impression left by all of his music (and, it goes without saying, by such explicitly programmatic works as *The Divine Poem, Prometheus,* or *The Poem of Ecstacy*). The little we know about his wish to unite sensory experience with religious thought is too amorphous as a frame of reference for meaningful comment.

Some of Scriabin's music, like Reger's, exhibits ultra-chromatic mixtures of pitch that warrant our well-established maxim: in the hands of a few of the most talented composers, music has truly reached a dramatic peak of development in harmony, certainly by the early stages of Schoenberg's career. But as with the music of Wagner and assorted colleagues, this harmonic complexity most often served a particular programmatic end, the exact nature of that end at times remaining covert.[29]

OTHER COMPOSERS OF THE 1880–1910 ERA

Other notable composers of that same time, however, found their musical uniqueness, their freshness of expression, without resorting to the tightly-packed chromaticism of Reger, Scriabin, or the Schoenberg of *Verklärte Nacht*. If one doubts the need to temper this received opinion that immoderate chromaticism (and thus a cowering tonality) was rampant during the thirty or so heady years of 1880–1910, then it is sobering to consider for a moment the not inconsiderable music composed by such contemporaries as Verdi, Rimsky–Korsakov, Franck, Mascagni, Fauré, Delius, Dvořák, Bizet, Tchaikovsky, Bruckner, Borodin, McDowell, Sibelius, Mahler,[30] Massenet, Elgar, Nielsen, and so on (not to mention Brahms, Debussy, Janáček, and Puccini).[31]

The music of these composers has proved to be persistently rewarding, more the sounds of creative voices with worthwhile things to say than adventurers who early in the century may have seemed to point more emphatically toward the future (like Charles Koechlin, Ferruccio Busoni, John Foulds).

The music of the times was not of one cloth. Certainly its dominating thread, in spite of the advanced tonal idioms of composers such as Wolf (whose idol was Wagner), Scriabin, or Reger, was not a disappearing tonality. Even major and minor scales (and church modes as well, long expired according to Schoenberg) were commonplace occupants of the textures created by these artists. Their music did not replicate the diatonic drabness of Calvinist hymns, but neither did it appear, without programmatic cause, as a chromatic Humpty-Dumpty, teetering on the verge of an irreparable fall.

NOTES

1. Schoenberg, *Style and Idea*, 216.
2. See for example Donald Grout's discussion of "the most remarkable Romantic achievements" in his short edition of *A History of Western Music*, 344. Luigi Rognoni says that "the chromatic universe was disintegrating" (*The Second Viennese School*, 15). Gary Wittlich (*Aspects of Twentieth-Century Music*, 388) claims that the century's end demanded "a radical revision of musical thought . . . a new musical dialectic."
3. I use the term *program music* here to refer to music whose composer utilizes any form of extramusical correspondence as a structural referent or precompositional guide for meaning. In this sense, a song's text or an opera's libretto justifies their inclusion under the rubric.
4. For instance, René Leibowitz, *Schoenberg and His School*.
5. Like the sudden stream of parallel diminished chords just before the ending of the D minor Prelude, Book I, *Well-Tempered Clavier*.

6. Lowinsky, *Tonality and Atonality in Sixteenth-Century Music.*

7. Andrew Porter finds a *Tristan* precursor in Bellini's 1833 opera *Beatrice,* and he claims the *Tristan* chord's prominence in Act III of Bellini's *Norma* (*New Yorker,* Nov. 14, 1988, 133).

8. Regarding Wagner as one of the three most influential "founders" of modern thought, Jacques Barzun emphasizes that *Tristan und Isolde* was finished during the same year (1859) as the publication of Marx's *Critique of Political Economy* and Darwin's *On the Origin of Species.*

9. Schoenberg, *Style and Idea,* 445. In Bartok's opinion Liszt, not Wagner or Strauss, was the true guide to the future. See Austin, *Music in the Twentieth Century,* 224.

10. Following the lead of Dika Newlin, who borrowed the term from Schoenberg's *extended tonality,* Donald Mitchell uses the term *progressive tonality* to describe music of Mahler and Carl Nielsen when it strays frequently to new tonics. See Mitchell, *Gustav Mahler: The Early Years,* 264–265.

11. In *Tannhaüser* through the death of Elisabeth, in *Dutchman* through Senta's sacrificial death.

12. Readers who know the opera and its dramatic-musical linkages may find this discussion redundant if not downright bromidic. It is included here because many people who know the opera have not had an opportunity actually to observe how chromaticism and diatonicism line up with their chosen programmatic matches.

13. In his notes to the Philips Records release of the 1976 Chereau production of the *Ring.*

14. By this I mean only that the twelve different notes occur in greater abundance within shorter periods of time.

15. Within pages 87–89, Breitkopf and Härtel piano-vocal score prepared by Hans von Bülow. References to the score refer to that edition, which is available in English and German texts.

16. My translation, immediate grasp of storyline the principal goal.

17. Especially noteworthy as an introduction to this complex work is the small *Opera Guide No. 6 (Tristan und Isolde)* produced by the English National Opera, Nicholas John, editor.

18. The number of separate motifs recognized depends, of course, on latitude allowed for the derivation of later patterns from earlier. Lining up leitmotif with its every dramatic match is a complication reminiscent of Arno Karlen's assessment of the history of syphilis: "a bog for those who love certainty and a delight to those who like detection" (*Napoleon's Glands,* 260).

19. Considering this book's main topic, it may be of interest that the unabbreviated pattern uses up eleven pitch-classes. Only B♭ is missing. I suspect no arcane dramatic cause for this omission. Let us note in passing that Gesualdo's "*Moro, Lasso, al Mio Daolo*" (Madrigals, Book VI) consumes exactly the same notes (again with the B♭ missing) in the first two measures.

20. Stuckenschmidt, *Arnold Schoenberg,* 73.

21. Better exemplars of loose tonal allegiances occur, of course, in two of Strauss's later dramatic works, *Salome* (1905), and *Elektra* (1909), but they make poor proof of the condition of late nineteenth-century music. They were composed around the time Schoenberg began his atonal explorations and probably were influential.

22. In Nietzsche's tract, *Von der Wissenschaft* lies within the fourth (and final) section.

23. Wagner's E♭ major triad in *Das Rheingold,* uninterrupted for 216 measures, alludes to the unchanging flow of the river's current.

24. Starting on page 28 of the Universal Edition pocket score.

25. Some of Scriabin's most innovative works have nonetheless led some writers, such as George Perle, to herald him as the first dodecaphonic composer.

26. This classical bent may explain Schoenberg's high opinion of Reger's music, which with Debussy's was performed often in the Zemlinsky-Schoenberg concerts.

27. And thus an occasional Reger passage sounds shockingly like an illustration from his 1903 treatise *Beitrage sur Modulationslehre.*

28. Alexander Ringer colorfully sized-up Reger's music—which he, like Schoenberg, considered to be the work of a genius—by saying that he "wallowed in the modulatory morass of his chromatic excesses" ("Arnold Schoenberg and the Prophetic Image in Music," 37). Most of our remarks about the chromaticism of Reger apply well to some of the later music of Belgian César Franck.

29. In this, Scriabin, like Schoenberg, was probably influenced by Mahler's concept of the *Inneres Programme*. In Reger, Schoenberg may have recognized a curious counterpart in what he calls his "application to 'absolute' music of Wagner's achievements in the realm of harmony" (*Structural Functions of Harmony,* 102).

30. The claim that Mahler led Schoenberg to his abandonment of tonality, made by both Newlin and Mitchell, is hardly credible. A composer like Mahler, who incorporates tonic or dominant (or both) pedal points in a great quantity of his textures is not on the brink of atonality, nor is he heading in that direction. I agree with O. W. Neighbors's assessment ("Arnold Schoenberg," *The New Grove Dictionary of Music and Musicians*) that Mahler's music "never influenced his own at all deeply, and his sympathy for it sometimes wavered." Furthermore, we have Schoenberg's testimony that Mahler's influence was rather in the opposite direction: "it is still possible that his strongly tonal structure and his more sustained harmony influenced me" (*Style and Idea,* 82).

31. Each of these composers wrote heavily chromatic music on occasion (as did Heinrich Schutz and Orlando Lasso). For example, parts of the last movement of Elgar's Cello Concerto, Opus 85, which is a late (1919) work, sound almost like the *Tristan* Prelude transcribed for solo cello and orchestra.

CHAPTER 13

The More Things Change, the More . . .

The evidence we considered in Chapter 12, drawn from music often cited to support allegations consistent with Schoenberg's views, leaves us with less than a convincing case for evolutionary progress, at least if the burial of tonality is to be the leading criterion. Yet clichés of music reporting of ensuing decades have led us to accept as truism that by 1900 tonality had been all but exhausted, like any other of the world's limited resources. This comfortable generalization settled in as incontrovertible fact, persisting over the years as a ground upon which our sense of musical styles has developed, in spite of contrary evidence all about us.

Having concluded, with Schoenberg, that the evolution of music had reached its ultimate chromatic development by 1900, conventional accounts proceeded to recognize and to enshrine only the "inevitable" music composed during the preceding century. This filtering process not surprisingly revealed a gradual but steady growth of chromaticism. A work that did not fit the approved prescription of so-many accidentals per measure might be plucked from the certified tree of Evolutionary Truth, victim of arrested development. In such a process, music found *historically representative* is imperceptibly transformed for us into music found *aesthetically superior,* adding one tenuous value judgment to another. The result in this case was an "official" progression running from Bach to Reger and Schoenberg. It is neat, but it is erroneous. It is poor history even if comforting theory.

The facts reveal a less monolithic story, one whose reinterpretation yields an alternative perspective. Arresting tonal confusion, or even mild ambiguity, when they occur at all in this music, are more handmaidens of programmatic posture than products of inexorable artistic progress.

SCHOENBERG'S RECOGNITION OF THE PROGRAMME'S POWER

Schoenberg was himself aware that extramusical motivations had a way of leading musical movement to its own tune. He recognized in this power a potential role in stylistic development. In his last book, the posthumous *Structural Functions of*

Harmony,[1] he noted that:

> a melody, if it followed the dictates of its musical structure alone, might develop in a direction different from that in which a text forces it. It might become shorter or longer, produce its climax earlier or later—or dispense with it entirely—require less striking contrasts, much less emphasis, or much less accentuation.[2]

And in his essay "Opinion or Insight" (1926) he paid homage to the innovations wrought in harmony and tonality by the will to compose "music as expression." He remarks there that

> this led to sudden and surprising modulations . . . strange chord progressions, interesting chords, and later to hitherto unexploited melodic steps, unusual progressions of intervals and other such things.[3]

We might add only that it was those evocative extramusical links—those textual ties, those ideational whispers—that were the principal cause of the patches of extraordinary chromaticism in music created just before his time. An individual composer's storytelling in tones, not a preordained universal evolving, led the way. Indeed, many of the most tonally wrenching passages of the *Faust Symphony,* of *Tristan,* and of *Zarathustra* are similar, in their crowded pitch content and consequent harmonic drama, to passages created by composers we have mentioned before, madrigalists Monteverdi, Marenzio, Gesualdo. They are passages in which harmonic cross-relations distort the clarity of a singular tonic or where brief phrases in one clear tonality are followed by one in a wholly different tonality.[4]

There is nothing modern, nothing particularly revolutionary or evolutionary about this. It is an old and perennially effective means for evoking images that transcend mere pitches and rhythms and chords. As most historians readily concur, the goals and resources of those Renaissance masters were not very much different. For them, too, chromaticism was a means to a thoroughly dramatic end. And their music similarly contrasted sharply with precedents, to the extent that the Monteverdi brothers felt compelled to explain why Claudio's madrigals in Books V and VI veered so precipitously from the "First Practice" of harmony that Zarlino had defined in 1558. As Giulio Cesare explains in the preface to Book VI, his brother's music harbors a more evocative relationship to its text, with poem as "mistress of the harmony" rather than the reverse. And in doing this, as Claude Palisca observes, "the composer has sacrificed musical consistency to mirror the poet's every image."[5]

And so it is that historian Christopher Headington's words about the sixteenth century can be as well applied, without emendation or reservation, to the dramatic touches of a Liszt, a Wagner, a Strauss, a Schoenberg:

> The Italian madrigal composers vied with one another in the portrayal of complex and extreme emotions. If the poem which was being set to music

spoke of dying love, it was no longer just sufficient to write quiet and solemn music: the music had to portray the full anguish of the unfortunate lover. Composers had to stretch the existing musical vocabulary to heighten its expressive power. They did so mainly by means of chromaticism.[6]

This earlier affinity for chromatic tone-painting certainly was not confined to Italy. We are reminded of English composer John Daniel's catchy exposé of 1606 shown in Example 50.

Chro - mat - ic tunes most   like my   pas - sions sound.

EXAMPLE 50. Chromatic phrase, John Daniel.

A PRINCIPAL ERROR

Regardless of what the true condition of musical development may have been early in this century, Schoenberg assumed personal responsibility, as he was fond of putting it, for drawing conclusions and mounting actions that would propel music toward its evolutionary destiny. At the time, he appears not to have grasped his own capital role, along with Reger, in bringing about what an unrepentant evolutionist might call a Wagner-Brahms mutation. He opted for Wagnerian chromaticism, but then he relentlessly adapted it to creations of Brahmsian autonomy, as well as to works with programmatic ties or elaborate texts. That he recognized this amalgam of antagonisms in Reger, along with its dangers, is made explicit in *Structural Functions of Harmony*. Speaking there of how his German contemporary had appropriated Wagner's harmonic audacities for non-programmatic uses he says,

> Because these were invented for dramatic expression, the application of these procedures in this way provoked an almost "revolutionary" movement among Wagner's successors.[7]

And with this particular Wagnerian successor, music lacking both pitch hierarchy[8] and explicit linkages to extramusical ideas became a fait accompli. In his zeal to model the future, Schoenberg far outstripped Scriabin and Reger.

He excised from music not just the "harmonic tonality" he inherited from his predecessors; his own ratification of a pitch democracy led also to a negation he may not even have recognized: the more elemental kind of pitch focus we discussed in Chapter 8, a tonal relatedness independent of chords, a more primitive hierarchical condition endemic to other perceptual modes as well as to audition and first clarified in the figure-ground statements of the Gestalt psychologists. This was a matter less easily disposed of, and as Wallace Berry has made clear it can be found as a vestigial remnant in some of the pre-dodecaphonic music of Schoenberg's most talented students, Berg (Op. 5) and Webern (Op. 7).[9]

And this was Schoenberg's principal error: renunciation of even the primal tonal archetypes bequeathed him by his full musical heritage, believing all the while that he was rejecting only the major-minor conventions of his immediate past. He did not understand the full ramifications of his renunciation, a denial that if followed rigorously entailed abandonment of the full range of structuring potentials of pitch. His transformation of music was motivated by the same hubris that in the world's myths spells the tragic downfall of heroes who try to call the shots of destiny.

Schoenberg thought he was fueling music's flight to the next plateau, in its ascent toward a musical heaven. He was in reality only fueling the ambitions of a singularly enormous talent and establishing a brief, strange interlude in an art's checkered history. It is true, as some contemporaries have said, that "he showed us the way." But, some eighty years later, we must recognize that his way fell short of becoming the next Golden Age so anxiously sought during the beginning of the twentieth century. Nor was it the inexorable "way" that music's hopscotching development had pointed toward in the long haul of history. As evolution, it was an ill-conceived, though passionately propagandized, mutation. It was an achievement far more radical than Schoenberg dreamed.[10]

In Search of Coherence

Schoenberg persistently maintained the expendability of tonality in its capacity for delineating large and small formal parts. He was correct in his conclusion, as history has borne out. Formal differentiation can be supplied through contrasts of timbre, textural differentiations, melodic contrasts, fluctuations of rhythmic densities—in sum, by quite enough properties to relieve tonality of that responsibility. We also know that formal relatedness or contrast need not depend on the stock key relationships of Baroque and Classic convention. One could have deduced this from examination of earlier musics in which the *particular ordering* of tonalities often is without plan, non-periodic, non-recurring, at times apparently even fortuitous.[11] And regardless, the kind of thematic orderings Schoenberg advocated as a replacement for tonality, an organicism achieved by fastidious motivic organization, can provide a kind of formal cohesion, a continuing sense of parts bearing kinship and of succeeding one another over a span of time. We are indebted to him for the concept of *Grundgestalt* as one way of characterizing the penetrating unity of many whole works, regretting only that he did not elaborate this helpful insight more fully.

We might even conjecture, following Schoenberg's claims, that non-tonally hierarchical pitch collections, such as a twelve-note row and its permuted orders, can supply ipso facto unity of a perceptually demonstrable kind.[12] But what music loses by this replacement (and Schoenberg always quickly noted that "every gain provides a commensurate loss," as if recognition healed the wound) is far greater than he bargained for.

Perhaps other processes for achieving local coherence and formal integrity make music without tonality possible. But such processes are not unique to music: pattern repetition, variation and metamorphosis and figure-ground distinctions operate in literature, in the visual arts, in the plastic arts, and in dance. What they replaced in music, which is the pitch perspective of tonality, could boast of more exclusive roots. Its archetypal source lies in an unparalleled phenomenon of our sensory processing of sound, the harmonic series. Its musical manifestation, as the projection in time of harmonic meaning, described for one style of music first by Schenker, can be regarded as nothing less than *the primary musical property,* the paradigmatic quality of the medium itself that renders sound uniquely malleable into the structures of music.

THE MOTIF AS FORMING UNIT

Motivic processes—transformation, return, recurrence—have been championed as an exclusive basis for musical coherence since Schoenberg proposed them as possible means for replacing tonality.[13] Some writers have even adopted the distinguishing category "motivic music," which in at least one respect (linguistic) is preferable to the regrettable "post-tonal" that began to infiltrate academic catalogues two decades ago.

It is revealing to make a comparison with literature, replacing a collection of motivic patterns with a cast of characters. Clearly, a rudimentary coherence can be achieved when dramatis personae are serially introduced, then their entrances and exits, their movements and blockings methodically intertwined as if unfolding a purely visual story. But imagine that these visual cues from speechless individuals are the totality of participating properties, the exclusive medium for relating later events to earlier, present event A to present events B and C, and so on. The product is skeletal; it lacks the motivating force, the flesh of reality that alone can engender drama or can even provide a credible basis for meaningful interaction. It falters from the absence of a narrative unity, whether explicable as propositional or non-propositional.

The mere display of personae lacks the potentiality of fusing action with the more encompassing condition of life. Just as dynamic situation—the venerable dramatic format of Conflict and Resolution—must provide reasons why characters move across a stage, successions of tones must be infused with a larger enveloping governance that can give meaning beyond themselves. As Jackendoff and Lerdahl argue,[14] no amount of compensatory injections—thematic, timbral, textural, or dynamic—are adequate replacements for the relatedness that comes from hierarchical structure. Or, turning to the words of Mark Johnson: "Whatever human rationality consists in, it is certainly tied up with narrative structure and the quest for narrative unity."[15]

It seems clear why tonality became for two centuries a dominating musical property. We need not wonder that in the preludes and sonatas and fugues and suites and symphonies—the "objectified," the "independent" musical genres of eighteenth-century Europe—elaborate conventions of key schemes became a presumed necessity of large-scale ordering. We can readily understand why this unprecedented torrent of music, works produced for the first time in history as autonomous objects for human contemplation separable from religious or political ritual, from dance or from any other direct link with an extramusical impetus, developed to an extravagant degree the use of tonality as an agent of form. Even when lacking extrinsic sources of meaning, whether in representational bodily movement, in established ritual, or in a scenario of human or animal action, music still could transmit meaning. It could project an embodied structure, and tonality made this eminently possible.

TRADING A VITAL LOSS FOR A COSMETIC GAIN

Our vantage point enables us to evaluate the logic of Schoenberg's arguments as well as the results of his musical decisions. Although our concern is with Schoenberg's theories and not with his compositions, hindsight provides a possible explanation for the comparatively greater success of his dramatic works, those with an explicit musical tie, works such as his songs and more extensive texted compositions like *Ewartung* (whose subtitle is "A Melodrama"), *Die Glückliche hand, Von Heute auf Morgen,* and *Moses und Aron.* Of the works he composed after his initial move into atonality, around 1907–1908, these externally driven pieces are more credible, more immediately meaningful than the non-programmatic works he composed later. Even the *Violin Concerto* (1936) and the *Piano Concerto* (1942), both of a genre suited to attract a public following, have failed after a half-century to establish a performance base with soloists, with orchestras, or with concert-going patrons.

The very early (and programmatic) *Verklärte Nacht,* whose tonality and texture and rhythmic life are heavily indebted to Wagner, is the most frequently performed of Schoenberg's works. The immense (and thus rarely performed) *Gurre-lieder,* in which Richard Norton finds synthesized the styles of every major composer of fin-de-siècle Western Europe, is often mentioned by musicians as one of the composer's masterworks, often when they have never actually heard a performance. And then the path-breaking *Pierrot Lunaire* is usually mentioned in a second breath, most often with stress on its historical significance, or something about its conceptual relationship to Stravinsky's *L'Histoire,* or its breaking of new vocal ground with its novel *Sprechgesang.*

The atonal and dodecaphonic works intended (and appropriately titled) to be understood in the Brahmsian tradition of non-representational music have fared poorly by comparison, even after the "new thus difficult" period of audience adjustment is well past. Serenades and the later string quartets (following No. 2) and sextettes as well as chamber symphonies and piano pieces seem, as a class, to have proved to be the less accessible and memorable works. It is one of the curiosities of modern music that he followed programs in composing many of these "objective" works, including the *String Trio*, Opus 45, but did not make those programs a part of the works' public performances, as perspectival aids to listeners.[16]

Nearly four decades ago sociologist John Mueller left open a decisive evaluation of Schoenberg's position in the performance scales of American orchestras with the question:

> Whether his music is a natural evolution from the chromaticism of *Tristan* . . . with the public taste in a deplorable cultural lag; or whether the composer was deceived by his own clever contrivance of an aesthetic theory which is simply too unpsychological to gain adherence, is another one of those temporarily insoluble questions which we so glibly pass on to a supposedly omniscient posterity to decide.[17]

Now, some forty years hence, we can only wonder just how long is posterity.

Schoenberg's consuming will to shape the course of music's history became a burden for every composer whose ultimate aim was to communicate with listeners but who at the same time wished to outmaneuver the "affliction of tonality." George Rochberg provides one of the most eloquent summations of this misjudgment in his book, *The Aesthetics of Survival*. He attributes the main problem to a simple mistake:

> The mistake would be . . . to believe . . . that given the security of preconceived abstract order, invention, clarity, and musical inevitability will automatically follow. Schoenberg was the first to fall into this trap of his own devising.[18]

Overrationalizing the process, in other words, runs the risk of losing the music.

To put the principal moral of our story into an appropriate historical frame: Wagnerian processes are not always amenable to Brahmsian forms and gestures and intentions. It was Schoenberg's most damaging error as a theorist to assume that they could be made so, and to conclude that the tonally perfidious music of the nineteenth century must of necessity give way to the uncharted seas of a non-hierarchical pitch world. There can be too much of a good thing. While stretches of tonal ambiguity may pique the fancy and ruffle the expectations, forced avoidance (or perhaps more apt is Glenn Gould's *legislated* avoidance) of pitch focus can nullify the projection of embodied meaning.

Today a larger part of Schoenberg's music seems destined to survive mainly in a confining academic purgatory, seldom to escape to the widespread acceptance he so passionately envisaged for it. His anomalous position in contemporary life is dramatically illustrated by an ever-widening gap that separates his image as "great composer" from the reality of neglect, in public performance, that prevails for all but a handful of his early works and transcriptions he made of others' music. His conviction that familiarity would breed eventual understanding and, ultimately, veneration, has not been justified. The Rejection-Acceptance-Assimilation-Endearment cycle for truly great music that shaped his aesthetic perspective appears to have been another case of unfulfilled prophecy. This is particularly unfortunate, for his will to achieve worldwide artistic veneration was at least equal to any other composer's in history. A good measure of his sense of professional insult came about because he was unprepared to acknowledge a simple cultural "law": one cannot be subversive and inoffensive at the same time.

American composer John Adams was four years old when Schoenberg died in 1951. His informal summary of the place a large segment of the Viennese master's oeuvre occupies in music today echoes the opinion of many contemporaries. In a reflection on the vicissitudes of musical communication and Schoenberg's lot, he observes:

> We thought his orchestral works would . . . become a part of the standard repertory. But they never did. His pieces . . . will never become assimilated like Schubert. They will permanently be avant-garde works, always difficult to approach.[19]

The future Schoenberg imposed on himself and on a body of music reminds us of George Bernard Shaw's line that "manufacturing destinies for other people is a dangerous game."

Evolution, Styles, and Non-Sequiturs

Inevitability is a value judgment. Even if rooted in the soil of acknowledged circumstances and high probability, it is nevertheless the product of interpretation, not a direct datum of the external world. Schoenberg's deeply held beliefs about the nature of history, coupled with a tenuous grasp of the music of history, left him unaware that shifts in musical style are not indubitably continuous and gradual; they often involve abrupt breaks, direct leaps to an opposing aesthetic persuasion. The separate pages of musical style, which we patiently dogear in our obsession for categories, frequently are products of anything *except* the stubborn perpetuation of a previous style. Had the ideals of the richly complex polyphony of the high Renaissance continued to dominate the minds of composers, the Italian Camerata would not have bloomed, and the rank amateurs who groped their way—false inferences, shabby pretenses, slippery history and all—into the invention of opera would never have succeeded. It was the ironic good luck of posterity that the contrapuntal skills of Count Giovanni de 'Bardi and Jacobo Peri left something to be desired; their technical liabilities turned out to be their creative assets.

Nor should we forget the revolutionary evolution that accompanied the death of J. S. Bach. The puerile creations of *Empfindsamer Stil* and *Galanter Stil* were scarcely perpetuations of the "old peruke's" contrapuntal magic. From his point of view that music probably would have been contemptuously dismissed as triflings of the modestly talented. And yet the monumentality that is Haydn, Mozart, Gluck, and Beethoven developed as a related strain from those less rigorously polyphonic essays in musical expression. The textural clarity of harmonized melody took over where labyrinthine counterpoint had outrun its course.

Even our own era holds an object lesson in how musical times manage to change. Who would have guessed that the arcane complexities of Total Serialism, assiduously cultivated in the decade after Schoenberg's death by Boulez and Babbitt, would be dethroned as the fashion of the day by—of all things—Minimalism? Who would have predicted that any serious composer after 1955 would dare to circulate a piece of music whose very title, *In C,* would reveal its *outré* disregard for the evolutionary plateau vaulted by Schoenberg almost a half-century before?

It would have taken a bold originality to imagine that the Serialisms and Total Serialisms cycled and recycled between the mid-1950s and the mid-1970s would be succeeded by melodic truisms founded in Rock of Ages harmony. And yet, Minimalism is with us today, even if it is an unlikely branching from the immediate past, even if it may be gone tomorrow.

Schoenberg died before convincing international vindication surfaced for him and for his seminal role in music's twentieth-century overhaul. It finally came most publicly within a decade after World War II, although the movement's seeds had sprouted some years before.[20] Perhaps it was best that vindication came posthumously. The way it turned out would not have pleased him.

NOTES

1. Published posthumously, 1954.
2. *Structural Functions of Harmony,* 76.
3. *Style and Idea,* 260.
4. In this sense perhaps Newlin's (and Mitchell's and Schoenberg's) *progressive tonality* should be applied more liberally than just to nineteenth-century music.
5. In *Baroque Music,* 12.
6. *History of Western Music,* 82.
7. *Structural Functions of Harmony,* 102.
8. Some people confidently find tonic chords—even functional harmonic progressions—in Schoenberg's atonal and serial music. For fascinating (and in my opinion unconvincing) discussion of these properties see Roy Travis, "Directed Motion in Schoenberg and Webern," and Will Ogden, "How Tonality Functions in Schoenberg's Opus 11, No. 1." George Perle's view (*Serial Music and Atonality,* 32) strikes me as far more consistent with the musical experience. As he says, "The abandonment of the concept of a root-generator of the individual chord is a radical development that renders futile any attempt at a systematic formulation of chord structure and progression in atonal music along the lines of traditional harmonic theory."
9. Berry, *Structural Functions in Music,* 90–93.
10. This point is hammered away by psychologist Robert Francès, *The Perception of Music.* See especially the section beginning page 117. As he observes, the "new syntax" was conceptually plausible

although perhaps not realizable in audition.

11. Musicians familiar with the mechanics of popular music and jazz of the mid-twentieth century know the irrelevance of *particular* key successions in attaining formal contrast and cohesion. Ordering keys in such musical "arrangements" simply by accommodating instrumental or vocal tessiture in no way reduces formal logic, attainment of finality, etc. A composition can end in a key wholly remote (tritone, semitone up or down) from the beginning key without hampering the unfolding of ideas or their logical cessation.

12. There is no shortage of writers who side with Francès (see n. 10 above) on this issue, who would not support the conjecture framed here. See Deutsch, "The Processing of Structural and Unstructured Tonal Sequences"; Krumhansl, Sandell, and Sargeant, "The Perception of Tone Hierarchies and Mirror Forms in Twelve-Tone Serial Music"; Ruwet, "Contradictions of the Serial Language"; and Dowling, "Recognition of Melodic Transformations: Inversion, Retrograde, and Retrograde Inversion." Also see the earlier note re Milton Babbitt's statement that other parameters are required to project row properties which are invariant under permutation, which means a tacit admission that the row alone lacks formative potential.

13. In his essay "My Evolution," Schoenberg recalls that at one time he, with Webern, Berg, and Hába, mistakenly thought even motivic features could be abandoned and still make music that would "remain coherent and comprehensible" (*Style and Idea*, 88).

14. Lerdahl and Jackendoff, *A Generative Theory*, 298.

15. Mark Johnson, *The Body in the Mind*, 172.

16. Since Schoenberg chose not to share their contents, they cannot be functionally programmatic. (For a thorough discussion of this interesting issue see Walter Bailey, *Programmatic Elements in the Works of Schoenberg*.) Schoenberg's paradoxical withholding of these background motivations is especially fascinating in the light of a comment he makes in his *Structural Functions of Harmony*. Speaking of the union of music and extramusical elements—the "drama, poem or story" of "descriptive music"—he says, on page 76, that

> their union thereafter is inseparable. Neither the text nor the music conveys its full significance if detached from its composition.

17. John Mueller, *The American Symphony Orchestra*, 58. This study included only the U.S., but it is my hunch that, by comparison with other twentieth-century masters, Schoenberg's dodecaphonic music fared no better in European capitals. A check of the performance log of radio station KUSC, Los Angeles, one of the most prestigious "classical music" stations in the country, is more current. It shows that during a four-month period, August–November, 1990, three Schoenberg works were programmed for four performances: two of *Verklärte Nacht*, and one each of *Pierrot Lunaire* and the *Chamber Symphony*, Opus 9.

18. Rochberg, *The Aesthetics of Survival*, 58.

19. As reported by Gregg Warner from an interview with John Adams, *Los Angeles Times*, February 14, 1989.

20. Doctoral dissertations about dodecaphonic and serial techniques and their histories began to appear in the mid-1950s with Ogden's (1955) from Indiana and Perle's (1956) from New York University. The English translation of Rufer's *Die Komposition Mit Zwolf Tonen* was published in 1954, and Anne Bassart's *Serial Music: A Classified Bibliography of Writings on Twelve-Tone and Electronic Music* came out first in the middle of the period in question, in 1961.

CHAPTER 14

The Schoenbergian Legacy

What the average music lover thought, in the decade following Schoenberg's death, about the hardcore dodecaphonic repertory has not been extensively documented. It may not even be cogent to our discussion. But it is clear that some of the most influential academics of the day were confident that illuminations of the subtleties of the twelve-note potential would remain a human priority for a very long time. The legacy of ordered atonality left by Schoenberg became an immensely complex network of pre-compositional operations expressible in strange new ways. Since it developed directly from the compelling methods he pioneered, it is an essential part of our story.

AESTHETIC POWER-BROKERING AND THE META-WORLD OF ACADEMIA

The post-Schoenberg/post-Webern era offers a fascinating case study of how a body of committed and talented individuals can develop, elaborate upon, and propound a shaky hypothesis (derived from Schoenberg's conclusions) until it dents the whole façade of an art. As a human condition it reveals an interesting modern parallel: the supreme bioethical dilemma of modern medicine, imposed because we now can sustain human life beyond traditional margins of vitality, is matched by an aesthetic dilemma centered in contemporary academe. The dilemma rose with the elevation of higher education following World War II, which gave academics an unprecedented voice in the background arbitrations of public values. What Professor X (of Harvard or Princeton or Stanford or MIT) has to say today about the world's aesthetic (or agricultural or psychiatric or economic) woes is heard broadly and in high places. It was not always that way. Thus when a prestigious coterie within the academic establishment took up the cause of Serialism in the mid-1950s, its voluble apologia seeped into market place as well as halls of ivy.

The full repertory—the music—of Serialism resisted firm transplanting onto the programmes of professional symphony orchestras and opera companies and the production schedules of recording companies.[1] But an elaborate mantra of dodeca-phonic extension—pitch notation newly interpreted through stock concepts and expressions of mathematical set theory—managed to arouse a certain awe in the intellectual and artistic communities for a corpus whose parts already had begun to slip into the grave of public neglect.

The flurry of enthusiasms of this period centered not around Schoenberg, whom Boulez had declared "dead," but around Webern. From the movement's inception in the United States, the newly-influential academic segment of the population became prominent, especially among themselves. In time it demonstrated how the lives of artworks (whose dependence on the auspices of higher education had in times past been negligible) could be sustained by artificial means and prolonged beyond normal expectancy, regardless of their direct aesthetic vibrancy.

The era's post-Viennese energy induced a remarkable production of analytical dissections and speculative tracts—more those than public performances of music.[2] The torrent of words and numbers and formulae unleashed about Schoenberg's methods, about their more thorough exploitation by Webern, and then about subse-quent extensions (like those of Boulez and Babbitt) to other musical dimensions, produced one of the most bountiful crops of verbiage ever harvested in the cause of an art.

The movement also harbored a hidden cul de sac for the unwary. Its participants produced a fair amount of theoretical "how to . . ." composers' shoptalk, which tended to be preoccupied with manipulation of notes as permutable collections, rather than with interpretive descriptions of phenomenal things. So the unassailable and unchanging concern of musicians for the art's aural ontology became secondary to the orderings of serialized particles.[3] *Permutations, reciprocal relativities, combinatori-ality, segmentation, source sets, derived sets, intersections, adjacencies, partitions, germ cells* (especially of the three-note Webernian genus), *aggregates, pitch qualia, hexachords, mathematical models, complementation modulus–12, pitch* (or *note*) *cells,* and the like dominated the literature of Serialism.

Several of these borrowed words were subsequently absorbed into the functional vocabularies of educated musicians. It is hard to imagine life without the handiness of the term *pitch class,* which so readily hurdles several linguistic barriers. But two decades later, the list as a whole appears jaded, with the aura of an extravagant lyric from last year's hit song.

The novel explications of serial ordering were at the same time intimidating and intoxicating. They were intimidating for an obvious reason: They demanded a broad and deep network of understandings alien to most musicians, even those of academic background. Before 1955 few had even heard the words *permutation* or *modulus-12,* let alone understood them. That *reordering* for the first, and *cycle of twelve elements* for the second, could have transmitted the same meaning would likely not have changed the explanatory habits of serial illuminati. Words have special powers:

permutation had an inimitable ring of profundity, and *modulus-12* was sheer magic. Both seemed to guarantee conceptual precision and mathematical certainty; both hinted at the flinty "rigor" of the hard sciences. Such terminology prompted a comforting fantasy in the 1960s and 1970s; it allowed us metaphorically to put on laboratory smocks and pretend to be "genuine scientists," the Einsteins of harmony.

THE RECALCITRANCE OF LANGUAGE

Musicians deal largely in incommensurables, with comparatives rather than with absolutes. Falsely assuming absolutes as the data of scientific disciplines, we detect a magical aura about scientific method and its accompanying cant, while scientists, equally misled about us, sometimes naively suspect rites of witchcraft in especially compelling musical performances. Each discipline uses, in its intramural communications, notation and jargon that is uncommonly difficult to follow without specialized experience. Each language is eminently suitable for those who use it; years of development have achieved the uniqueness demanded for the communication of unique things. And so when a member of one group writes for colleagues in ways that call upon the explicative skills assumed within the other, a degree of presumptuousness—let us even call it insolence—is betrayed. Bewilderment rather than enlightenment most often ensues.

Were Kepler's attempts to explain planetary motions via musical relationships any more ill-considered than musicians' transmogrifications of musical things into the language of mathematics? Informative languages are not imposed ex cathedra; they develop gradually by the common consent of users. As a group, musicians, for obvious and justifiable reasons, are not fluent in the languages of mathematics, of symbolic logic, or of chemical formulae. And yet around 1960 they found themselves confronted, in the literature of their discipline, by hidden tongues. It was an academic avant-garde action in the twilight of Schoenberg's revolution, and it predictably could only exacerbate the radical alienation begun earlier with Schoenberg's institutionalized abandonment of tonality.

Eager to understand, yet modestly equipped for instant translations, bright musical minds were alternately enchanted and repelled by explanations like the following, which tells us how eight measures of music can be "reduced to the following pitch scheme":[4]

1. Two rotational arrays based on sets of size 2 arrays related by T.

$t = 0$		$t = 1$		
0	2	1	3	= 0, 1, 2, 3 total pc content of "generating" lines.
0	10	1	11	

2. Two rotational arrays based on sets of size 4, arrays related by T. The "generating" line of the first array is the reordering of the pitch classes of the two "generating" lines of A.

t = 0				t = 2				
0	1	3	2	2	3	5	4	= 0, 1, 2, 3, 4, 5 total pc content of
0	2	1	11	2	4	3	1	"generating" lines.
0	11	9	10	2	1	11	0	
0	10	11	1	2	0	1	3	

3. Two rotational arrays based on sets of size 6, arrays related by T. "Generating" line is reordering of all the pitch classes of the two tetrachord "generating" lines.

t = 3						t = 9						
3	4	0	2	1	5	9	10	6	8	7	11	= all 12 pcs in
3	11	1	0	4	2	9	5	7	6	10	8	"generating"
3	5	4	8	6	7	9	11	10	2	0	1	lines.
3	2	6	4	5	1	9	8	0	10	11	7	
3	7	5	6	2	4	9	1	11	0	8	10	
3	1	2	10	0	11	9	7	8	4	6	5	

The possibilities for both large and small scale connection which this procedure makes possible should be obvious.

This is unarguably one kind of rendering of the music illustrated, a reduction of internal consistency and incontestable accuracy—of a sort—that describes with precision a note-generating process.

Although quite different in surface features, a similar explanatory stance informs Milton Babbitt's extensive discussion of his composition *Relata I*. It opens with the promising statement that he "as an analyst, shall attempt to discover and formulate that which [he], as a listener, would like to know."[5] But our optimism is short-lived. We soon conclude that Babbitt, as listener, wants to know things that are improbably knowable through audition; and even were they knowable, they likely would be only tenuously consequential (of things musical). We read that

From the standpoint of aggregate structure, the second section is a pitch-class retrograde of the first, while from the standpoint of the set structure of the instrumental lines, it is a pitch-class inversion, but it must be emphasized and understood . . . that since aggregate structure does not define the orderings of its component parts, the total pitch progression of the second section is by no means a retrogression of the first section, and since the component timbral lines are timbrally reinterpreted on the basis of combinatorial connection, neither is the linear pitch progression.[6]

Reproduction here of the notated excerpts accompanying these descriptive words would be only redundant; they confirm what the words ably suggest: the author assumes perceptual solvency for some intractably abstract note-orderings (systematic though they be) of some registrally undefined (as series components) pitch classes. One's difficulty in penetrating to meaning here is not solely a product of the sentence's Faulknerian structure.[7]

Babbitt's explanation pays no heed to how the crush of time might cause a listener to transform the heard embodiments of these already abstract units (the pitch classes) and their revised coagulations (the variously permuted orders) into a progression of cohering elements, parts which relate in some manner as structure. Subsequent mention of such palpable things as clarinets and violins gives only temporary encouragement to the baffled reader. As the guided tour continues:

> Again, the overall transformational relation is revealed most explicitly at the corresponding midpoint, which in this section represents a reduction from the (I^2) with which it opens, and is combinatorially presented totally linearly by the doubling of clarinet 2 and violin 4, and similarly opens the second part of the section, a chamber orchestra-like part, which is most obviously characterized by greater timbral and linear homogeneity than has appeared thus far in the work. The pitch class dyadic associations, which determine harmonic contingencies in the small, are literally revealed at the end of the section with the return of the (6^2) partition.[8]

Formidable number lists, postulations in the phrases of formal logic, and misguided assignments of assumed meaning to humbling abstractions (like the Is and Ts and Rs of twelve-note sets) were not the only barriers erected during the period that followed in Schoenberg's wake. The very language of Serialism and of related theoretical generalization became at times sublimely baroque, especially when old ideas were couched in terrifyingly new sentences. Thus one author, in the spirit of linguistic clarification (with the help of philosopher Nelson Goodman) could explain for his readers "The Role of 'Sounds' in 'Music.' "[9]

> "A concretum is a *fully* concrete entity in that it has among its qualities at least one member of every category within some sense realm. It is a minimal concrete entity in that it contains nothing more than one quale from each such category." . . . "Sounds" are the concreta associated with music. But we are limiting our system to the description of relations among *pitch* and *time-order* qualia, or at most pitch-time-order quale

complexes as (at least *partial*) "musical structures," rather than relations among the associated sounds themselves.

It was just these kinds of exposés and clarifications that led one of the most astute music minds of the twentieth century, Ernst Krenek, to file a lengthy complaint, a tiny part of which we reproduce here:

> I have covered several sheets of music paper with experiments, exercises, and examples trying to penetrate the meaning of his discourse. . . . I gave up in frustration. . . . I am afraid that the use of this language . . . has reached a point of diminishing returns: the possible increment of scholarly prestige (not to speak of snob appeal) is compensated by the loss of communicability.[10]

Whatever may or may not be the merit of Krenek's complaint, let us be clear on one thing: our principal concern is not with the relative complexity, the appropriateness, or even with the accuracy of languages and symbolic representations as they occur in the serial-related literature. As scholars, Rogers, Boretz, and Babbitt are obligated to use the language that best communicates their ideas. That their explanatory means may at times strike us as self-indulgently opaque perhaps tells as much of our own limitations as of theirs. We cannot fault Kant for not reading like Rousseau.

Our concern, on the contrary, is more with message than with massage. Harboring the implicit assumption that there should be tight correspondences between concepts and percepts in any music theory, we persist in asking the same old question once again: How do these ideas and the processes they represent relate to music as heard, and if they are not intended to bear relations to heard phenomena, where did this quaint perspective originate?

NEW TEMPTATIONS FOR OLD SINS OF OMISSION

The first postulate of the theorem of music may rightfully be pitched sound, but a necessary condition of that postulate is extension in time. It should be axiomatic that talk about pitches as structural beings without reference to their deployment in time is mere idle chatter. Yet the critical and analytical literature of our musical past largely ignores this unarguable fact. And the analytical formalism[11] of Serialism that followed Schoenberg fostered the promotion of this barren perspective until it became one of the supreme mismemes of theoretical history. While a durationless pitch is an unfortunate aberration, *pitch class,* as referential *datum,* dissolves into a Never-Never-Land of nothingness—it lacks extension in the two critical dimensions of sound, pitch and time.

Schoenberg took over the one-sided explanatory freight of his theorist-predecessors without sufficient critical examination of its content. Its implicit message was that pitch (and especially pitch deployed as harmony) is for all practical purposes synonymous with music. And then, in moving as a composer from the chromatic maneuverings of his most influential precursors to the equitable treatment of the twelve notes, he pushed this mistaken assumption to unprecedented heights. Its ultimate end came after him, of course, in works of "total serialization." When durations themselves became subject to serial ordering, whatever residue of conscious or intuitive rhythmic control that may have persisted in dodecaphonic music was negated. There is no greater mark of indifference than relegating something, whether people or tones, to "automatic control."

It is especially interesting in this light to note that Schoenberg's pre-serial works frequently exploit rhythm, timbre, and/or texture as de facto controlling properties, yet his theoretical formulations deny them the controlling roles he assigned pitch orders. And his development of the twelve-note method confirmed that theoretical blind spot. In this respect, as Charles Rosen observes, his Serialism was "a grave step backwards from the vision of his earlier work."[12]

THE EMPTY MONADS OF SERIAL DESCRIPTION

Our concern with the literature of Serialism is not what most critics of the past have focused upon, that the language is foreign and/or excessively complex. If true, those circumstances are mere inconveniences. New languages can be learned; complexity can be unravelled and surmounted. The real problem has to do with what the language is about, what it attempts to describe, what it testifies to be the issues of musical reality.

We can detect a chain that links serial explications of the 1960s and 70s, as well as Schoenberg's ideas, to the music theory of the previous two centuries in Europe: they share this obsession for pitch as the expense of rhythm[13] and every other possible structuring agent of music. The majority of these theorists behaved as if music were the direct product of disembodied pitch, as if descriptions of its distributions (whether as major triads or as combinatorial hexachords) are tantamount to descriptions of the musical whole. Timbre, texture, and rhythm are allowed as fellow travelers, but the nature and goal of the journey is uncontestably determined by pitch mappings. This part-whole confusion endures today, along with the romantic notion of atonality as the musical analogue of total political freedom.[14]

This curious imbalance of Western theory is especially pronounced in the analyses and conceptual discussions of serial theory, 1955–75. As the excerpts we have sampled reveal, they suffer unconfirmed links (tenuous at best, non-existent at worst) with the cognitive stuff that makes acoustical signal into music. The literature of Serialism is filled with discussions of the shadows of already-diffuse things, abstractions twice-removed from sounds in time. Abstraction is piled on abstraction when Babbitt tells us further that in his *Relata I:*

> the inversionally related . . . lines of this underlying "polyphony" how-
> ever, though still maintaining hexachordal combinatoriality, do not pre-
> serve this dyadic relationship; clearly they could have been so chosen . . .
> but the final pair was chosen to function as a linear summation of the
> "simultaneous" dyads.[15]

We assume, I believe, that we are being told something about how to prepare for or to imagine encounters with palpable sounds. But these words beat no paths for us to data of audition in the mind's ear, to "the way it sounds." Every element refers to an abstraction, the base-abstraction of all which is pitch class. Observe:

a. The "inversionally related . . . lines" refers to an operation of abstraction (inversion within modulus-12 rather than contoural inversion) upon a collection of impalpables (pitch classes);

b. the "hexachordal combinatoriality" preserved refers to the non-duplicative second hexachord derived by It^9, which is an abstraction (inversion/transposition via modulus 12) of the abstraction that is "set of pitch classes";

c. the "dyadic relationship" that is not preserved refers to the abstraction of paired elements that is not duplicated in the original pitch-class hexachord (abstraction) and its It^9 permutation (further abstraction);

d. the "linear summation of the 'simultaneous dyads' " refers to the abstraction of orchestral parts sounding (in temporal relationships unspecified except as to succession), the abstraction of which is the yield of six pitch class pairs from the combinatorially related hexachords.

EXAMPLE 51. Pitch class pairs, S and It^9 (Babbitt, *Relata I*).

While in human discourse the usual goal of description is concreteness, setting up direct ties with sensate objects or feelings that can nudge essences to the surface of consciousness, the descriptive literature of Serialism abounds in abstraction. It favors words and phrases whose links are instead with configurational obscurities, which are themselves constituted from disembodied monads.

Since we are fed words about words, we cannot know whether the elements as stipulated play a formative role—not to mention a catalytic role—in the musical passage under scrutiny, so this presumed objective is beside the point. These ordered entities are certainly there, residing as tabulated "in the notes." (The analyses of Serialism tend to be reassuringly precise and thorough and error-free in this respect.) But like the *talea* and *colore* of isorhythmic motets, like the Golden Sections allegedly embedded in works from antiquity through Bartók, and like the balancing power claimed for the subdominant degree of the major-minor tonal systems, these instances of "what is there in the notes" lead dubious lives.

Indeed, these highly literate but regrettably obscure statements take off from the same misconception that hounded claims made in defense of Schoenberg's twelve-tone methods, especially those made in an attempt to gain respect through pseudo-associations with a respected past. For example, Rufer erroneously invokes the memory of Bach and Beethoven, unaware that inversions and retrogressions of collections of *pitch classes* cannot be compared with the same operations applied to collections of (contourally fixed) *pitches*.

> The use of these mirror forms [referring to R. I, RI used by Schoenberg in his Op. 31 *Variations for Orchestra*] was a commonplace among the masters of the polyphonic age of music; in J. S. Bach's last works, the *Art of the Fugue* and the *Musical Offering,* they often determine the entire musical development, and Beethoven also used them in his last creative period.[16]

OF BORDERS, BICYCLES, AND INSIGHT

There is a homely yet piquant story that neatly ties together Wittgenstein's warning at the beginning of this volume, that truly fundamental things are often the hardest to recognize, and this pervasive exclusivity that Western theory has bestowed on pitch (or pitch-class) content. It is about a small boy who arrives at the U.S.–Mexico border pushing a bicycle. A filled bag rests in the basket attached to his bike's handlebars. Instantly suspicious, the customs guard demands:

"So what's in the bag?"

"Sand."

"C'mon now boy. Whatcha got in there?"

"Nothin' but sand, Sir. Honest."

Whereupon the cockily impatient guard grabs the bag, methodically pouring a load of sand onto the tarmac. Embarrassed but temporarily bested, he motions boy and bicycle ahead, to pass the checkpoint.

The same incident, with minor variants, recurs several times in subsequent weeks, a bag of sand providing the leitmotif of continuing mystery. The persistent guard's suspicions and curiosity mount with each encounter. And at last, having emptied the most recent bag of sand, he is reduced to primal exasperation, shouting:

"For God's sake, boy! What *are* you smuggling?"

To which the overwhelmed child replies: "Bicycles, sir."

Music theory has kept its figurative head in the sand of pitch through its recent history, ignoring all the while that no reckoning of musical content, regardless of how ravishingly precise and how elegantly expressed, can ever account for music's structure so long as it treats of pitch as a web of disembodied tone, especially as sound elements that are without the boundaries of time. Pitch is incapable, in and of itself, of creating structure.

CONCEPTS VERSUS PERCEPTS: A POST-SCHOENBERG CONCERN

Discussions of how one might rationalize putting this note with that note can certainly be worthwhile, especially for novice composers. No danger need be imminent so long as participants in the dialogue remind themselves that they run the risk of talking about the fabrication of hypothesized structures rather than about the reality of audible structures, about presences which although indisputably existent are arguably relevant. It was an awareness of this risk that led Edward T. Cone to observe that Schoenberg might as well have composed his *Fantasy* Opus 47 as the mirror inversion of the original, so far as one analyst's painstaking demonstration of its continuity was concerned. In such descriptions, backwards and upside down works as well as their obverse.[17] And perhaps there was an even more disturbing possibility to acknowledge: Was it not possible that such perceptually empty talk could be a party to the fabrication of perceptually unconnected music?

Fears of just this pitfall did cross the minds of some of the principals of Serialism during those loquacious days. Thus Henri Posseur finds in Boulez's *Structures* (1952) passages describable as Brownian Movements, which in this case refers to "movements lacking (from the observer's viewpoint) in all individual signification and therefore offering a high degree of resistance to unified overall apprehension and to distinct memorization." And to press home his point Posseur reminds us that statements made by Boulez himself, around the same time, confirm his conclusion: some compositional means can produce apparently unfruitful results, "a sort of non-measurable asymmetry implying their own imperceptibility."[18]

From another side of the intellectual fence, wise musician-physicist John Backus, not one entranced by pseudo-scientific prattle or empty compositional strategies, concluded that the "composition by numerology" processes invoked by Boulez in the same *Structures* might nonetheless spark the beginning of a veritable golden-egging goose. His reaction (within the context of exposing the pretensions of the journal *Die Reihe*) included a happy prospect. Minimal investments could yield maximum profits: "By using different numerical rules—using a knight's moves, for example, rather than a bishop's move along the diagonals—music for centuries to come could be produced."[19]

And Peter Westergaard found perplexing anomalies between apparent intent and apprehendable product in Babbitt's *Composition for Twelve Instruments* (1958). He was unable to discover how some of the composer's scrupulously invested pitch-rhythm orderings might yield perceptual dividends. Although numerous passages harbor cunning pitch-rhythm complementations, not all are potentially perceptible as such (and thus seem not to warrant incorporation). About one particular set of complementations Westergaard demurs, in the end, with the frank conclusion that "I see no way for the ear to perceive either order or content."[20]

These were rare and disarmingly candid (and at the time too-lamely acknowledged) insights into a reality tucked beneath a vast numerological security blanket. An intimidating system of note orderings obscured the perceptual vacuousness of the musical body. One can only wonder Who really cared what it actually sounded like?

Who actually cared who listened (as Babbitt once asked), so long as it could produce reams of publishable analytical comment? To reread today some of these daunting chronicles of set permutations is to be reminded of the sly impudence of Bertrand Russell's remark that mathematics is the subject in which we never know *what* we are talking about.

Edward T. Cone early played wise cynic in frequent inward probings of his own, especially in weighing the concept/percept equation. He has consistently shown special sensitivity for how some musical matters seem to defy certain analytical demonstration. In a paper first delivered in 1967 he expressed the fear that disregard for these non-analytical values led some scholars to write "not about actual compositions, but about abstractions derived from composition."[21]

Some dozen years after Cone wrote, it was clear that an astonishing part of the rich corpus of analytical guides to set-analytic potentials could deteriorate into much ado about nothing musical,[22] in spite of the daunting language and awesome symbolism in which it was couched. Wary (and perhaps weary as well) of the uncontested assumptions that plagued such work, a few writers followed Cone in urging analytical realism, begging caution in reconciling concepts with percepts. In this spirit in 1974 William Benjamin could regret that

> Analysts have sometimes assumed that any relation which holds among the simple, abstract, entities named in the theory, that is, among pitch-class sets, can be said to hold among the actual entities which represent these abstractions in those contexts.[23]

The roots of this concept-percept tension are manifestly traceable to Schoenberg's controlling assumptions and even to some aspects of his compositional habits. For instance, the insecure perceptual basis of his "solution" can be detected in the way he perpetuates the mythic symmetry of tonality by exploitation of inversional sets.[24] In this he derives abstraction from pure myth: the very idea of dominant and subdominant as "upper" and "lower" balances for tonic was itself a hapless fiction motivated by conceptual ambition rather than perception. One can only marvel that such an idea persists, when the duplicative nature of the pitch spectrum, by octaves, renders meaningless the "higher" and "lower" or "above" and "below" designations of tonal degrees.[25] But the idea of systemic symmetry was nonetheless entrenched in nineteenth-century music theory (another gift from Rameau) as a background assumption, even after the undertone series evaporated as an experiential datum.

THE MUSICAL META-WORLD

It is informative and appropriate that one of the emergent buzzwords of the post-war period was *meta-* (as in *meta-language, meta-theory,* and even *academic meta-novel*). Today we can appreciate the ironic propriety of this prefix's gradual absorption, never widespread, into the burgeoning vocabulary of music theory.[26] When used in the sense of "beyond" or "transcending," it revealed a grave ontological flaw: perhaps what was talked about transcended music entirely. Just as medieval questions of angel populations on pinheads transcended the observable data of vision, so the mid-twentieth-century tapestries of set permutations exceeded the data of aural perception. At their worst they were mere tiptoeings through the tautologies of set theory, modulus 12. On occasion the naive incredulous child of Hans Christian Anderson's parable would have been wholly in order to tell the new suit of clothes: "There is no Emperor!"

And this was what became of Schoenberg's profound tamperings with music's basis. If tonality was a mere way-station on the road to non-hierarchical chromaticism, perhaps all other paradigms of tonal order (except that persistent old octave, whose primacy the *method* could not ignore) are equally ephemeral. If pitch defers to meaningful structuring on terms independent of habits of audition, then why not any and all other discriminable musical properties as well? So Schoenberg's lifelong struggle to sustain what he confidently thought was the predestined child of evolution led with impeccable logic to full syntactic breakdown. It led ultimately to numerically posed propositions whose pertinence to music is no more defensible than the ritual of bullfighting is to agriculture.

SUPER-RATIONALISM MEETS DADA: THE ODD COUPLE

It was at this point that the super-rationalism of the Schoenberg-Webern-Boulez-Babbitt wing of the art began its unanticipated flirtation with the whimsically-mystical Tzara-Cocteau-Satie-Cage stream of Dada. It sometimes appeared, during the decade of the 1960s, that products of the one—enormously complex in concept and execution—resembled the other, whose principal measure was a cool "Let happen what happens!" But this was illusory, only superficially true. The elaborate machinery of Total Serialism did not actually spawn the same kinds of sound structures as free improvisation (whatever that may mean for skilled performers) or by collections of "random sounds" or by rigorously controlled throws of *I Ching* dice.

Both products share a lack of concern for (and thus attention to) predictable audible structure.[27] For both musics a sense of structure becomes largely dependent on the listener's will to image part-whole relationships, since composed hierarchy is byproduct rather than goal. The predictable structural void each commonly achieves (Was this the structural silence Posseur found in Boulez's *Structures?*) nonetheless was sufficient cause for the popular generalization that the two therefore "sound alike."[28] (Which is a bit like saying that the rainbow stain of oil on my garage floor and the first page of my income tax return look alike because they both lack linear perspective.) It is important to remember that statements made about one compositional approach were frequently as apt for the other. Although speaking of composers of experimental music like himself, John Cage's explanations of the desire to achieve separation from the act of choice, from direct responsibility for the heard product, are often revealing of some motivations of Serialism, especially the total Serialism championed for a brief period by Boulez and Babbitt. As Cage puts it, his colleagues "find ways to remove themselves from the activities of the sounds they make."[29] Analogously, confederates of analytical formalism allow musical explanations to apply exclusively to materials and processes, without responsibility to reflect audible hierarchical structures in time.

THE REIFICATION OF SONIC NOTHINGNESS

From another perspective, explanations like those of Rogers and Babbitt are fully accurate and appropriate, achieving respectable verisimilitude with the objects of their concern. Perhaps the truth is that what they describe is in fact what we might call *Urgrundgestaltmusik,* music for which there is no message-bearing surface, no *Vordergrund* for auditory contemplation. Perhaps it is music whose aesthetic import is consciously and necessarily concealed in deeper machinations, in the kinds of concealed ties Schoenberg valued so highly. If this perspective is reasonable, then Babbitt rightly describes his *Relata I* as the whirlings and spewings and gyrations of conceptual phantoms, the combinatorial hexachords and inversionally transposed and segmented pitch class sets of Serialism, whose audible surface is that of perceptual stasis. The action lies in deeper recesses of structure, not where we seek it because we found it there in Palestrina and Mozart. And those who fail to recognize and yield to those concealed truths simply lack the skills of the adequately prepared.

The examples of analytical formalism we have sampled revived, through their extraordinary derivations from Schoenberg, the disarming fiction that is *Musica Mundana.* The explications from this analytical annex describe meta-music, music whose sound, as Boethius taught us, "does not reach our ears." It is music of an icy purity reverberating in a Pythagorean heaven, a music that can afford to be perfect because it disdains the time-bound stuff of *Musica Instrumentalis,* to which we mortals move.

BARING SOME ROOTS TO RESOLVE A PARADOX

This fresh perspective can also resolve a perplexing paradox. It has to do with the apparent inherent contradiction of an academic mix, that of dodecaphonic super-rationalism living harmoniously in the same houses with Schenkerian prescriptives. As can now be seen, it turns out that they do, deep down, possess heretofore unrecognized bonds, affinities strong enough to justify cohabitation if not marriage. Although the stuffings of their *Urlinien* and *Bassbrechungs* are different, they grow from the same soil of hidden interior structures. They both depend upon *Ur* sets—one the twelve-note row, the other the harmonic triad—for their being. And each (the row in one, the triad in the other) preempts the analytical stage, in thus flaunting control over the musical object itself. Music and justifying theory both derive from a radical preoccupation with background. Their main difference is that the music/analytic essays of Serialism pay scant attention to levels of structure closer to the perceptual interception; for them the *Background* of Schenkerian reductionism has become the solitary musical stratum, Foreground, Middleground, and Background rolled into one.

Schoenberg's goal to boost music's evolutionary progress to a still higher plateau led to this. His will to ensure what he believed to be a Germanic domination that began with J. S. Bach, and his obsession to free music of its expendable trappings (thereby attaining the purity of expression Kraus and Loos had taught him to admire) led to the most elemental rent in history of any art's fabric. The separation, begun in the twentieth century and intensified by the excesses of Serialism's heady era, widens even today. It is an unbridged chasm that divides people within the practice, the commerce, and the pedagogy of the art.[30]

Unlike the notable disputes of the eighteenth century, the Rameau-Rousseau *guerre des bouffons* or its Gluck-Piccini *querelle célèbre* sequel, the division initiated by Serialism was motivated by more than petty national tastes or linguistic conventions. Unlike the Brahms-Wagner "War" precipitated in the nineteenth century by Hanslick, it is more than a dispute over stylistic territories or aesthetic abstractions. This still-festering standoff, now some eighty years old, puts the musical substance itself on the line. It forces us to decide whether music is even answerable to perceptual hierarchies, whether its kinetics require that small sound events cohere in ways that create experientially larger sound events, whether, indeed, the ultimate description of music is not wholly circumscribed by the ultimate of solipsistic utterance: "There are sounds."

Notes

1. Transmission to a broader public seemed inevitable, however, when Boulez in 1969 became principal guest conductor of the Cleveland Orchestra, later (1971) to replace Bernstein as Music Director of the New York Philharmonic. But the Boulez-Gotham conjunction did not produce the expected bumper crop of serial music concerts.

2. This unprecedented epiphany of dodecaphonic theorist-composers coincided in time (and matched in volubility) the enshrinement in the visual arts of what Tom Wolfe called in 1975 the period of "the painted word," when, as he says, "art theory became an essential accompaniment to the art work" (*The Painted Word*, 37).

3. In this it was antithetical to Schoenberg's own warning, made in a letter to Rudolf Kolisch of July 27 1932, that one must never be concerned for "how it is done," but rather for "what it is."

4. Rogers, "Some Properties of Non-Duplicating Rotational Arrays," 98–99.

5. Babbitt, "On *Relata I*," 2.

6. Ibid., 15.

7. We must not forget the doubtful status assigned by empirical research into perception on such complex pitch orderings (even when registrally and rhythmically defined). See earlier, 84.

8. Babbitt, "On *Relata I*," 17.

9. Boretz, "Sketch of a Musical Syntax (Meta-Variations II)," 61. The internal page reference is to Nelson Goodman's *The Structure of Appearance*. Note well that "Sounds" and "Music" in this context refer to non-realized, conceptual things rather than to audible ones, so they must be confined to the meta-world of quotation marks. They are what as children we called "play-like."

10. Ernst Krenek, "Some Current Terms," in response to Milton Babbitt's "Twelve-Tone Invariants as Compositional Determinants." The object of Krenek's remarks is eminently comprehensible although relentlessly abstract.

11. *Analytical Formalism* is Leonard B. Meyer's coinage.

12. Charles Rosen, *Arnold Schoenberg*, 96.

13. This is not to overlook Hauptmann's unique discussions in *Harmony und Metrik,* which manage to complete his dialectical excursion but do not shed much light on the nature of rhythm (or meter).

14. Composer Mel Powell reflects both when he repeats a popular post-Schoenbergian metaphor: "I subscribe," Powell asserts, "to atonality because it's egalitarian. It cancels hierarchy and creates anarchy, the ideal musical state." *Los Angeles Times,* April 14, 1990.

15. Babbitt, "On *Relata I*," 8.

16. Rufer, *Composition with Twelve Tones,* 82.

17. Cone, "Beyond Analysis," 74. He is referring to Forte's *Contemporary Tone Structures,* 110–127.

18. P. 102. Posseur concludes, nonetheless, that these conditions are not fatally damaging to the essence of Boulez's piece, that the composer's *true* intention was to manifest the essential irreversibility of time, to negate all periodicity (which, come to think of it, seem like strange things for composers to be up to). It was Boulez's way, Posseur suggests, "of removing music from the out-of-date rhetoric" that remained from the music of Schoenberg and Webern. He imputes to the musical product what is perhaps the most provocative unintentional (?) insult ever hurled at a composition, saying (103) that *Structures* achieves a "truly structural silence." Or perhaps *silence* here is analogous to the *flatness* so rhapsodically touted by art critics Clement Greenberg and Harold Rosenberg, during the 1960s, as the essential element of abstract expressionist painting. Or, it may also have been what Stravinsky-Craft meant (*Dialogues and a Diary,* 128) in referring to Boulez's *Structures* as "the essence of static."

19. John Backus, "*Die Reihe:* A Scientific Evaluation," 170.

20. Peter Westergaard, "Some Problems Raised by the Rhythmic Procedures in Milton Babbitt's *Composition for Twelve Instruments,*" 118.

21. Edward T. Cone, "Beyond Analysis," 90.

22. For gentler suggestions of about the same conclusion see Meyer, *Music, the Arts and Ideas;* Lerdahl and Jackendoff, *A Generative Theory of Music;* and Serafine, *Music as Cognition.*

23. William E. Benjamin, "Ideas of Order in Motivic Music," 24.

24. This practice is brilliantly documented by Lewin, "Inversional Balance as an Organizing Force in Schoenberg's Music and Thought," who more readily accepts the conceptual/perceptual role granted the subdominant by tradition than I find reasonable.

25. For compelling empirical confirmation that the dominant/subdominant balance of power originated in pure myth, see Brown, "The Interplay of Set Content and Temporal Context in a Functional Theory of Tonality Perception," 229–230, who concludes that there is a "vast difference between primary scale degrees four and five, in spite of the fact . . . that the tones as well as the chords built upon them are considered to have an equivalent relationship to the tonic in structural models of tonal relationships."

26. A definitive exposition of the meta-principle is Benjamin Boretz's dissertation (Princeton). Extended excerpts appear in volumes of *Perspectives of New Music* through 1972.

27. Leonard B. Meyer arrived at *anti-teleological* to represent the byproduct, in his classic essay "The End of the Renaissance."

28. Leo Treitler questioned this tenuous view as early as 1965 ("Musical Syntax in the Middle

Ages," 76) and it figures even earlier as a recurring concern of Meyer ("End of the Renaissance," for example). I do agree with George Rochberg, nonetheless, that the *aesthetic product* of random and totally serialized compositions at times might sound similar, especially when performers well-versed in the latter are the improvisers creating the former.

29. In *Silence*, 10.

30. As Samuel Lipman remarks ("Music and Musical Life: The Road to Now," 29), the era of concocting (on whatever basis) sounds "which impressed only their inventors as music is an era which would now seem past in every way, were it not for the damage it did and continues to do) in the academy." Very few young composers (under 35) compose serial music today. It is as déclassé now as it was chic in 1970. The atonal-dodecaphonic-serial movement lives on today mainly in the theses and dissertations of second- and third-generation serial music scholars and composers.

BIBLIOGRAPHY

Adorno, Theodor W. *Philosophy of Modern Music*. Trans. Anne G. Mitchell and
    Wesley V. Blomster. New York, 1973.
Aldrich, Putnam. "An Approach to the Analysis of Renaissance Music," *Music
    Review* 30 (1969): 1–21.
Allport, Floyd H. *Theories of Perception and the Concept of Structure*. New York,
    1955.
Anderson, Warren. *Ethos and Education in Greek Music*. Cambridge, 1966.
Appollonio, Umbrio, ed. *Futurist Manifestos*. Trans. Robert Brain et al. New York,
    1973.
Aristotle. *Problems*. Trans. W. S. Hett. Cambridge, 1924.
———. *The Basic Works of Aristotle*. Ed. Richard McKeon. New York, 1941.
Augustine. *De Musica Libri Sex*. Trans. R. Catesby-Taliaferro. Annapolis, Md.,
    1936.
Austin, William. *Music in the Twentieth Century*. New York, 1966.
Averbach, E. and Coriell, A. S. "Short Term Memory in Vision." *Bell System
    Technical Journal* 40 (1961): 309–328.
Babbitt, Milton. "On *Relata I*. " *Perspectives of New Music* 9 (1970): 1–22.
———. "Since Schoenberg." *Perspectives of New Music* 12 (1973): 3–28.
———. "Some Aspects of Twelve-Tone Composition." *The Score* 12 (1955): 53–
    62.
———. "The Structure and Function of Music Theory." In *Perspectives on Contem-
    porary Music Theory,* ed. Benjamin Boretz and Edward T. Cone. New York,
    1972.
———. "Twelve-Tone Invariants as Compositional Determinants." In *Problems of
    Modern Music,* ed. Paul Henry Lang. New York, 1960.
———. "Who Cares If You Listen?" *High Fidelity Magazine* 8.2 (1958): 38–40.
Bachem, A. "Note on Neu's Review of the Literature on Absolute Pitch." *Psycholog-
    ical Bulletin* 45 (1948): 161–162.

————. "Time Factors in Relative and Absolute Pitch Determination." *Journal of the Acoustical Society of America* 26 (1954): 751–753.

Backus, John. "*Die Reihe:* A Scientific Evaluation." *Perspectives of New Music* 1 (1962): 160–171.

Bailey, Walter. *Programmatic Elements in the Works of Schoenberg.* Ann Arbor, Mich., 1984.

Baird, J. W. "Memory for Absolute Pitch." In *Studies in Psychology, Titchener Commemorative Volume.* Worcester, 1917.

Barbera, André. "Octave Species." *Journal of Musicology* 3 (1984): 221–228.

Barzun, Jacques. *Darwin, Marx, Wagner.* Boston, 1941.

Bassart, Anne. *Serial Music: A Classified Bibliography of Writings on Twelve-Tone and Electronic Music.* Berkeley, Ca., 1961.

Beardslee, David C. and Wertheimer, Michael, eds. *Readings in Perception.* Princeton, N.J., 1958.

Benjamin, Walter. *Reflections.* Trans. Edmund Jephcott, ed. Peter Demetz. New York, 1978. ·

Benjamin, William E. "Ideas of Order in Motivic Music." *Music Theory Spectrum* 1 (1979): 23–34.

Bentley, Eric, ed. *Shaw on Music.* New York, 1955.

Bergland, Richard. *The Fabric of Mind.* New York, 1985.

Bernstein, Leonard. *The Unanswered Question.* Cambridge, 1976.

Berry, Wallace. *Structural Functions in Music.* Englewood Cliffs, N.J., 1976.

Bessler, Heinrich. *Bourdon und Fauxbourdon.* Leipzig, 1950.

Bingham, W. Van Dyke. "Studies in Melody." *Psychological Review Monograph* 12 (1910): 1–88.

Blackwood, Easley. *The Structure of Recognizable Diatonic Tunings.* Princeton, N.J., 1986.

Boethius, Anicus Manlius. *Fundamentals of Music.* Trans. Calvin Bower (*De Institutione Musica*). New Haven, Conn., 1989.

Boomsliter, P. and Creel, W. "The Long Pattern Hypothesis in Harmony and Hearing." *Journal of Music Theory* 5 (1961): 2–31.

Boretz, Benjamin. "The Construction of Musical Syntax (I)." *Perspectives of New Music* 9 (1970): 23–42.

————. "Sketch of a Musical System (Meta-Variations, Part II)." *Perspectives of New Music* 8 (1970): 49–111. Additional installments from this Princeton dissertation appear in issues of the same journal through 1972.

Boretz, Benjamin, and Cone, Edward T. *Perspectives on Contemporary Music Theory.* New York, 1972.

Bosanquet, R. H. M. *An Elementary Treatise on Musical Intervals and Temperament* (1876).

Bose, Fritz. "Der Musik der Uitito." *Zeitschrift für vergleichende Musik wissenschaft* II. Musical Supplement (1934): 1–40.

Bower, Calvin. "The Modes of Boethius." *Journal of Musicology* 3 (1984): 252–263.

Bowers, Faubion. *The New Scriabin*. London, 1974.

Brown, Helen. "The Interplay of Set Content and Temporal Context in a Functional Theory of Tonality Perception." *Music Perception* 5 (1988): 219–250.

Brown, Helen and Butler, D. "Diatonic Trichords as Minimal Tonal Cue-Cells." *In Theory Only* 5 (1981): 39–55.

Bruckner, Anton. *Vorlesungen über Harmonie und Kontrapunkt an der Universitat Wien*. Ed. Ernst Schwangara. Vienna, 1950.

Bruner, Jerome. "Going Beyond the Information Given." *Contemporary Approaches to Cognition: A Symposium Held at the University of Colorado*. Cambridge, 1957.

———. *On Knowing*. Cambridge, 1964.

———. "On Perceptual Readiness." *Psychological Review* 64 (1957): 123–152.

Bruner, Jerome and Minturn, A. L. "Perceptual Identification and Perceptual Organization." *Journal of General Psychology* 53 (1955): 21–28.

Brunswick, Mark. "Tonality and Perspective." *The Musical Quarterly* 29 (1943): 226–258.

Bukofzer, Manfred. *Music in the Baroque Era*. New York, 1947.

Burns, E. M. and Ward, W. D. "Categorical Perception—Phenomenon or Epiphenomenon: Evidence From the Perception of Melodic Intervals." *Journal of the Acoustical Society of America* 63 (1978): 456–468.

Busoni, Ferruccio. "Sketches of a New Aesthetic of Music." Trans. Theodore Baker. In *Three Classics in the Aesthetics of Music*. New York, 1962.

Butler, David. "Describing the Perception of Tonality in Music: A Critique of the Tonal Hierarchy Theory and a Proposal for a Theory of Intervallic Rivalry." *Music Perception* 6 (1989): 219–242.

———. "Response to Carol Krumhansl." *Music Perception* 7 (1990): 325–338.

Cage, John. *Silence*. Middletown, Conn., 1961.

Carterette, E. C. and Friedman, M. P., eds. *Handbook of Perception* IX. New York, 1978.

Castellano, M. A., Bharucha, J., and Krumhansl, C. L. "Tonal Hierarchies in the Music of North India." *Journal of Experimental Psychology: General 113* (1984): 394–412.

Chailly, Jacques. "Le Mythe des modes grecs." *Acta Musicologica* 28 (1956): 137–163.

Clarke, Eric F. and Krumhansl, Carol. "Perceiving Musical Time." *Music Perception* 7 (1990): 213–252.

Cohen, Morris A. *A Preface to Logic*. New York, 1944.

Cone, Edward T. "A Budding Grove." *Perspectives of New Music* 4 (1965): 38–46.

Cook, Nicholas. "The Perception of Large-Scale Tonal Closure." *Music Perception* 5 (1987): 107–206.

Crocker, Richard. "Discant, Counterpoint, and Harmony." *Journal of the American Musicological Society* 15 (1962): 1–21.

Dahlhaus, Carl. *Richard Wagner's Music Dramas*. Trans. Mary Whittal. London, 1979.

————. *Schoenberg and the New Music*. Trans. Derrick Puffett and Alfred Clayton. London, 1987.

————. "Tonality." In *The New Grove Dictionary of Music and Musicians,* ed. Stanley Sadie, 15. London, 1980.

————. *Untersusuchungen über die Enstehung der Harmonischen Tonalität*. Kassel, 1968.

Danielou, A. *The Rāgas of Northern Indian Music*. London, 1968.

Del Mar, Norman. *Richard Strauss,* I. New York, 1962.

Descartes, René. *Compendium of Music*. Trans. Walter Robert. Rome, 1961.

Deutsch, Diana. "Delayed Pitch Comparisons and the Principle of Proximity." *Perception and Psychophysics* 23 (1978): 227–230.

————. "Facilitation and Repetition in Recognition Memory for Pitch." *Memory and Cognition* 3 (1975): 263–266.

————. "The Octave Illusion and the What-Where Connection." In *Attention and Performance* VIII, ed. R. Milkench. Hillsdale, N.J., 1980.

————. "The Processing of Structured and Unstructured Tonal Sequences." *Perception and Psychophysics* 28 (1980): 381–389.

————. "Two Issues Concerning Tonal Hierarchies: Comments on Castellano, Bharucha, and Krumhansl." *Journal of Experimental Psychology: General 113* (1984): 413–416.

————, ed., The *Psychology of Music*. London, 1982.

Deutsch, Diana and Boulanger, Richard. "Octave Equivalence and the Immediate Recall of Pitch Sequences." *Music Perception* 2 (1984): 40–51.

Deutsch, Diana, Kuyper, William L., and Fisher, Yuval. "The Tritone Paradox: Its Presence and Form of Distribution in General Population." *Music Perception* 5 (1987): 72–92.

Dickenson, George. "A Comparison of the Impulses at Work in the Rise and Decline of Tonality." *MTNA Bulletin* 17 (1920): 20–30.

Dill, Heinz J. "Schoenberg's George-Lieder: The Relationship Between the Text and the Music in Light of Some Expressionist Tendencies." *Current Musicology* 17 (1974): 91–95.

Dowling, W. J. "Assimilation and Tonal Structure: Comments on Castellano, Bharuca, and Krumhansl." *Journal of Experimental Psychology* 113 (1984): 417–420.

————. "Melodic Information Processing and Its Development." In *The Psychology of Music,* ed. Diana Deutsch. London, 1982.

————. "Recognition of Inversions of Melodies and Melodic Contours." *Perception and Psychophysics* 9 (1971): 348–349.

————. "Recognition of Melodic Transformations: Inversion, Retrograde and Retrograde-Inversion." *Perception and Psychophysics* 12 (1972): 417–421.

————. "Scale and Contour: Two Components of a Theory of Memory for Melodies." *Psychological Review* 85 (1978): 341–354.

Dowling, W. J. and Bartlett, J. C. "The Importance of Interval Information in Long Term Memory for Melodies." *Psychomusicology* 1 (1981): 30–49.

Dowling, W. J. and Fujitani, D. S. "Contour, Interval, and Pitch Recognition in Memory for Melodies." *Journal of the Acoustical Society of America* 49 (1971): 524–531.

Dunsby, Jonathan. "Schoenberg and the Writings of Schenker." *Journal of the Arnold Schoenberg Institute* 2 (1977): 26–33.

Erickson, Robert. "New Music and Psychology." In *The Psychology of Music,* ed. Diana Deutsch. London, 1982.

Eschmann, Carl. *Changing Forms in Modern Music.* Boston, 1945.

Forte, Allen. *Contemporary Tone Structures.* New York, 1955.

———. "The Magical Kaleidoscope: Schoenberg's First Atonal Masterwork, Opus 11, No. 1." *Journal of the Arnold Schoenberg Institute* 5 (1981): 127–168.

———. "Schoenberg's Creative Evolution: The Path to Atonality." *The Musical Quarterly* 64 (1978): 133–176.

———. "Sets and Non-Sets in Schoenberg's Atonal Music." *Perspectives of New Music* 11 (1972): 43–64.

———. *The Structure of Atonal Music.* New Haven, Conn., 1973.

Francès, Robert. *"Recherches expérimentales sur le perception des structures musicales." Journal de Psychologie* 45 (1954): 78–96.

———. *The Perception of Music.* Trans. W. Jay Dowling. Hillsdale, N.J., 1988.

Freitag, Eberhard. "German Expressionism and Schoenberg's Self-Portraits." *Journal of the Arnold Schoenberg Institute* 2 (1978): 164–172.

Friedheim, Philip. "Rhythmic Structure in Schoenberg's Atonal Compositions." *Journal of the American Musicological Society* 19 (1966): 59–72.

Friedrich, Otto. *Before the Deluge.* New York, 1972.

———. *Glenn Gould.* New York, 1989.

Gass, William H. "Vicissitudes of the Avant-Garde." *Harper's Magazine,* October, 1988: 64–70.

Gerhard, Roberto. "Tonality in Twelve-Tone Music." *Score* 6 (1952): 23–25.

Gleason, Harold and Becker, Warren, eds. *Examples of Music Before 1400.* Bloomington, Ind., 1984.

Gould, Glenn. *The Glenn Gould Reader.* Ed. Tim Page. New York, 1984.

Greeno, J. G. and Senior, H. A. "Processes for Sequence Production." *Psychological Review* 81 (1972): 187–196.

Gregory, R. L. "Choosing a Paradigm for Perception." In *Handbook of Perception* I, ed. Carterrette and Friedman. New York, 1974.

Grout, Donald. *A History of Music in Western Civilization* (short edition). New York, 1964.

Guilford, J. P. and Hilton, R. A. "Some Configurational Properties of Short Musical Melodies." *Journal of Experimental Psychology* 16 (1933): 32–54.

Hall, Donald and Hess, Joan Taylor. "Perception of Music Interval Tuning." *Music Perception* 2 (1984): 166–195.

Hall, Joseph W., III and Peters, Robert W. "Pitch for Nonsimultaneous Successive Harmonies in Quiet and Noise," *Journal of the Acoustical Society of America* 69 (1981): 509–513.

Hamao, Fusako. *The Origins and Development of Schoenberg's Twelve-Tone Method.* Yale University Ph.D. dissertation, 1988.

Harvey, Dixie Lynn. *The Theoretical Treatises of Josef Hauer.* University of North Texas Ph.D. dissertation, 1980.

Hauptman, Moritz. *Die Natur der Harmonik und Metrik.* Berlin, 1853.

Headington, Christopher. *History of Western Music.* New York, 1976.

Helmholtz, Hermann. *On the Sensations of Tone* (1863). Trans. Alexander Ellis. New York, 1954.

Hibberd, Lloyd. "Tonality and Related Problems in Terminology." *The Music Review* 22 (1961): 13–20.

Hindemith, Paul. *The Craft of Musical Composition,* I. Trans. Arthur Mendl. New York, 1942.

———. "Methods of Music Theory." Trans. Arthur Mendl. *The Musical Quarterly* 30 (1944): 20–28.

Hochberg, J. "Organization and the Gestalt Tradition." In *Handbook of Perception* I, ed. Carterette and Friedman. New York, 1974.

Hopkins, G. W. "Schoenberg and the Logic of Atonality." *Tempo* 94 (1970): 15.

Hoppin, Richard. *Medieval Music.* New York, 1978.

Hornbostel, Erich von. "African Negro Music." *Africa* 1 (1928): 30–62.

Humphreys, L. F. "Generalization as a Function of Method of Reinforcement." *Journal of Experimental Psychology* 25 (1939): 361–372.

Hutchison, W. and Knopoff, L. "The Acoustical Component of Western Consonance." *Interface* 7 (1978): 1–29.

Hyde, Martha M. "Musical Form and the Development of Schoenberg's Twelve-Tone Method." *Journal of Music Theory* 29 (1985): 85–143.

Ives, Charles. *Essays Before a Sonata.* Ed. Howard Boatwright. New York, 1961.

Jackendoff, Ray and Lerdahl, Fred. *A Deep Parallel Between Music and Language.* Bloomington, Ind., 1980.

Jairazbhoy, N. A. "Factors Underlying Important Notes in North Indian Music." *Ethnomusicology* 16 (1972): 63–81.

Janik, Allan and Toulmin, Stephen. *Wittgenstein's Vienna.* New York, 1973.

John, Nicholas, ed. *Tristan und Isolde* (English National Opera Guide No. 6). London, 1986.

Johnson, Mark. *The Body in the Mind.* Chicago, 1987.

Johnson, S. C. "Hierarchical Clustering Schemes." *Psychometrika* 32 (1967): 241–254.

Jones, M. R. "Dynamic Pattern Structure in Music: Recent Theory and Research." *Perception and Psychophysics* 41 (1987): 621–634.

Karlen, Arno. *Napoleon's Glands.* New York, 1984.

Kaufmann, Walter. *The Rāgas of North India.* Bloomington, Ind., 1968.

Keller, Hans. "Response to Tischler on Mahler." *Music Survey* 4 (1952): 433–434.

Kerman, Joseph. *Contemplating Music.* Cambridge, 1985.

Kessler, Edward J., Hansen, Christa, and Shepherd, Roger N. "Tonal Schemata in the Perception of Music in Bali and in the West." *Music Perception* 2 (1984): 131–165.

Koestler, Arthur. *The Sleepwalkers*. New York, 1959.

Koffka, Kurt. *Principles of Gestalt Psychology*. New York, 1940.

Kohler, Wolfgang. *Dynamics in Psychology*. New York, 1947.

———. *Gestalt Psychology*. New York, 1947.

———. "Relational Determination in Perception." In *Cerebral Mechanisms in Behavior,* ed. L. A. Jeffries. New York, 1951.

Kramer, Jonathan D. "Studies in Time and Music: A Bibliography." *Music Theory Spectrum* 7 (1985): 72–106.

Krenek, Ernst. *Music Here and Now*. New York, 1940.

———. "Schoenberg the Centenarian," trans. Paul Pisk. *Journal of the Arnold Schoenberg Institute* 1 (1977): 87–91.

———. "Some Current Terms." *Perspectives of New Music* 4 (1966): 81–84.

Krumhansl, Carol L. "Acquisition of the Hierarchy of Tonal Functions in Music." *Memory and Cognition* 10 (1982): 243–251.

———. "Perceptual Structures for Tonal Music." *Music Perception* 1 (1983): 28–62.

———. "The Psychological Representation of Musical Pitch in a Tonal Context." *Cognitive Psychology* 11 (1979): 346–374.

———. "Tonal Hierarchies and Rare Intervals in Music Cognition." *Music Perception* 7 (1990): 309–324.

Krumhansl, Carol L. and Castellano, M. A. "Dynamic Processes in Music Perception." *Memory and Cognition* 11 (1983): 325–334.

Krumhansl, Carol L. and Kessler, E. J. "Tracing the Dynamic Changes in Perceived Tonal Organization in a Spatial Representation of Musical Keys." *Psychological Review* 89 (1982): 334–368.

Krumhansl, Carol L., Sandell, Gregory J., and Sargeant, Desmond C. "The Perception of Tone Hierarchies and Mirror Forms in Twelve-Tone Serial Music." *Music Perception* 5 (1987): 31–78.

Krumhansl, Carol L. and Shepherd, R. N. "Quantification of the Hierarchy of Tonal Functions Within a Diatonic Context." *Journal of Experimental Psychology: Human Perception and Performance* 5 (1979): 579–594.

Kurth, Ernst. *Romantische Harmonik und ihre Krise in Wagners "Tristan."* Berlin, 1923.

Lath, Makund. *A Study of "Dattilam": A Treatise on the Sacred Music of Ancient India*. New Delhi, 1978.

Leewenberg, E. L. "A Perceptual Coding Language for Visual and Auditory Patterns." *American Journal of Psychology* 84 (1971): 307–349.

Lefebvre, Vladimir A. "The Fundamental Structures of Human Reflexion." *Journal of Social and Biological Structures* 10 (1987): 129–175.

Leibowitz, René. *Schoenberg and His School*. Trans. Dika Newlin. New York, 1947.

Levin, Flora. *The Harmonics of Nichomachus and the Pythagorean Tradition*. University Park, Pa., 1975.

Lenneberg, Eric H. "Language, Evolution, and Purposive Behavior in Cultural History." In *Essays in Honor of Paul Radin*, ed. S. Diamond. New York, 1960.

Lerdahl, Fred and Jackendoff, Ray. *A Generative Theory of Tonal Music*. Cambridge, 1983.

Lewin, David. "Inversional Balance as an Organizing Force in Schoenberg's Music and Thought." *Perspectives of New Music* 6 (1968): 1–21.

Lipman, Samuel. "Music and Musical Life: The Road to Now." *The New Criterion*, special issue, 1985: 23–37.

List, Kurt. "Schoenberg and Strauss." *Kenyon Review* 7 (1945): 52–58.

Lowensky, Edward. *Tonality and Atonality in Sixteenth-Century Music*. Berkeley, Ca., 1961.

MacDonald, Malcolm. *Schoenberg*. London, 1976.

Maegaard, Jan. *Studien zur Entwicklung des Dodekaphonen Satzes bei Arnold Schoenberg*. Copenhagen, 1972.

Malm, William P. *Music Cultures of the Pacific, the Near East, and Asia*. Englewood Cliffs, N.J., 1967.

Malmberg, C. F. "The Perception of Consonance and Dissonance." *Psychological Monographs* 25 (1918): 93–133.

Margolis, Howard. *Patterns, Thinking, and Cognition*. Chicago, 1987.

Mathieson, Thomas J. "Harmonia and Ethos in Ancient Greek Music." *Journal of Musicology* 3 (1984): 264–285.

Mead, Andrew. "The State of Research in Twelve-Tone and Atonal Music." *Music Theory Spectrum* 11 (1989): 40–48.

Medawar, Peter. *Pluto's Republic*. New York, 1982.

Merriam, Alan. *The Anthropology of Music*. Evanston, Ill., 1964.

Meyer, Leonard B. *Emotion and Meaning of Music*. Chicago, 1956.

———. "The End of the Renaissance?" *Hudson Review* 16 (1963): 169–186.

———. *Explaining Music*. Berkeley, Ca., 1973.

———. *Music, the Arts, and Ideas*. Chicago, 1967.

Meyer, Max. "Contributions to a Psychological Theory of Music." In *University of Missouri Studies*. Columbia, 1901.

Meyer-Baer, Kathi. "Psychologic and Ontologic Ideas in Augustine's *De Musica*." *Journal of Aesthetics and Art Criticism* 11 (1953): 224–230.

Mitchell, Donald. *Gustav Mahler: The Early Years*. Berkeley, Ca., 1980.

———. *Gustav Mahler III: Songs and Symphonies*. Berkeley, Ca., 1985.

———. *The Language of Modern Music*. London, 1966.

Moore, B. C. J., Peters, R. W., and Glasberg, R. W. "Thresholds for The Detection of Inharmonicity in Complex Tones." *Journal of the Acoustical Society of America* 77 (1985): 1861–1867.

Mueller, John. *The American Symphony Orchestra.* Bloomington, Ind., 1951.

Musgrave, Michael. "Schoenberg and Theory." *Journal of the Arnold Schoenberg Institute* 4 (1980): 34–40.

Narmour, Eugene. "Some Major Theoretical Problems Concerning the Concept of Hierarchy in the Analysis of Tonal Music." *Music Perception* 1 (1983): 129–199.

Neisser, Ulrich. *Cognitive Psychology.* New York, 1967.

———. *Cognition and Reality.* San Francisco, 1976.

Nettl, Bruno. *Music in Primitive Culture.* Cambridge, 1956.

Newlin, Dika. *Bruckner, Mahler, Schoenberg,* revised ed. New York, 1978.

———. "Why is Schoenberg's Biography so Difficult to Write?" *Perspectives of New Music* 12 (1974): 40–42.

Nietzsche, Friedrich. *The Birth of Tragedy and the Case of Wagner.* Trans. Walter Kaufmann. New York, 1967.

———. *The Will to Power.* Trans. Ludovici. New York, 1940.

Norton, Richard. *Tonality in the Music of Western Culture.* University Park, Pa., 1984.

Odo of Cluny. *Enchiridion Musices.* In *Source Readings in Music History,* ed. Oliver Strunk. New York, 1950.

Ogden, Will. "How Tonality Functions in Schoenberg's Op. 11, No. 1." *Journal of the Arnold Schoenberg Institute* 5 (1981): 169–181.

Ortmann, Otto. "On the Melodic Relativity of Tones." *Psychological Monograph* 35 (1926): 1–47.

———. "Tonal Determinants of Melodic Memory." *Journal of Educational Psychology* 24 (1933): 454–467.

Poggioli, Renato. *The Theory of the Avant-Garde.* Trans. Gerald Fitzgerald. Cambridge, 1968.

Palisca, Claude. *Baroque Music.* Englewood Cliffs, N.J., 1968.

———. "Introductory Remarks on the Historiography of the Greek Modes." *Journal of Musicology* 3 (1984): 221–228.

Parncutt, Richard. *Harmony: A Psychoacoustical Approach.* Berlin, 1989.

———. "Revision of Parncutt's Psychoacoustical Model of the Root(s) of a Musical Chord." *Music Perception* 6 (1988): 65–94.

Perle, George. *Serial Composition and Atonality.* Berkeley, Ca., 1963.

Perloff, Marjorie. *The Futurist Movement.* Chicago, 1986.

Pikler, Andrew. "The Diatonic Foundation of Hearing." *Acta Psychologica* 11 (1955): 432–445.

Piston, Walter. "More Views on Serialism." *Score* 23 (1958): 46–49.

Planchart, Alejandro. "A Study of the Theories of Giuseppe Tartini." *Journal of Music Theory* 4 (1960): 32–61.

Plato. *Ion.* In *The Dialogues of Plato,* vol. 1. Trans. B. Jowett. New York, 1937.

Plomp, R. *Aspects of Tone Sensation.* London, 1976.

———. "Detectability Threshold for Combination Tones." *Journal of the Acoustical Society of America* 37 (1965): 1110–1123.

———. "The Ear as a Frequency Analyzer," *Journal of the Acoustical Society of America* 36 (1964): 1628–1636.

Popper, Karl. *Conjectures and Refutations*. London, 1963.

———. *Unended Quest*. London, 1974.

Powers, Harold. "Modes." In *The New Grove Dictionary of Music and Musicians*, ed. Stanley Sadie, 12. London, 1980.

Raessler, Daniel M. "Schoenberg and Busoni: Aspects of Their Relationship." *Journal of the Arnold Schoenberg Institute* 7 (1983): 7–27.

Rahn, John. *Basic Atonal Theory*. New York, 1980.

Raksin, David. "Life with Charlie." *Quarterly of the Library of Congress*, Summer, 1983: 234–253.

Rameau, J.-Philippe. *Treatise on Harmony*. Trans. Philip Gossett. New York, 1971.

Randel, Don. M. "Emerging Triadic Tonality in the Fifteenth Century." *Musical Quarterly* 57 (1971): 73–86.

Ratner, Leonard. *Classic Music*. New York, 1980.

Reese, Gustave. *Music in the Middle Ages*. New York, 1940.

Reich, Willi. *Schoenberg*. Trans. Leo Black. New York, 1971.

———, ed. *Schopferische Konfessionen*. Zurich, 1910.

Restle, F. "Theory of Serial Pattern Learning: Structural Tries." *Psychological Review* 77 (1970): 481–495.

Restle, F. and Brown, E. R. "Serial Pattern Learning." *Journal of Experimental Psychology* 83 (1970): 120–125.

Reti, Rudolph. *Tonality in Modern Music*. New York, 1962.

Riemann, Hugo. *Handbuch der Harmonielehre*. Leipzig, 1906.

———. *History of Music Theory, III*. Trans. William Mickelson. Lincoln, 1977.

———. *Harmony Simplified*. Translation of *Vereinfachte Harmonielehre* by H. Bewegung. London, 1893.

Ringer, Alexander. "Arnold Schoenberg and the Prophetic Image in Music." *Journal of the Arnold Schoenberg Institute* 1 (1976): 26–38.

Ritsma, R. J. "The Octave Deafness of the Human Ear." *IPO Reports* 1 (1966): 15–17.

Ritsma, R. and Engel, F. L. "Pitch of Frequency Modulated Signals." *Journal of the Acoustical Society of America* 36 (1964): 1637–1644.

Rivera, Benito. "Harmonic Theory in Musical Treatises of the Late Fifteenth and Early Sixteenth Centuries." *Music Theory Spectrum* 1 (1979): 80–95.

Rochberg, George. *The Aesthetics of Survival*. Ann Arbor, Mich., 1984.

———. "Reflections on Schoenberg." *Perspectives of New Music* 11 (1973): 56–83.

———. "The Harmonic Tendency of the Hexachord." *Journal of Music Theory* 3 (1959): 208–230.

———. *The Hexachord and Its Relation to the Twelve-Tone Row*. Bryn Mawr, Pa., 1955.

Rogers, John. "Some Properties of Non-Duplicating Rotational Arrays." *Perspectives of New Music* 7 (1968): 80–102.

Rognoni, Luigi. *The Second Viennese School.* Trans. Robert W. Mann. London, 1977.

Rosch, E. "Cognitive Reference Points." *Cognitive Psychology* 7 (1975): 532–547.

Rosen, Charles. *Arnold Schoenberg.* New York, 1975.

Rowell, Lewis. *Thinking About Music.* Amherst, Mass., 1983.

Rufer, Joseph. *Composition with Twelve Tones.* Trans. Humphrey Searle. New York, 1954.

———. *The Works of Arnold Schoenberg.* Trans. Dika Newlin. London, 1962.

Rumelhart, David E. "Schemata." In *Perspectives of Cognitive Science.* Hillsdale, N.J., 1981.

Ruwet, Nicholas. "Contradictions of the Serial Language." In *Die Reihe, Speech and Music.* Bryn Mawr, Pa., 1972.

Ryle, Gilbert. *The Concept of Mind.* Chicago, 1949.

Sachs, Curt. *The Rise of Music in the Ancient World.* New York, 1943.

———. *The Wellsprings of Music.* New York, 1965.

Samson, Jim. *Music in Transition: A Study of Tonal Expansion and Atonality.* New York, 1977.

Schoenberg, Arnold. *Harmonielehre,* rev. ed. Vienna, 1922.

———. *Fundamentals of Musical Composition.* Ed. Gerald Strang and Leonard Stein. London, 1967.

———. *Letters.* Trans. Wilkins and Kaiser, ed. Erwin Stein. London, 1964.

———. *Models for Beginners in Composition.* New York, 1942.

———. *Structural Functions of Harmony.* Ed. Humphrey Searle, London, 1954.

———. *Style and Idea.* Trans. Leo Black, ed. Leonard Stein. Berkeley, Ca., 1975.

———. *Theory of Harmony.* Trans. Roy Carter. Berkeley, Ca., 1978.

Schorske, Carl. *Fin-de-Siecle Vienna.* New York, 1986.

Schwarz, Boris. "Arnold Schoenberg in Soviet Music." *Perspectives of New Music* 4 (1965): 86–94.

Scruton, Roger. "Analytical Philosophy and the Meaning of Music." *Journal of Aesthetics and Art Criticism* 66 (1987): 169–176.

Shackford, Charles. "Some Aspects of Perception." *Journal of Music Theory* 5 (1961): 162–202.

Simms, Bryan. "Choron, Fetis, and the Theory of Tonality." *Journal of Music Theory* 19 (1975): 112–139.

Simon, H. A. "Complexity and the Representation of Patterned Sequences of Symbols," *Psychological Review* 79 (1972): 369–382.

Simon, H. A. and Kotovsky, K. "Human Acquisition of Concepts for Sequential Patterns." *Psychological Review* 70 (1963): 534–546.

Slonimsky, Nicholas. *Perfect Pitch.* New York, 1988.

———. *Music Since 1900,* 3rd ed. New York.

Smith, Joan Allen. *Schoenberg and His Circle.* New York, 1986.

Smith, Leon R. *An Investigation of the Inherent Qualities of Musical Intervals as Definers of Melodic Tonality.* Indiana University Ph.D. dissertation, 1967.

Solomon, Jon. "Toward a History of Tonoi." *Journal of Musicology* 3 (1984): 242–251.

Sperling, G. "The Information Available in Brief Visual Presentations." *Psychological Monographs* 74.11 (1960).

Spratt, John F. "The Speculative Content of Schoenberg's *Harmonielehre.*" *Current Musicology* 2 (1971): 83–88.

Sternberg, Michael. "Traditions and Responsibility." *Perspectives of New Music* 1 (1962): 154–159.

Stravinsky, Igor and Craft, Robert. *Dialogues and a Diary.* London, 1968.

Stroh, Wolfgang Martin. "Schoenberg's Use of Text: The Text as a Musical Control in the 14th *Georgelied,* Op. 15." *Perspectives of New Music* 4 (1966): 35–44.

Strunk, Oliver, ed. *Readings in Music History.* New York, 1950.

Stuckenschmidt, H. H. *Arnold Schoenberg.* Trans. Humphrey Searle. New York, 1977.

Suchoff, Benjamin. "Ethnological Roots of Béla Bartók's Musical Language." *World of Music* 29 (1987): 1–20.

Szabalszi, Bence. *A History of Melody.* New York, 1965.

Tenney, James. *A History of Consonance and Dissonance.* New York, 1988.

Teplov, B. M. *La Psychologie des aptitudes musicales.* Translated from the original Russian by J. Deprun. Paris, 1966.

Terhardt, Ernst. *"Oktavspreizung und Tonhohenverschiebung bei Sinustönen,"* *Acoustica* 22 (1970): 345–351.

———. "The Concept of Musical Consonance: A Link Between Music and Psychoacoustics." *Music Perception* 2 (1984): 276–295.

———. "Pitch, Consonance, and Harmony." *Journal of the Acoustical Society of America* 55 (1974): 1064–1069.

———. "The Two-Component Theory of Musical Consonance." In *Psychophysics and Physiology of Hearing,* ed. Evans and Wilson. London, 1977.

———. *"Zur Tonhöhenwahrnehmung von Klangen* I. Psychoacustische Grundlagen." *Acoustica* 26 (1972): 173–186.

———. Ibid., II: 187–199.

Terhardt, Ernst, Stoll, G., and Seewann, M. "Algorhithm for Extraction of Pitch and Pitch Salience from Complex Tone Signals." *Journal of the Acoustical Society of America* 71 (1982): 679–688.

Terhardt, Ernst and Zick, M. "Evaluation of the Tempered Tone Scale in Normal, Strached (sic.) and Contracted Intonation." *Acoustica* 32 (1975): 268–274.

Thomson, William. *A Clarification of the Tonality Concept.* Indiana University Ph.D. dissertation, 1952.

———. "Functional Ambiguity in Musical Structures." *Music Perception* 1 (1983): 3–27.

———. "Hindemith's Contribution to Music Theory." *Journal of Music Theory* 9 (1965): 52–71.

————. "The Problem of Tonality in Pre-Baroque and Primitive Music." *Journal of Music Theory* 2 (1958): 36–46.

Tillyard, H. J. W. *The Hymns of the Octoechus,* I. Copenhagen, 1940.

Tischler, Hans. "Mahler's Impact on the Crisis of Tonality." *Music Review* 12 (1951): 114–115.

Tittel, Ernst. "*Wiener Musiktheorie von Fux bis Schoenberg.*" In *Beitrage zur Musiktheorie des 19 Jahrhundert,* ed. Martin Vogel. Regensberg, 1966.

Travis, Roy. "Directed Motion in Schoenberg and Webern." *Perspectives of New Music* 4 (1966): 85–89.

Treitler, Leo. "Musical Analysis in an Historical Context." *Symposium of the College Music Society* 6 (1966): 75–88.

————. "Musical Syntax in the Middle Ages: Background to an Aesthetic Problem." *Perspectives of New Music* 4 (1965): 75–85.

Tuchman, Barbara. *The Proud Tower.* New York, 1966.

Updike, John. *Hugging the Shore.* New York, 1984.

Van der Werf, Hendrik. *The Chansons of the Troubadors and Trouveres.* Utrecht, 1972.

Vernon, P. E. "Auditory Perception: The Gestalt Approach." *British Journal of Psychology* 25 (1934): 123–139.

Ward, W. D. "Subjective Musical Pitch." *Journal of the Acoustical Society of America* 26 (1954): 369–380.

Wason, P. C. "Realism and Rationality in the Selection Task." In *Thinking and Reasoning,* ed. J. S. B. Evans. London, 1983.

Wason, Robert W. *Viennese Harmonic Theory from Albrechtsberger to Schenker and Schoenberg.* Ann Arbor, Mich., 1985.

Wellesz, Egon. *Arnold Schoenberg.* London, 1971.

————. *A History of Byzantine Music and Hymnography.* Oxford, 1949.

————. "The Origins of Schoenberg's Twelve-Tone System." *Lecture Notes from the Library of Congress.* Washington, D.C., 1958.

Wertheimer, M. "*Untersuchungen zur Lehre der Gestalt II.*" *Psychologische Forschung* 4 (1923): 301–350.

Westergaard, Peter. "Some Problems Raised by the Rhythmic Procedures in Milton Babbitt's Composition for Twelve Instruments," *Perspectives of New Music* 4 (1965): 109–118.

White, B. "Recognition of Distorted Melodies." *American Journal of Psychology* 73 (1960): 100–107.

White, Pamela. *Schoenberg and the God Idea.* Ann Arbor, Mich., 1985.

————. "Schoenberg and Schopenhauer." *Journal of the Arnold Schoenberg Institute* 8 (1984): 39–57.

Wilcox, John. "The Beginnings of the *L'Art Pour L'Art.*" *Journal of Aesthetics and Art Criticism* 11 (1953): 360–377.

Wingell, Richard. "Anonymous XI and Questions of Terminology in Theoretical Writings of the Middle Ages and Renaissance." *Music Theory Spectrum* 1 (1979): 121–128.

Winnington-Ingram, R. P. "Ancient Greek Music: A Survey." *Music and Letters* 10 (1929): 326–352.

———. "Aristoxenus and the Intervals of Greek Music." *Classical Quarterly* 26 (1932): 195–202.

———. *Mode in Ancient Greek Music.* Cambridge, 1936.

Wittlich, Gary, ed. *Aspects of Twentieth Century Music.* Englewood Cliffs, N.J., 1975.

Yasser, Joseph. *A Theory of Evolving Tonality.* New York, 1932.

Zarlino, G. "On the Modes" (*Le Istitutione Harmoniche,* Book IV). Trans. Vered Cohen. New Haven, 1983.

INDEX

Boldface numbers indicate extended discussion

Adam St. Victor, 149
Adams, John, 180
Adler, Oskar, 43
Adorno, Theodor, 2, 34, 71
Affekt, 35
Aldrich, Putnam, 115n
Alia Musica, 105, 115n
Allen, Woody, 19
Allport, Floyd, 118, 128n
Ambitus, 57, 115n, 140
Analytical formalism, 188
Anderson, Warren, 89n, 115n
Apel, Willi, 108
Appearance-Reality dichotomy, 26n, 31
Aristotle, 37n, 111, 146
Aristoxenus, Aristoxenian, 116n
Aron, Pietro, 57
Art: as battle, 36; as escape, 24; as truth, 37n
L'art pour l'art, 10, 20, 21
Atonal, atonality, 12n, 29, **50,** 53n, 76n, 157; "legislated," 17, 179; triadic, 76n, 156; as analogue of egalitarianism, 189
Auffassungseinheit, 60, 87,90
Augustine, St., 126
Auskomponierung, 87
Austin, William, 76n, 171n
Averbach, E. (and Coriell), 125
Askenase, Stefan, 28

Babbitt, Milton, 42, 85, 118, 181, 182n, 184, **186,** 188, **189,** 192, 195

Bach, J.S., 6, 13, 156; C-sharp Minor Prelude, *WTC* I, 143; C Major Prelude, *WTC* I, 170n
Bachem, A., 151n
Bailey, Walter, 182n
Baird, J.W., 151n
Banchieri, Adriano, 156
Bardi, Giovanni dé, 180
Bartók, Béla, 13, 171n
Barzun, Jacques, 17, 26n, 171n
Bassart, Anne, 182n
Bassbrechung (Schenkerian), 195
Beardslee, David C. (and Wertheimer), 113
Beethoven, Ludwig Van, 37n, 137, 156, 163
Bellini, Vincenzo, 171n
Benét, Stephen Vincent, 9
Benjamin, Walter, 26n
Benjamin, William, 86, 193
Berg, Alban, 15, 182n
Bergland, Richard, 61
Bernstein, Leonard, 138
Berry, Wallace, 176
Bingham, Van Dyke, 11
Bitonal, bitonality, 25n, 167; in modes, 59
Bizet, Georges, 170
Blaze, Françoise-Henri-Joseph, 5
Boethius, 59, 65, 106, 128n, 151n, 195
Bologna, Jacobo da, 146
Boretz, Benjamin, 62, **187,** 188, 197n
Borodin, Alexander, 170

Borrowed chords, 61
Bosanquet, R.H.M., 54
Bose, Fritz, 103
Boulez, Pierre, 161, 181, 184, 192, 194, 196n; *Structures* (1952), 192, 194, 197n
Bower, Calvin, 106
Brahms, Johannes, 22, 37n, 170, 178, 179; "Brahms-Wagner War," 6
Braque, Georges, 10
Brown, Helen, 63, 96, 116n, 197n
Bruckner, Anton, 44, 135, 170
Bruner, Jerome, 86
Bukofzer, Manfred, 80, 89n
Busoni, Ferruccio, 8, 11, 170
Butler, David, 114n
Buxtehude, Dietrich, 138
Byzantine liturgy, 108

Cage, John, 118, 194, 195
Calvinist determinism, 9
Camerata, 180
Carillo, Julian, 13, 14, 25
Casella, Alfredo, 11
Castellano, M.A. (et al.), 101, 114n, 115n
Chailly, Jacques, 116n
Chant, Gregorian, plainchant, 13, 55, 90n, 104, 119
Chaplin, Charlie, 22
Chopin, Frédéric, 7, 8
Christ, Christian, Christianity, 39, 61
Christ, William B. (et al.), 114n

This book was set in Linotron Times. Times is a modified book version of the original Times New Roman, a newspaper typeface, commissioned in 1931 to be designed under the supervision of Stanley Morison for the London *Times*.

Printed on acid-free paper.